Disability and the Labor Market

Economic Problems, Policies, and Programs

MONROE BERKOWITZ AND
M. ANNE HILL, EDITORS

ILR Press
New York State School of
Industrial and Labor Relations
Cornell University

Cover design by Kathleen Dalton

Library of Congress number: 86-19131
ISBN: 0-87546-125-5

Library of Congress Cataloging in Publication Data
Disability and the labor market.

  Papers presented at a meeting on the economics of
disability held in Washington, D.C. on April 9 and 10,
1985; sponsored by the Bureau of Economic Research of
Rutgers University.
  Bibliography: p.
  Includes index.
  1. Handicapped—Employment—United States—Congresses.
I. Berkowitz, Monroe, 1919–   . II. Hill, M. Anne.
III.Rutgers University. Bureau of Economic Research.
HD7256.U5D56   1986   331.5′9′0973   86-19131
ISBN 0-87546-125-5

Copies may be ordered from
ILR Press
New York State School of
Industrial and Labor Relations
Cornell University
Ithaca, NY 14851-0952

Printed by Braun-Brumfield in the United States of America
5 4 3 2 1

CONTENTS

TABLES AND FIGURES

Figures

PREFACE

This volume contains papers presented at a meeting on the economics of disability held in Washington, D.C., on April 9 and 10, 1985. The meeting was sponsored by the Bureau of Economic Research of Rutgers University, and funded by the U.S. Department of Education, Office of the Assistant Secretary for Special Education and Rehabilitative Services, and the National Institute of Handicapped Research. Additional funds for this and subsequent meetings were provided by the National Council on Compensation Insurance and the Health Insurance Association of America.

The April meeting covered a broad range of issues such as control of health care costs, economics of mental retardation, long-term care, and mental illness. This volume contains only the papers concerned with the economic analysis of disability and the labor market.

The authors have benefited from the lively discussion at the meeting and the comments of the discussants. Although these are not reproduced here, the cogent comments and the questions raised by persons in the audience are reflected in the changes made by the authors in the papers they prepared for the meeting. We acknowledge our debt of gratitude to those persons who chaired the sessions and to the discussants.

We are particularly grateful to Kenneth McLennan, who not only chaired the session on private sector initiatives but provided much-needed advice and guidance as to the choice of contributors.

Each of the chairs helped make the meeting a success. All were responsible for our getting through the agenda in the allotted time. Elizabeth Boggs, Government Affairs Committee of the Association for Retarded Citizens, and more widely known as the parent of developmental disabilities legislation in the United States, chaired the session on special programs. John Burton, professor at the New York State School of Industrial and Labor Relations at Cornell University and a noted expert in the field of workers' compensation, chaired the session on labor force participation of disabled persons. Donald E. Galvin, former state administrator of vocational rehabilitation and now a professor of health studies at Michigan State University, chaired the session on international experience. Martha A. McSteen, Acting Commissioner for Disability of the Social Security Administration, was kind enough to chair the final session on the outlook for change. Alton Hodges, Deputy Director of the National Institute of Handicapped Research (NIHR), introduced the program.

The discussants commented on the papers in their sessions and helped set the tone for the discussion that followed. These discussants were Martin Gerry, Fund for Equal Access to Society, Washington, D.C.; Paul Dziedic, Department of Services for the Blind, Olympia, Washington; James Chelius, Rutgers University; Thomas Bellamy, University of Oregon; Tom Nerney, Disability Institute, Washington, D.C.; David Braddock, University of Illinois; Richard Butler, Brigham Young University; Donald O. Parsons, Ohio State University; Gerben Dejong, Institute for Rehabilitation and Disability Management, National Rehabilitation Hospital; Charles F. Soule, Paul Revere Life Insurance Co.; Patricia Owens, Social Security Administration; Frank Bowe, Architectural and Transportation Barriers Compliance Board; and Guy Stubblefield, International Association of Machinists.

We wish to acknowledge our debt to Madeleine Will, Assistant Secretary for Special Education and Rehabilitative Services, who originally suggested these inquiries into the economics of disability. Douglas Fenderson, then Director of NIHR and now at the University of Minnesota, and John Clark, consultant to NIHR, worked diligently in the planning stages to assemble the group of economists and to select the topics. Many other members of the NIHR staff helped at various stages of the process.

Our thanks go to Leslie Dean for her patient typing of the manuscript and its many revisions, to Susan Hill for her tireless assistance in the copy-editing process, and to Helene Handaly for her assistance with the administrative details associated with this project.

Needless to say, the views expressed by the authors are theirs alone and are not the views, policies, or positions of the NIHR or the Department of Education. The authors and the editors bear full responsibility for any errors or omissions.

Monroe Berkowitz
M. Anne Hill

1 · DISABILITY AND THE LABOR MARKET: AN OVERVIEW

Monroe Berkowitz and M. Anne Hill

Disability imposes individual and social costs. With the onset of a potentially disabling condition, an individual experiences both economic and psychic losses as he or she faces restricted choices. The individual may suffer pain, incur increased medical costs, lose income, and face societal prejudice. Society may lose the output of an otherwise productive worker and use its resources for medical care and rehabilitation. A firm may lose its investment in the hiring and training of that worker.

Although the losses caused by disabling conditions extend far beyond the world of work, the essays in this volume focus primarily on disability and the labor market. Disability is said to occur when an individual is unable to perform some social role because of a mental or physical condition. While work is perhaps the most important social role that many of us perform, there are other dimensions of disability. The medically impaired child may be prevented from playing or going to school, the adult may be forced to restrict his or her work around the home, the retired person may find that he or she is unable to engage in a favorite recreational activity because of a physical condition. Although these types of disability are obviously important, we do not consider them in this volume but concentrate instead on the relationship between medical conditions and the decision to work or not to work in the labor market.

What do economists have to contribute to our understanding

of work disability? We would argue that the contribution is potentially large. The economist's approach serves to emphasize that disability is much more than a medical phenomenon. Work disability that eventually involves some withdrawal from the labor market begins with the onset of a medical condition, but it cannot be understood without some inquiry into a host of socioeconomic variables, including the state of the labor market.

Withdrawal from the labor market may signal eligibility for some form of income maintenance benefit. At the federal level, the premier income maintenance program is the Social Security Disability Insurance (SSDI) program, which has been challenged by the administrative problem of determining eligibility for benefits. The heart of this problem does not lie simply in the diagnosis and classification of medical conditions or in how to determine whether a person with a given medical condition should be allowed to collect benefits. The economist argues further that the need from an economic standpoint is to understand those factors that determine when and under what conditions persons with given medically defined conditions will apply for and receive these benefits. In chapters 2 and 3, these incentive and disincentive issues are explored. These are almost traditional issues for the economist, but there are other facets of the disability issue where some further contributions to understanding can be made.

Social Security Disability Insurance is a relative newcomer to the social insurance field. It was preceded by the pioneering and still thriving workers' compensation insurance program which can be found in each state. These insurance programs share common problems even as they deal with different constituencies. Chapter 4 in this volume examines the lessons the workers' compensation program may have for dealing with the problems that affect the administration of SSDI.

The economist is concerned not only with the effects of income maintenance programs on labor supply, but with the incremental costs these programs impose on firms. Using workers' compensation costs as an example, chapter 5 examines the employment effects of these costs, especially how such additional costs may affect an industry's demand for labor.

A virtual revolution has taken place in our understanding of the work capabilities of severely handicapped individuals, particularly mentally retarded persons. Persons formerly consigned to institutions are now finding their way into the workplace. One pathway to work has been through various transitional or supported work programs. While the economist has little to contribute to the design of such programs—they exist in a multiplicity of forms—we can apply some of the traditional public finance tools to examine the efficiency of the expenditures of these public funds. Chapter 6, based on recent data, analyzes the results from a wide sample of such ongoing programs.

A portion of our public funds (about $2 billion in 1982) is spent on efforts to restore disabled workers to the workplace. Are such efforts worthwhile in an economy that exhibits some unemployment? Do rehabilitated workers simply displace other workers who consequently join the ranks of the unemployed? Chapter 7 subjects the phenomenon of possible job displacement to an economic analysis.

Government has intervened in the labor market to aid disabled persons in at least two ways that are examined in chapters 8 and 9. One of these interventions is a law compelling certain government contractors to make reasonable accommodations so that impaired persons can work. The second prohibits discrimination against handicapped workers. These are natural areas for inquiries by lawyers, but there are obvious economic dimensions to such rules and regulations, and such dimensions are examined here.

The final chapter in this book compares U.S. disability policy with that of Sweden and the Netherlands. The structure of disability benefits payments can be compared across nations, as can such variables as the percentage of gross national product spent on disability programs. It is both sobering and reassuring to recognize that most of the problems with which we are concerned, whether they be disincentive effects or problems of opening up labor market opportunities for disabled persons, are present in other countries as well.

The economist's concern with disability begins with the recognition that our country faces considerable losses because of disability. While we cannot measure with any accuracy the costs to disabled persons of their diminished well-being, we *can* estimate the expenditures of various programs and policies targeted to serve disabled workers. Between 1970 and 1982, estimated disability expenditures for the population aged 18 to 64 more than doubled, from $60.6 billion to $121.5 billion in real 1982 dollars (see table 1.1). These costs increased as transfer payments and medical care payments escalated. We estimate that total cash transfers for disability in fiscal 1982 amounted to more than $67 billion, with an additional estimated $51.2 billion being spent on medical care. Between 1970 and 1978, the number of Social Security Disability Insurance (SSDI) recipients nearly doubled, from 1.5 million to 2.9 million (Reno and Price 1985), prompting legislative action in 1980 and 1984.

In this chapter, we set forth our terminology of disability, present some estimates of the numbers of disabled persons, describe various programs designed to serve disabled persons, and provide estimates of their current expenditures. We then examine in more detail the implications of these programs for the functioning of the labor market. Following this, we summarize the contents of the chapters in this volume, and in the final section we draw some policy implications from these papers and offer suggestions for future research.

DEFINITIONS AND CONCEPTS

The field of disability research is rife with terminological confusion. In discussing disability issues, we must clarify these concepts as much as possible, but we realize that the distinctions made by researchers are not always followed by legislators and administrators. Our solution is to begin by setting forth what have come to be some accepted distinctions among researchers and those persons engaged in surveys of disabled persons. We then point out how usages depart from these ideal concepts. These conceptual distinctions follow Nagi (1969) and Haber (1985).

Disability is the loss of the ability to perform socially accepted or prescribed tasks and roles due to a medically definable *condition*. Perhaps the person's body has been invaded by a bacillus leading to a diagnosis of tuberculosis, or a traumatic incident has led to an injury to the spinal cord, with resulting paraplegia. The sequence leading to disability begins with this physical, mental, or emotional condition that is the state of active pathology. In some relatively few cases, the condition leaves a person with some residual *impairments*, that is, some

TABLE 1.1
Disability Expenditures for
the Population Aged 18 to 64,
1970–82
(current and real dollar amounts in millions)

Year	Transfer Program Payments		Medical Care Payments		Costs of Direct Services		Totals	
	Current Dollars	1982 Dollars	Current Dollars	1982 Dollars	Current Dollars	1982 Dollars	Current Dollars	1982 Dollars
1970	15,230	37,793	7,968	19,773	1,053	2,613	24,251	60,179
1975	31,470	56,341	16,158	28,928	2,308	4,132	49,936	89,402
1976	35,533	60,146	19,547	33,087	2,554	4,323	57,634	97,555
1977	41,411	65,847	22,821	36,287	2,887	4,591	67,119	106,725
1978	45,700	67,532	27,353	40,420	2,877	4,251	75,930	112,204
1979	52,188	69,184	31,651	41,959	3,344	4,433	87,183	115,577
1980	58,335	68,160	36,399	42,529	3,395	3,967	98,129	114,656
1981	64,068	67,903	44,051	46,688	3,415	3,619	111,534	118,210
1982	67,377	67,377	51,197	51,197	2,950	2,950	121,524	121,524

Source: M. Berkowitz, 1985a, tables 7, 9, and 11.

physiological, anatomical, or mental loss or abnormality that persists after the condition has stabilized. The tubercular patient is left with damage to the lungs; the person with an injured spinal cord is left with perhaps complete severance of the spinal cord. A person who suffered a myocardial infarct is left with some heart-muscle damage. In some cases (again, relatively few) these residual impairments cause a person to have *functional limitations*. Because of these physical impairments, the person is unable to lift, carry, or walk or has not the strength or endurance to perform certain tasks. An emotional impairment may leave the person in such a state that he or she is simply unable to relate to fellow workers. As a consequence of these functional limitations, some persons may perform their expected roles only with extreme difficulty; hence we classify them as being *disabled*.

To determine whether a person has a physical condition, an impairment, or a functional limitation, we need only examine that person. But to determine whether someone has a disability may be a more complex task, since the inability to perform an expected or prescribed role may be due to a functional limitation as it interacts with a whole host of other factors in that person's environment. When considered in this way, it is obvious that disability, as opposed to the condition, impairment, or functional limitation, is a socioeconomic phenomenon and not a medical one. We return to this point again and again because it lies at the heart of the inquiries with which the economics of disability is concerned.

In discussing the continuum from condition to disability we must recognize that there is a time dimension. A person acutely ill with the flu and suffering its chills, aches, and fever has no difficulty in identifying the physical condition and impairment. That person is completely functionally limited and certainly disabled in the sense that no role can be filled except that of the supine patient. But these episodes are self-limiting and usually of short duration. It is when the condition leaves the person with more or less permanent impairments and functional limitations that we become involved with disability issues. We confine our attention here to permanent or long-term disabilities, usually those that last six months or longer. Any dividing line must be arbitrary, and we recognize that long-term disabilities begin with short-term episodes.

Although these distinctions are relatively clear-cut, disability definitions still differ in real-world usage. The World Health Organization (1980) uses "disability" to mean what we have called "functional limitation," and the term "handicap" to denote what we have called "disability." Their concepts, if not their terminology, are similar, however, to the more traditional terms we employ. Far more serious confusion arises because of entrenched but inconsistent usages in various programs. The definition of "handicapped" in the Rehabilitation Act of 1973 (P.L. 93–112) comes close to our concept of disability, but it pertains not only to a person who has an impairment that limits a major life activity, but also to a person with a record of such impairment or a person who is regarded as having such an impairment. Persons with physical and mental impairments that began at birth or developed early in life may benefit from services under the Comprehensive Service and Developmental Disabilities Amendments of 1978, although that concept fits more neatly under our definition of impairments. Under most state workers' compensation laws, a person will be examined after the medical condition has stabilized. If left with some physical impairment or functional limitation, the person may be eligible for a weekly cash benefit. But whether the amount of that benefit is rated according to the extent of the physical impairment or according to some measures of functional limitation, it is likely to be called a permanent partial *disability* benefit. When it is awarded on the basis of the actual loss of wages due to an inability to perform all the duties of a job, then it conforms to our concept of disability.

Workers' compensation cases are concerned with a person's ability or inability to work, which is obviously only one of the many roles a person fills in daily living. It is the inability to perform that role—a work disability—with which we will be most concerned. This is not to say that other aspects of a person's life are not of equal importance; but "work disability" is intimately connected with eligibility for some of the benefit programs. Also, most of our information about the prevalence of disability comes from labor market or social security surveys that define disability as some variant of the inability to work. For example, the Social Security Administration surveys define "disability" as a limitation in the kind or amount of work (or housework) resulting from a chronic health condition. (Haber 1985 provides a digest of the various surveys that include disability-related questions.)

As a consequence of these differences of definition, disability statistics suffer from measurement problems. We cannot count the number of disabled persons with any degree of precision, though we could count the number of persons with a particular condition or impairment. While estimates of the number of persons with particular conditions or impairments—e.g., spinal cord injuries (Kurtzke 1975) or multiple sclerosis (Inman 1983)—may not be fully accurate, they can be improved by better surveys and more accurate diagnoses. With disability, however, we depend upon surveys that ask respondents whether they are limited in the amount or kind of work they can do by reason of a health condition.

One obvious problem with these surveys is that a person's answer may be influenced by his or her individual circumstances. Claiming a medical condition to be the reason for nonparticipation is socially acceptable; it may be tempting to assert a health reason for nonparticipation when other factors may be responsible. This problem is particularly troublesome for persons in older age groups. Among older workers, it may be impossible to distinguish between withdrawals from the labor force because of disability and withdrawals for other reasons.

Whether a person suffers from a health condition is, in part, accidental or random, but individuals' differing attitudes toward risk will affect the incidence of accidental injuries and the onset of certain illnesses. A degree of choice is involved in whether a person with a certain condition and certain functional limitations becomes disabled or not.

Facing such a choice, individuals do not respond to their condition in a vacuum. As they strive to regain the level of satisfaction they enjoyed prior to the onset of their condition, they will be greatly influenced not only by their personal characteristics but also by labor market conditions and the public policies and programs that impinge on their decisions. Their basic choices will depend on the level of transfer payments available to them and on the conditions of eligibility for these payments.

THE NUMBERS OF DISABLED PERSONS

Given these choices, we expect the total number of persons who identify themselves as disabled to change with shifting economic conditions. We explore the implications of the effects of such changes below, but in this section we detail the information reported on numbers of persons disabled. The aggregate numbers give us some idea of the dimensions of the overall problem, and delving into the composition of the disabled population can tell us a good bit about the nature of the disability process. We begin by examining the "severely disabled" (defined as those not working or not working regularly). Haber (1985) estimates on the basis of the 1978 Survey of Disability and Work that 5.8 percent of the noninstitutional population aged 18 to 64 can be classified as disabled. (While this estimate is higher than that found in the 1980 census—4.4 percent of the population aged 16 to 64— the disability surveys use more specialized personnel and have the advantage of more refined screening questions.) In 1983, the non-institutional population aged 18 to 64 was approximately 142 million. Using the 5.8 percent prevalence figure, we estimate that 8,353,000 persons were classified as disabled in this restricted meaning of the term.

Table 1.2 presents information on the prevalence of a work disability across sex, race, age, and schooling categories. These data are drawn from the March 1982 Current Population Survey (CPS) (U.S. Bureau of the Census 1983), which has a more liberal definition of disability. The CPS classifies individuals as having a work disability if they have a health problem that prevents or limits their work; if they have a disability related to military service or have left a job for health reasons; if they did not work in the previous week due to a long-term illness or disability that prevents the performance of any kind of work; if they did not work at all the previous year due to illness or disability; if they are under age 65 and covered by Medicare; or if they are under age 65 and a recipient of Supplemental Security Income (SSI). While this is a much broader measure than that for the "severely disabled" (as defined above), and leads to a higher overall prevalence of work disability (8.9 percent of all persons aged 16 to 64), the direction of the differences across the age and education groups are likely to be similar.

The prevalence of a work disability increases systematically with age. While only 5.4 percent of men aged 25 to 34 report the presence of a work disability, it is five times as likely for men aged 55 to 64 to report a disability (26.2 percent).

Among men and women of a given age, the prevalence of a work disability decreases dramatically with years of schooling. For

TABLE 1.2

Prevalence of a Work Disability
by Sex, Race, Age, and
Years of Schooling, 1982
(by percentage of total noninstitutional population in category)

Age and Years of Schooling	Male			Female		
	All Races	White	Black	All Races	White	Black
25 to 34 years old	5.4	5.2	8.3	4.7	4.1	8.5
8 years or less	15.7	15.3	21.0[a]	14.7	15.1	18.6[a]
9–12 years	6.4	6.1	9.7	5.2	4.5	9.6
13 years or more	3.5	3.4	4.4	2.9	2.6	5.1
35 to 44 years old	7.4	7.0	11.8	6.8	6.1	12.4
8 years or less	17.8	17.5	20.0[a]	17.8	15.7	26.9
9–12 years	7.9	7.1	9.3	7.1	6.4	12.9
13 years or more	4.7	4.8	3.4	3.8	3.9	3.8
45 to 54 years old	12.8	12.4	18.5	11.7	10.3	22.8
8 years or less	38.0	36.2	47.6	38.8	35.9	53.2
9–12 years	25.9	25.2	34.4	19.7	18.5	34.2
13 years or more	18.1	17.5	29.5[a]	14.2	14.0	18.3[a]

Source: U.S. Bureau of the Census 1983, calculated from table 9, pp. 9–14.
[a]Figure has low statistical reliability.

example, among men aged 35 to 44, 17.8 percent with fewer than nine years of schooling report a work disability, as against 4.7 percent of those who have completed at least one year of college. Nearly 16 percent of all women aged 35 to 44 with fewer than nine years of schooling report a work disability, while only 3.8 percent of those with some college do so.

With few exceptions, it is more likely for a black man or woman of a given age and level of schooling to report a work disability than a white counterpart. Finally, while white men experience a greater prevalence of work disabilities than do white women, in most age groups black women are more likely to have a work disability than are black men.

That the prevalence of a disability increases with age is not surprising. Both morbidity and potentially disabling conditions (such as visual and hearing impairments, circulatory and respiratory conditions) increase with age. More troubling is the apparently strong negative relationship between schooling and the prevalence of a work disability. The early onset of a disabling condition could lead an individual to shorten his or her time in school, and persons with less formal schooling may work in jobs that involve greater risks of occupational injury or illness. But the strong relationship cannot be explained without recognizing that individuals with less education face restricted occupational choices. The same condition that may force a grade-school-educated manual laborer to withdraw from the labor force may only be an inconvenience to a professional person. We reach the same conclusion as we did earlier. Disability cannot be explained by examining a person's medical condition alone. The contributions in this volume emphasize the role of demographic and socioeconomic variables in explaining the number of disabled persons. One influential factor will be the benefits an impaired person might receive. Aspects of the several benefit programs that form the disability system are examined in the next section.

DISABILITY PROGRAMS AND POLICIES

There are myriad disability-related programs and policies. These programs differ in terms of their eligibility criteria (their definition of "disability"), the extent to which receipt of benefits is dependent on a means test, the limits on the level of market earnings allowed for continuation of benefits, and the degree to which these benefits are taxable. These programs also differ in the philosophy of their response toward disabled persons. Haveman, Halberstadt, and Burkhauser (1984) characterize these responses as either "ameliorative" or "corrective." Among ameliorative government programs are those that provide payments for income support and medical care. Corrective responses are geared to enhance the individual's ability to return to work and to reduce or remove the effects of an impairment. Provision of training through vocational rehabilitation, sheltered workshops, programs for job accommodation, and employment subsidies, for example, involves corrective responses.

We identify the various programs and estimate the expenditures of these programs for the long-term disabled population of working age (18 to 64). In order to estimate the expenditures, we separate these programs into three basic types: cash transfers, medical care programs (which are for the most part ameliorative) and direct service programs (which incorporate corrective responses). We are not able to estimate the costs of all the corrective responses, especially the costs of workplace accommodations and the costs of affirmative action that are incurred by individual firms. (The cost estimates provided in this section and the methodology for deriving them can be found in M. Berkowitz 1985a.)

CASH TRANSFERS

We divide transfer-payment programs into three categories according to the rationales for paying benefits. These categories are social and private insurance, indemnity, and income support. Social and private insurance programs maintain incomes of persons who have had their usual and regular stream of earnings interrupted because of the disability. Tort and no-fault remedies indemnify persons who have been wronged, and income support programs prevent persons from suffering the destitution that could result from their disabling condition.

Social and private insurance. Social insurance programs originated with the passage of the Social Security Act of 1935. Social Security Disability Insurance (SSDI), with its compulsory coverage of the working population, is the prototype social insurance program. SSDI, the largest and most important government program targeted to the long-term disabled population, makes cash payments to covered workers who become disabled and also to the dependents of those disabled workers. Payments are based on an individual's earnings history and are not dependent on a needs or means test. SSDI pays benefits on the basis of impairments (whether or not the applicant meets the so-called medical listings) but always with the insistence that the person demonstrate disability by almost total withdrawal from the labor force. To collect SSDI benefits, then, an applicant must demonstrate both the withdrawal from the labor force and its connection with the chronic condition. As SSDI benefits are not taxable, benefits can exceed predisability take-home pay for some disabled workers (see Reno and Price 1985). Some $18.8 billion was paid out in fiscal 1982.

There are also a host of private insurance programs, ranging from policies purchased by individuals to group plans offered by employers. Private insurance programs provided nearly $18 billion in disability-related transfers in fiscal 1982, an amount approximately equal to total SSDI payments.

Indemnity. Nearly seventy-five years ago, we began workers' compensation programs designed to compensate workers for injuries arising out of or in the course of employment. These programs provide cash benefits, medical care, and rehabilitation services. Workers' compensation expenditures for such injuries in fiscal 1982 amounted to $7.3 billion.

Disabled persons may also receive funds if they are involved in accidents in which some other party is at fault. If it can be proved that the other driver involved in an automobile accident is negligent, the driver or his or her insurance company must pay. Under both fault and no-fault schemes, automotive bodily injuries accounted for $4 billion in disability transfer payments in fiscal 1982. Veterans' compensation accounted for an additional $6.1 billion, with indemnity transfers resulting from other bodily injuries amounting to $5.9 billion.

Income support. We transfer funds to those persons who can demonstrate that they are without sufficient resources. With the passage of the social security act, the federal government paid monthly benefits to "needy" persons in specific categories, including blind and permanently and totally disabled persons. Today, these programs are combined into the Supplemental Security Income (SSI) program, with disability transfers of $4.2 billion in fiscal 1982. To receive SSI benefits, a disabled person must pass a "needs" test to show that assets and income are below a specified level.

In addition, veterans who can demonstrate need are eligible for a veteran's pension. More than $1.2 billion was paid to such veterans in fiscal 1982. Finally, our largest welfare program, Aid to Families with Dependent Children (AFDC), also has on its rolls some recipients who live in households headed by a disabled person. Disability-related AFDC transfers accounted for nearly $1.8 billion in fiscal 1982.

Total cash disability transfers in fiscal 1982 were as follows: social insurance, $18.8 billion; individual and employer-provided insurance, $18 billion; indemnity payments, $23.3 billion; and income support, $7.3 billion—for a total of $67.4 billion.

MEDICAL CARE

As with transfer payments, we can divide medical care costs into categories that depend on the reason for payment. The social insurance category includes only the Medicare program, which since 1973 has covered SSDI recipients after a two-year waiting period. In 1982, Medicare paid out in hospital and supplementary medical insurance payments of $9.8 billion to persons receiving SSDI benefits or to those qualifying for the special end stage renal disease program.

Individuals may insure against the contingency of a disabling condition by purchasing a private policy, by subscribing to one of the Blue Cross or Blue Shield plans, or by having this type of coverage provided through the employer. While it is relatively easy to estimate the total expenditures of private insurers and the Blue plans, it is less straightforward to estimate the proportion of the total paid for medical care usage by disabled persons because of their impairments or underlying chronic condition. It is difficult to separate such expenditures from the usual expenditures incurred because of acute conditions. We estimate that private and employer-provided insurance paid $23.4 billion in fiscal 1982 for disability-related medical expenses.

Indemnity medical payments include those in the veterans' programs, the federal and state workers' compensation programs, and tort settlements. The total in this category was $6.4 billion for fiscal 1982.

Finally, the prominent program in terms of income support is Medicaid, which paid nearly all of the $11.7 billion in income support for medical care in fiscal 1982.

The total medical care payments in fiscal 1982 were as follows: social insurance, $9.8 billion; private and employer-provided insurance, $24 billion; indemnity, $6.4 billion; and income support, $11.7 billion—for a total of $51.9 billion.

DIRECT SERVICES

Direct services provided to disabled persons include rehabilitation and vocational education, food stamps, services provided by various veterans' programs, and employment assistance programs.

1. *Rehabilitation and vocational education.* Each of the states has one or more agencies that provide vocational rehabilitation (VR) services

to eligible clients under a joint federal-state VR program. Some VR services are provided only upon a demonstration of need; others are available regardless of the client's income. These are neither insurance nor indemnity programs, although workers' compensation recipients may be among the rehabilitation clients. The usual and historical rationale for providing rehabilitation services is that they are a good investment, the claim being that one dollar spent on rehabilitation will yield more than one dollar in benefits.

2. *Veterans' programs.* Among the veterans' programs are a separate VR program, programs to supply adapted vehicles, housing, and prosthetic appliances, and various programs to provide domiciliary care. These direct service programs cost about $406 million in 1982.

3. *Services for persons with specific impairments.* Historically, the government has provided services to blind and deaf persons, and in more recent years has extended the provision of services to the mentally ill and to persons afflicted with developmental disabilities. In fiscal 1982, approximately $141 million was spent on these programs, with the largest amount, some $52 million, allocated for the developmental disabilities programs.

4. *General federal programs.* These programs include food stamps and social services provided under title XX of the social security act— Social Service Programs for Individuals and Families. For both programs, we must estimate the amount spent on disabled persons. We assume that some disabled persons are eligible for these services as a result of their disabling condition and that they would lose their eligibility for these services if their physical or mental condition improved. However, this would not always be the case since their poverty could survive their disabling condition. In 1982, we estimate that $663 million was spent on food stamps received by families of disabled persons and that about $405 million was spent on social services, for a total of about $1.1 billion.

5. *Employment assistance programs.* We include here the programs for handicapped persons working for the federal government, as well as the various employment or jobs programs such as the Comprehensive Employment and Training Program (CETA) and its successors and predecessors. In some of these programs that are designed to return people to the labor market or to encourage their initial entry, a specific

dollar amount is set aside to serve handicapped persons. In other programs, it is necessary that we estimate the amounts spent on disabled persons. We estimate that for all of these employment assistance programs, approximately $300 million was spent for services to disabled persons in fiscal 1982.

The total expenditures for direct services for fiscal 1982 were as follows: vocational rehabilitation and education, $1.1 billion; veterans' programs, $0.4 billion; services for persons with specific impairments, $0.1 billion; general federal programs, $1.1 billion; and employment assistance programs, $0.3 billion—for a total of $3 billion.

Our estimate of $3 billion for all direct services probably understates the total, since we do not capture the costs associated with the many private sector accommodations for disabled employees. Neither do we include the expenditures of community groups, which have been especially active in mental health and mental retardation activities.

ANTIDISCRIMINATION LEGISLATION

Numerous federal and state laws have been implemented to prohibit discrimination against and to promote the employment of handicapped persons. The most important of these is the Rehabilitation Act of 1973 (P.L. 93–112), as amended in 1978. Sections 501, 503, and 504 are particularly relevant in this regard.

Section 504 prohibits discrimination on the basis of handicap in federal employment, while section 501 prohibits such discrimination in any program or activity receiving federal assistance. Section 504 also mandates affirmative action in the hiring of handicapped persons by the federal government. Section 503 requires businesses with federal contracts of $2,500 or more to engage in affirmative action to employ qualified handicapped persons, who are defined as those persons capable of performing a given job with a "reasonable accommodation" to their handicap.

EXPENDITURE TRENDS

We have made crude estimates of disability expenditures. The amounts, however, may be less important than the trend in these expenditures.

Consider for a moment our division of expenditures into the broad categories of transfers, medical care, and direct services (see table 1.1). We would argue that the obvious way to reduce transfer payments and medical care costs is to prevent disabilities in the first place, or, failing that, to rehabilitate disabled persons—that is, restore them to the labor market or to their highest level of functioning. This is the presumed purpose of the direct services.

Our best estimate is that, in 1970, 4.2 percent of all disability expenditures went for direct services of all kinds. Most of the disability dollar, some 64 percent, went for transfers, and the remainder, 33 percent, for medical care. Admittedly, the categories cannot be directly compared, but by 1982 the proportion spent for direct services was an even smaller share of the total disability dollar. Largely due to the rapid increases in medical care payments, the proportion of total disability expenditures for direct services had shrunk from 4.3 percent to 2.4 percent.

The bulk of these direct service expenditures is for rehabilitation, either via the joint federal-state program or for the veterans' programs. Are these programs effective? That is, if we spent more dollars on rehabilitation, would we spend fewer dollars on transfers? Although we suspect an affirmative answer to these questions, that would be difficult to prove. One seemingly reasonable proposition is that any disability policy that assumes that all persons with a given level of impairment are unable to work may be both inefficient and wasteful of human resources.

Implications for the Labor Market

At one time, compensation for accidents at the workplace was our only disability program. We now face a bewildering variety of programs providing for transfers, medical care, and other direct services to disabled persons. These programs range from those with inherent work disincentives to those oriented toward rehabilitating and employing disabled workers.

Some programs for disability benefits create incentives to reduce labor supply effort. In 1982, monthly benefits averaged $413 for all disabled workers and $812 for workers with families (Reno and Price 1985). Lando, Farley, and Brown (1982) found that nearly one-fourth of newly disabled workers were receiving more in SSDI benefits than they had earned while working. Burkhauser and Haveman (1982, 54–55) provide a clear example of the strength of these disincentives. Consider a worker whose SSDI benefits are $400 per month and whose impairment has improved sufficiently that he or she could earn $750 per month if working full time. Recipients of SSDI benefits are eligible for benefits as long as they are not capable of substantial gainful activity (SGA, defined currently as the ability to earn $300 per month, or $610 per month for blind persons). That is, the non-blind worker in question could earn up to $300 and retain SSDI benefits of $400 per month. However, earning an additional dollar above the SGA level would result in the loss of $400 in SSDI benefits. An individual must earn $700 (SGA + $400) at a minimum in order to make up the lost income. If the worker can command monthly full-time earnings of only $750 in the labor market, he or she is in effect gaining only $50 by choosing to work full time.

Clearly, the receipt of cash transfers constitutes a potential disincentive to a person's returning to work. In evaluating the seriousness of that problem, we can estimate with some degree of confidence the amount of cash transfers a person might receive. However, SSDI recipients are also eligible for Medicare, and any forecasts of future medical care payments are clouded with uncertainty since they are dependent both on program eligibility and on a person's medical condition, which may change over time. While a disabled person may be persuaded to give up a monthly SSDI check for labor market earnings, he or she may be more cautious about relinquishing Medicare eligibility, given possible future medical liability.

The Disability Amendments of 1980 (P.L. 96–265) changed somewhat the nature of these disincentives. For participants in a vocational rehabilitation program, SSDI benefits became payable after recovery if the individual's continued receipt of benefits would increase the likelihood of a return to work. The trial work period during which an individual can continue to receive benefits was extended to twelve months, and the term during which the person could receive Medicare benefits was lengthened to thirty-six months.

ASPECTS OF THE ECONOMICS OF DISABILITY:
CHAPTER SUMMARIES

Many problems with SSDI eligibility stem from our inability to define in an unambiguous way who we will allow to be classified as disabled for benefits purposes and who we will not. Carolyn L. Weaver, in chapter 2, traces the development of the Social Security Disability Benefits Reform Act of 1984 (P.L. 98–460). She recounts in detail recent controversies in social security disability policy and in the application of various SSDI benefits eligibility criteria.

Weaver links together issues of incentives and benefits adequacy with administration and enforcement within the Social Security Administration (SSA). She attributes the growth in the number of SSDI beneficiaries not only to changes in the relative value of SSDI benefits but also to changes on the administrative side. These changes include more lenient application of eligibility criteria, cutbacks in federal reviews of the state agencies that administer the SSDI program, and a reduction in the number of reviews of continuing eligibility.

By examining the SSDI benefits supply system within the framework of an insurance paradigm, Weaver highlights some of the most serious problems with this program. It is impossible to insure against an event that is both difficult to measure and is a function of individual characteristics apart from the impairment and implied functional limitations.

Weaver concludes that a social insurance program must possess a viable structure of benefits and eligibility criteria. The costs of the program must be reasonably predictable, the program must be administered in such a way that the outcomes are consistent and replicable, and the standards of disability within the law must be explicit.

In chapter 3, Jonathan S. Leonard addresses one of the fundamental puzzles in the economics of disability: Why do two persons, each with identical functional limitations, behave so differently in the labor market? Among the key problems are those of measurement surrounding "disability." If we had better measures of the number of persons who are prevented by their mental or physical condition from making certain motions, from lifting, carrying, walking, or stooping, from relating to others on the job, from enduring a day's stint at the workplace, and so on, we could begin to distinguish more carefully between the health and the nonhealth reasons that make similarly impaired persons behave so differently in the labor market. Empirically, there is a strong negative relationship between the level of SSDI benefits provided and the labor supply of "disabled" persons. If we could define disability in medical terms alone, we would expect to see no relationship between the economic incentives and disability.

To address this question, Leonard critically reviews the economic literature on the relationship between SSDI benefits (and eligibility) and the labor supply of disabled persons. The studies on which Leonard reports all agree on the direction but not the magnitude of this effect. In time-series regressions, Leonard (1979) finds that a $100 increase in average real monthly SSDI benefits leads to reductions in labor force participation of 4 percentage points for nonwhite men and of 3 percentage points for white men. Parsons (1980a, 1980b) finds an elasticity of nonparticipation with respect to the replacement rate of 0.63, where the replacement rate is the ratio of expected SSDI benefits to predisability earnings. Slade (1984) reports somewhat higher estimates, with his elasticity of nonparticipation with respect to the replacement rate being 0.81. Haveman and Wolfe (1984a) estimate the lowest elasticity of nonparticipation with respect to expected SSDI benefits at 0.06.

There is also empirical evidence that the number of SSDI beneficiaries is positively related to the level of benefits. Treitel (1979a) and M. Berkowitz, Johnson, and Murphy (1976) find that as the replacement rate increases, the likelihood that a recipient of SSDI benefits will leave the benefit rolls declines. Leonard (1979) estimates that a 10 percent increase in expected SSDI benefits will increase the number of SSDI beneficiaries by 3.5 percent. Halpern and Hausman (1984) also model the decision to apply for SSDI benefits, but find that potential applicants are more responsive to benefits levels than to the probability of acceptance into the SSDI program. Lando (1979) estimates across states a strong positive relationship between the number of disabled persons and the local unemployment rate.

In chapter 4, John D. Worrall and Richard J. Butler report on the effects that workers' compensation (WC) benefits may have on an individual's labor supply. A number of studies have found injury rates and claims frequency to vary directly with the levels of WC benefits.

Butler (1983) finds that the average elasticity of the frequency of disability claims with respect to WC benefits is 0.4. In an updated study (Worrall and Butler 1984), the elasticity estimates exceed one. Ruser (1984) estimates an elasticity of 0.35 for injury rates with respect to WC benefits; Butler (1983) reports an average elasticity of one. These studies imply that a 10 percent increase in the level of WC benefits leads to increases in injury rates and the frequency of WC claims of between 3.5 and 10.0 percent. Worrall and Butler (1985), Butler and Worrall (1985), and Worrall et al. (1985) estimate hazard rate models, examining the effect of WC benefits on the duration of the nonwork spells of injured workers. They find the duration of disability to vary directly with WC benefits and inversely with the wage.

These studies show how changes in the levels of disability benefits compared to the wages that persons can earn will influence the propensity to apply for benefits. The evidence is drawn from the older workers' compensation program, but the lessons apply to the newer social security program as well. Clearly, individuals who are "impaired" can become disabled as the economic incentives change. For some persons with identifiable physical and mental conditions, disability benefits have become a ticket out of the labor force. The direction of the estimated effects of both SSDI and WC benefits on labor supply is the same; the estimates are of the same order of magnitude and with few exceptions are quite large, with "supply" elasticities ranging from 0.35 to 1.00.

While disability benefits clearly affect the labor supply of individuals, James Lambrinos and David Appel argue in chapter 5 that workers' compensation benefits also affect labor demand. To the extent that employers bear the cost of workers' compensation, product prices will rise, and output and employment will fall. Lambrinos and Appel measure the potential magnitudes of these changes across industries. They compute upper-bound estimates of the employment effects of the workers' compensation program in eleven industries across thirty-eight states.

The workers' compensation rate is determined on the basis of an industry's injury experience and costs. Lambrinos and Appel assume that employers absorb the full cost of workers' compensation coverage and shift these costs forward to consumers by increasing product prices. As the product prices rise, output and consequently employment will fall. The extent to which employment declines as WC costs increase depends on the sensitivity of output demand to changes in the output price, on labor's share in total cost, and on the substitutibility in production of other inputs for labor. The upper-bound estimates of decreases in employment resulting from workers' compensation range from 0.92 percent in the stationery industry to 5.86 percent in the liquor industry.

This research is a first look at the issue and should be extended to model jointly labor supply and labor demand considerations, incorporating all the various disability-related benefits that impaired workers may receive.

Even as there are people trying to get out of the labor force, there are others struggling to get in. Some of these persons have never worked. An increasing number of developmentally disabled persons without any work history are entering the labor market in positions ranging from competitive jobs to supported work and transitional work (Wehman and Hill 1982).

In chapter 6, Craig Thornton and Rebecca Maynard examine in detail two program models designed to increase the job opportunities of disabled persons: transitional employment and supported employment. Transitional employment serves as a bridge to employment for persons who are in schools or sheltered workshops, or are unemployed, by providing short-term services that place and train those persons in competitive jobs. Supported employment is targeted toward more severely impaired persons who may be unable to remain employed without ongoing assistance. Thornton and Maynard outline some of the costs and benefits of these programs and analyze the potential of these programs to enhance the employment prospects of disabled persons.

There have been many small programs fielded across the country and two statewide programs carried out in Washington and Massachusetts. Generally, the placement rates, starting wages, job tenure, and costs per placement indicate that these programs can successfully move even those persons with severe disabilities into employment. However, there has been little rigorous evaluation of the performance of these programs. One exception is the U.S. Department of Labor's Structured Training and Employment Transitional Services (STETS) demonstration, which focused on transitional employment services for mentally retarded young adults. The STETS program included an evaluation component with eligible applicants randomly assigned to a treatment group that was provided services and a control group that was prevented from receiving services. The evaluation of the STETS program concluded that while these services did not increase *overall* employment activity, they did significantly raise the proportion of participants who held regular competitive jobs relative to the number holding jobs in sheltered workshops. The services also increased average weekly earnings of all participants.

It is likely that the number of transitional and supported work programs will increase as more developmentally disabled persons come out of the school system. Thornton and Maynard's overview of the evaluation of such programs points the way to needed policy to assure a wise allocation of funds.

One hypothetical cost of rehabilitation and employment programs is the potential displacement of able-bodied workers. In chapter 7, Robert S. Smith analyzes the circumstances under which these new entrants or reentrants may simply displace able-bodied workers. Smith treats the job displacement issue in general, with particular reference to those government programs designed to assist disabled persons in their employment efforts. If employers are ignorant of the productive potential of the employees, or if disabled persons cannot secure their own funding for vocational rehabilitation and, as a result, miss out on employment opportunities, then government intervention is warranted and this increases the general social welfare. In perfectly functioning labor markets, the wages of able-bodied workers may be reduced as otherwise unemployed disabled persons join the labor force; however, the losses imposed on the able-bodied by an increase in labor supply will be offset by employer gains in profit. Only if there is significant unemployment can displacement occur.

The physically or mentally impaired person may face a number of obstacles in the labor market. Steps at the factory door may bar access to all those in wheelchairs. Persons who cannot stand for long periods of time may not even be considered for positions whose job specifications require this mode of working. Personnel offices may enforce rules that require unreasonable physical or mental qualifications, or may refuse to consider applications from persons with records of particular impairments.

As mentioned above, portions of the amendments to the Rehabilitation Act of 1973 deal with the problems of discrimination against handicapped persons. The legislation and the rules and regulations issued under it are necessarily controversial as administrative agencies and courts decide what are bona fide occupational qualifications and what should be regarded as evidence of discriminatory practices. Such legislation, as well as similar enactments providing for access to transportation and public buildings, lies at the heart of the concern of the disability rights activists who see society and not themselves as being disabled. Their demand is that barriers be removed and attitudes changed so that they can compete on an even basis.

Economic analysis may help us understand whether the intended effect of the legislation is likely to come about. Two chapters deal with these issues. Frederick C. Collignon treats the accommodations issue in chapter 8, and William G. Johnson, in chapter 9, focuses on discrimination. Collignon describes the legislation regarding reasonable accommodation. He points out some of the economic incentives to accommodate handicapped workers that employers may face. Collignon reports on the results of a Berkeley Planning Associates survey responded to by 367 federal contractors. These firms employed 512,000 workers, 19,200 of whom had potentially disabling conditions. Most of the accommodations made by the surveyed firms required little cost and minimal adjustments by the employers. More than half of all accommodations cost nothing. Only 8 percent of these accommodations cost more than $2,000. Larger firms appeared more likely to recruit handicapped workers and also to undertake expensive accommodations. Collignon's review excludes those firms that are not federal contractors and therefore not legally liable to accommodate handicapped workers. As a result, we cannot judge the relative effect of the legislation on the accommodations made by the surveyed firms. It is unclear whether accommodations made by nonfederal contractors, in the absence of a legal requirement, follow a similar pattern as among the surveyed firms of the same type and size.

Johnson analyzes, from an economic viewpoint, the likely consequences of those sections of the Rehabilitation Act of 1973 that prohibit discrimination against handicapped workers. One shortcoming of the act is the implicit assumption that "impairment" automatically defines minority group status but does not affect productivity.

Clearly, an impairment may render a worker virtually incapable of performing one job, yet have no effect on that worker's productivity in another. Johnson explores this subtlety and applies economic models of discrimination to the case of impaired persons. He outlines three potential sources of discrimination (prejudice, statistical discrimination, and monopsony power) and the impact that discrimination may have on the employment opportunities of handicapped persons. To the extent that impaired workers face discrimination in the labor market, their job opportunities and their potential earnings will be lowered. Consequently, both the incentives to finding jobs and the benefits of vocational rehabilitation will be reduced.

Johnson questions the extent to which title V of the act can work to reduce the effects of discrimination against impaired workers. If discrimination arises from prejudice, competitive market forces should eliminate the ill effects. Statistical discrimination and monopsony power, however, result from market failure and may require government intervention. Johnson argues that the effectiveness of the act will be limited by the failure to capture the distinctions between discrimination based on race, on sex, and on impairment. All else equal, race and sex do not affect productivity, while an impairment can in many cases limit productivity. The effect of an impairment on an individual's work depends on the nature of the job and the work environment. Consequently, courts must decide these discrimination cases based on narrow rather than on precedential issues.

The same disability issues faced in the United States are faced in other countries as well. In chapter 10, Richard V. Burkhauser analyzes U.S. disability policy in the context of the experience in the Netherlands and Sweden. In recent years, these countries, like the United States, have experienced rather dramatic increases in disability expenditures. Burkhauser compares the disability programs and policies in the three countries, especially their disability benefit structures and the relative emphasis on income transfers as against supported work. While both the Netherlands and Sweden are committed to providing employment for disabled workers, the United States decreased funds for supported work programs as the 1970s ended. The disability benefit schemes appear to be more generous in the two European countries than in the United States. Burkhauser compares the ratio of the number of disability transfer recipients to the number of active labor force participants, and finds this ratio in Sweden in 1980 to be considerably higher than in the United States, with the ratio in the Netherlands being more than twice as high as in the United States. The methods of handling disability policies and programs in the Netherlands and Sweden may provide lessons for the formulation of our own domestic policy.

POLICY IMPLICATIONS AND SUGGESTIONS FOR FUTURE RESEARCH

Taken together, these chapters form the basis of what can be called the economic model of disability, but, as Weaver shows in her analysis of the 1984 social security amendments, the U.S. Congress seems to have been singularly unimpressed by such a construct. By emphasizing medical improvement as the criterion for removal of beneficiaries from the SSDI rolls, the legislators have seemed to downplay the role of demographic, human-capital, and socioeconomic variables that the economists stress. Perhaps the economic model, which seems to explain various disability phenomena, is not well understood. Possibly, it has not yet been developed with sufficient certainty and precision. The essays in this volume are designed to remedy these problems. We seek to explain the economic model of disability and to explore its several aspects. Traditionally, labor supply issues have dominated this field. Without in any way denigrating their central importance, the authors of these contributions also explore issues in the demand for labor, problems of job displacement, and evaluation of programs for new entrants, as well as discrimination and accommodation issues that affect the structure of the labor market.

Disability policy has not been developed in the United States in a unified and coherent fashion. Unlike the attack on poverty in the 1970s, or the current attention to the problems of aging, disability policy has not been the subject of concentrated concern. If the experience of Europe is any harbinger of the future, increased attention may be paid to disability issues in coming years.

Socioeconomic analysis in the area of disability requires a data base. The last comprehensive survey took place in 1978 and is now woefully outdated. Sponsored by the Social Security Administration, the survey was confined to adults of labor force age, thus precluding the gathering of information on children and retired persons. The decennial census contains some disability questions, but these are confined to self-perceptions of the disability state—whether a person feels that he or she is limited in the amount and kind of work performed—and it tells us nothing of the relationship between that state and the existence of impairments and functional limitations. Bits and pieces of information that become available from the National Health Interview Surveys and the new Survey of Income and Program Participation will help, but cannot substitute for a full-scale survey that will allow the researcher to trace the pathways to disability and help us understand how to deal with it.

No survey will ever attain its maximum potential use until we learn more about how to measure functional limitations in a reliable and efficient manner. It is one thing to define and refine the concepts of impairment and functional limitations; it is another to devise the questions to measure these limitations or their counterparts, residual functional capacities, in some unambiguous way. A great deal more work needs to be done in this area.

Since disability causes such obvious losses, it seems both socially and economically prudent to invest some funds in prevention. To derive the optimal expenditures for prevention and rehabilitation requires an accurate fix on the losses that disability causes. Additional research needs to be done on the nature and the extent of these losses. Methodological inquiries, as well as the empirical work, need to be done. Given the permanent or at least long-term nature of disability, the costs of illness models need substantial modification if they are to be adapted to meet the needs of measuring disability losses. Here again, new survey data would enable the researcher to substitute real information for informed guesses.

Prevention requires a good deal more information than simply knowing how much it is rational to spend. The methods and techniques in this area can benefit from an economic as well as a clinical analysis. Which types of intervention yield which kinds of benefits? Do employers have sufficient incentives to prevent the worker who is currently on a short-term sickness benefit program from moving to the long-term rolls and eventually to the Social Security Disability Insurance program? If early intervention is indicated to prevent long-term disability, is it possible to identify potential candidates for the long-term benefits in some cost-efficient manner?

The chapters in this volume touch on only some of these issues, but are relevant to all of them. Each chapter concentrates on an aspect of the total problem, and illustrates something of the work that has been done and the results to date. Our purpose will be served if these contributions aid and inform the policy maker and the administrator charged with responsibilities in the disability area in both the private and public sectors. At the same time, we hope that the obvious work still to be done stimulates the economists and other social scientists to see this area as a fruitful one for further research.

2 · SOCIAL SECURITY DISABILITY POLICY IN THE 1980s AND BEYOND

Carolyn L. Weaver

In the spring of 1981, the Reagan administration implemented a new requirement in the law that all beneficiaries of Social Security Disability Insurance (SSDI) be reviewed at least once every three years to assess their continuing eligibility for benefits.[1] The purpose of this little-noticed and, at that time, noncontroversial provision was to remove from the benefit rolls those people who were not disabled within the meaning of the law, and to ensure that the federal government carry out its obligation to provide for the accuracy of the benefit rolls. During the previous decade, the number of people added to the rolls each year had reached an historic high and the rate at which people left the rolls had reached an historic low, together helping to fuel a four-fold increase in spending (Committee on Finance 1982; Treitel 1979a). The responsibility for this unprecedented growth was believed to lie, in no small measure, with work disincentives and inadequate administrative control.

Congress got everything it bargained for when it approved the review requirement in 1980, if not more. Applying the same eligibility criteria to individuals undergoing review as to those newly applying

---

I wish to acknowledge Robert J. Mackay, Dave Koitz, Robert J. Myers, James R. Swenson, and Charles E. Soule for their many helpful comments, and Gil Fisher and Patricia Owens for their help in compiling data.

1. This requirement, contained in the 1980 Disability Amendments (P.L. 96-265), applied to beneficiaries with nonpermanent impairments. Those with permanent impairments were to be reviewed less frequently.

for benefits, the Social Security Administration (SSA) found one out of two people reviewed ineligible for benefits. In the span of thirty-six months, during which time just over a million reviews were conducted, some 480,000 people were found ineligible and, for many of them, benefits were stopped.[2]

In the ensuing uproar, the entire governing structure of the SSDI program was challenged. Between the actions of administrative law judges (ALJs) and federal judges, SSA's decisions to terminate benefits were reversed in over 200,000 cases. The states—entrusted to administer SSDI—stopped abiding by federal laws and rules, sometimes halting reviews, and sometimes conducting reviews under self-styled eligibility criteria. And the courts, in a series of decisions, ruled against the secretary of the Department of Health and Human Services on the very rules used for determining eligibility. As one member of Congress was prompted to say in the spring of 1984, legislation was "critical to the continued functioning of the social security disability insurance program" (Rostenkowski, *Congressional Record*, 27 March 1984, p. H1958). That legislation was the Social Security Disability Benefits Reform Act of 1984, which became law on October 9, 1984.

It is the purpose of this paper both to trace the development of the 1984 social security disability legislation and to provide some insight into the difficult policy issues faced by Congress. I argue that to properly understand recent legislative developments and to appreciate the policy issues that are likely to lie ahead, it is fruitful to examine SSDI from an economic perspective, drawing on the economics of insurance as the framework for analysis. Such a perspective links issues of incentives and benefit adequacy—the focus of the economics literature to date—with often neglected issues of administration and enforcement. Moreover, it provides a comprehensive view of the incentive problems that are likely to plague the design of a socially valuable (and financially viable) disability program, incentive problems that lie on both the beneficiary side and the provider side.[3]

---

2. Data supplied by the SSA and contained in U.S. Congress 1983. Early in 1983, legislation became effective that permitted individuals found ineligible for benefits to elect to receive payments pending appeal to an administrative law judge. Prior to this, benefits ceased three months after a finding of ineligibility.

3. As discussed below, economic research on SSDI and the issue of incentives has tended to focus on work incentives and the labor supply decision of the severely impaired.

BACKGROUND

As most observers of disability policy are aware, the genesis of the 1984 legislation was a little-noticed provision in the Disability Amendments of 1980 (P.L. 96-265) known as the "periodic review" requirement. Originating in the House Ways and Means Committee, the provision was a simple one, stating that all SSDI beneficiaries except those with permanent impairments must be reviewed at least once every three years to assess their continuing eligibility for benefits. It was one of a half-dozen or so provisions designed to tighten administrative control and thereby improve accountability and uniformity in the administration of the SSDI program (Social Security Administration 1981a; Koitz 1980; Committee on Finance 1982, 31–45).

In marked contrast to more recent experience, Congress in the 1970s was faced with what seemed to be runaway growth in the SSDI program. Between 1970 and 1978, the number of workers on the rolls nearly doubled, from 1.5 million to 2.9 million, and expenditures quadrupled. By 1980, some 4.7 million Americans, including workers and their dependents, were receiving monthly cash benefits at a cost of $16 billion. In the span of just a decade, the cost of the program for the average earner increased more than 50 percent.[4]

Many factors were cited for the explosion of costs and caseload, most notably the disincentives to work for those on the rolls, the enticement of high benefit levels for those still at work, and lax administration.[5] In the early-to-mid-1970s, social security retirement and disability benefits rose substantially and, from a work incentive standpoint, reached levels that were likely to have a strong influence on

---

4. Actually, the tax *rate* increased more than 50 percent, from a combined employee-employer rate of 0.95 percent to 1.50 percent between 1969 and 1979 (U.S. Congress 1982; Social Security Administration 1981b).

5. Other factors included increased public awareness of SSDI and increased workload resulting from the introduction of the black lung program in 1970 and SSI in 1974; increased allowances by administrative law judges during the late 1960s; and the administrative use of a medical improvement standard as a prerequisite to terminating disability recipients during the period 1969–76. Over the longer term, important determinants of growth were the liberalization of the program by Congress and the courts along with the growth of the insured population. On the dimensions and possible causes of growth, see Bayo, Goss, and Weissman 1978, Lando and Krute 1976, Lando, Coate, and Kraus 1979, Treitel 1979, U.S. Congress 1982, 25–29, and Burkhauser and Haveman 1982, 41–48.

the decision of an impaired person to work or not work. According to one study, a worker with median earnings in 1976 could expect to receive disability benefits equal to about 90 percent of after-tax earnings (U.S. Congress 1982, 26). In another study, one-fourth of newly disabled workers were found to be receiving more in benefits than they earned while working (Lando, Coate, and Kraus 1979). The increasingly favorable relation between benefits and earnings, and the relative decline in the return to work, made the SSDI program an attractive escape hatch during the high unemployment years of the 1970s.[6]

Adding to the value of gaining (or the cost of losing) benefit status was the availability of protection under the Medicare program. Beginning in 1972, disabled workers on the rolls for at least twenty-four months were made eligible for full Medicare coverage. With this provision in place, the disability beneficiary who considered rehabilitation and return to work faced an extremely high marginal tax rate since work, even part-time, generally rendered him or her ineligible for cash benefits and Medicare (after a nine-month trial work period).

On the administrative side, three key developments were thought to be contributing to the explosion of the benefit rolls: (1) a more lenient application of eligibility criteria, with a growing tendency to grant benefits on the basis of the more subjective elements of the disability determination; (2) a sharp cutback in federal reviews of state agency decisions; and (3) a sharp cutback in reviews of continuing eligibility. In 1970, for example, about 39 percent of the people added to the rolls had benefits awarded on the basis of a mental or physical disability severe enough to "meet the listings."[7] Three years later, that proportion had fallen to 29 percent, with the balance being accounted for by people whose benefits were awarded based on an impairment

---

6. SSA conducted a number of studies in the 1970s demonstrating a significant relationship between unemployment and the applicant rate. See Lando, Coate, and Kraus 1979, Hambor 1975, and Lando and Krute 1978. See Marvel 1982, Parsons 1980a, 1984b, Leonard 1979 and M. Berkowitz et al. 1982 for empirical analyses of the effect of economic variables on the decision to apply for SSDI (or the effect of SSDI on male labor force participation).

7. That is, having a specific medical impairment of such severity that inability to work is presumed, as opposed to one where a judgment must be made as to comparable medical severity or one of less severity which, when vocational factors are judged, is still determined to be disabling.

of comparable severity or, failing that, on the basis of nonmedical, vocational factors. Inaccurate allowances by states, moreover, were much less likely to be detected and corrected by federal examiners. Whereas before 1972, SSA followed a practice of verifying the accuracy of 70 percent of state agency decisions, it subsequently adopted a policy of reviewing only 5 percent of allowances and only after the claimant had begun receiving benefits. In addition, by the mid-1970s, something less than 5 percent of beneficiaries were being reviewed annually to assess continuing eligibility (U.S. Congress 1982, 25–29, 49–51, 76–78, 110–11). Together, these developments were likely to produce more erroneous allowances and continuances and a higher proportion of decisions which could not be replicated.

Perhaps not surprisingly, the SSDI program saw a record high number of people applying for and being granted benefits during the 1970s, and a record low rate of "recovery." Between 1967 and 1976, the number of people applying for benefits jumped from around a half million to over 1.2 million, and the number of workers (not counting dependents) newly awarded benefits rose from 280,000 to 552,000 annually (Lando and Krute 1978, 10; U.S. Congress 1982, 21, 27–28). Over the same period, the number of beneficiaries who left the rolls due to recovery, which was already extremely low, fell sharply, from about 30 per 1,000 beneficiaries in 1967 to 15 per 1,000 beneficiaries in 1976 (Treitel 1979a, 5). The adverse trend in recovery was particularly disturbing in light of the fact that recent legislative and administrative changes were tending to bias the mix of beneficiaries toward those with less severe impairments and greater recovery prospects.

The 1980 legislation was designed to deal headlong with these problems (U.S. House of Representatives 1980; Koitz 1980; Social Security Administration 1981a). Among other important changes, the legislation attempted to deal with work incentives by placing a lower cap on the benefits a family could receive and a lower limit on the number of years of low earnings young workers could drop in computing benefits, thereby helping to ensure that benefits would not exceed predisability earnings. For beneficiaries participating in vocational rehabilitation programs, benefits were made payable even after medical recovery in cases where participation was believed to increase the probability of permanently returning to work. For disabled persons who return to work, the trial work period was lengthened, allowing automatic re-enrollment during the twelve months after benefits ended and extending Medicare protection for thirty-six months. Also, for beneficiaries who attempted to return to work and subsequently refiled for benefits, waiting period provisions were made more lenient. In the Supplemental Security Income program (SSI), a new initiative was undertaken in permitting, on a temporary basis, severely disabled recipients to continue receiving at least a partial cash payment while working.[8] Albeit modest in scope, these work incentive provisions were unparalleled in the history of the social security disability programs.

To deal with lax administration, the legislation mandated eligibility reviews of existing beneficiaries at least once every three years. Also, the legislation directed the secretary of the Department of Health and Human Services to review a significant proportion of allowances by state agencies (prior to the payment of benefits) and to establish a program for reviewing ALJ decisions.

This significant and broadly supported piece of legislation was signed by President Carter on June 9, 1980. Somewhat paradoxically, the growth of SSDI had already begun to slow, with the number of workers added to the rolls each year falling by a quarter between 1977 and 1979.

EXPERIENCE UNDER THE REVIEW REQUIREMENT

The task of administering the 1980 amendments fell to the next administration, which moved quickly to implement the eligibility reviews. As part of President Reagan's first budget, it was announced that the reviews would be initiated several months earlier than required by law, in March 1981 rather than the first of the next year. Citing a recent General Accounting Office report (1981) which indicated that as many as 20 percent of those on the rolls were not disabled within the meaning of the law, the administration argued that there were potentially large sums of tax dollars being diverted to ineligibles and

---

8. Also, changes were made in the treatment of impairment-related work expenses, and work incentive demonstration projects were authorized.

that the extra time would help ease the burden of completing the massive task ahead.[9]

Absent any congressional or administrative directive to the contrary, the administration determined that continuing eligibility would be assessed in the same way that eligibility for a new applicant was assessed—based on the laws, regulations, secretarial rulings, and directives in effect at the time of review. Cases would be selected for review by SSA and sent to the state disability offices, where the reviews would actually be conducted.[10] The effect of the reviews was felt quickly. Within six months, some 67,000 people, or one out of two reviewed, were found ineligible for benefits and removed from the rolls.[11] A year later, another 160,000 people had been removed from the rolls, and by the end of 1983, some 480,000 people had been found ineligible for benefits. The proportion of reviews resulting in cessation remained high, averaging close to 50 percent during the entire period. By 1983, the total number of SSDI beneficiaries had actually fallen from 4.7 million, just three years earlier, to 3.8 million.[12]

Even if every decision had been "correct," this would have been

---

9. For general background material on the experience under the periodic review requirement, see U.S. House of Representatives 1982, U.S. Congress 1982, Committee on Finance 1983, and Koitz 1983.

10. Two points should be noted. First, the new law did not alter the government's obligation to periodically verify continuing eligibility or specify under what conditions those reviews were to be conducted; it simply mandated a minimum *frequency* of reviews. Second, prior to the 1984 legislation, there was no distinction in the law (pertaining to eligibility) between individuals filing for benefits and those already on the rolls. Eligibility was defined in terms of ability to perform substantial gainful activity. From 1969 to 1976, an administrative procedure was followed that required a showing of medical improvement as a prerequisite for terminating benefits to people who could perform substantial gainful activity. This was replaced by the procedure of performing eligibility reviews *as if* beneficiaries were new applicants, by simply determining ability to perform substantial gainful activity, which was the procedure adopted by the Reagan administration.

Originally, SSA targeted reviews on error-prone cases, which led to a higher termination rate than would have resulted with random selection of cases. SSA abandoned this practice in 1983.

11. Prior to legislation enacted in 1983, benefits ceased three months after a finding of ineligibility. Under legislation enacted in January, 1983 (P.L. 97-455), benefits were made payable beyond a finding of ineligibility to individuals who appealed their cases to ALJs. Data supplied by SSA and contained in Committee on Finance 1983, 6, 23–26.

12. This also reflected the slowdown in new awards which commenced in the late 1970s, and the curtailment of certain dependents' benefits in 1981.

an extremely difficult situation politically. There were over two million seriously disabled people who were going to have their eligibility verified, some of whom were improperly granted benefits (or no longer disabled), and some of whom were not. Most were in their fifties and sixties, and many had been on the rolls for years, having never been reviewed. Because of the strict definition of disability in the law, which also applied to the SSI program, many of those found ineligible could well have quite serious mental or physical impairments. Support and medical protection—under SSDI, SSI, Medicare and Medicaid—were being threatened under a program that had come to be viewed by many as "early retirement."

Adding to the difficulty, a finding of ineligibility could result not only from a change in the individual's condition or a previous error by the agency, but also from the growing specificity of the regulations defining disability. In 1979, the medical listing of disabling impairments was updated—not having been previously modified since the 1960s—to provide greater specificity and to reflect advances in medical technology. With changing criteria, people allowed benefits at one point in time could and would be found ineligible at a later point in time, even without any change in their condition. There was no inherent reason for these revisions to create difficulties; the problem lay in the infrequency of such revisions and the fact that beneficiaries had not been forewarned that they had an obligation to regularly reestablish eligibility under standards reflecting the *current* state of medical and vocational knowledge.

What happened to the people found ineligible for benefits? Most appealed their cases, and most who appealed had benefits reinstated by yet another decision maker acting on behalf of the federal government. In the twelve months ending October 1, 1982, 41,000 cases were heard by ALJs, and benefits were restored to 25,000 people. Ten to twenty thousand cases proceeded all the way to federal court. By the end of 1983, *half* the people found ineligible for benefits since March 1981 had been reinstated to benefit status at some level of appeal. By that time, there were over 150,000 disability cases pending before ALJs, with the average time to a hearing decision having reached six months, and 42,000 cases clogging the federal court system.[13]

---

13. Data supplied by SSA and contained in U.S. Congress 1983. The reasons for the different decisions rendered at the various levels of appeal are discussed below.

LEGISLATIVE STALEMATE

The worse the situation seemed to get, the less likely it appeared that Congress would enact remedial legislation. Hearings were held—in the House Ways and Means Committee Subcommittee on Social Security, the Senate Finance Committee, the Senate subcommittee on oversight, and even the committees on aging in the House and Senate. Efforts to draft legislation, however, were unsuccessful. One failed attempt at reform followed another and, by the spring of 1984, the one temporary relief measure to have made its way through Congress expired.[14]

There were a number of reasons for legislative stalemate, not the least of which was the cost of most major proposals. Any bill that slowed the review process or made it more difficult to remove individuals from the rolls had large budgetary consequences, and it was a time of record federal deficits and fragile social security financing.[15] Short of a well-defined solution to a well-defined problem, "reform" could carry a price tag of *billions* of dollars. Also, the administration was working to improve the disability review process. Face-to-face

---

14. Early in 1982, the House Ways and Means Subcommittee on Social Security drafted a bill (H.R. 6181, which amended a bill—H.R. 5700—originally introduced by Reps. Pickle and Archer) that was approved by the Ways and Means Committee and never considered by the full House. Its emphasis was on modifying the appeals process so as to achieve better evidence and thus better decisions earlier in the process. In the fall of 1983, the Ways and Means Committee drafted another bill (H.R. 3755, originally reported as part of H.R. 4170), different in most major respects from the bill drafted a year earlier. Its emphasis was on changing eligibility standards for those on the rolls. On the Senate side, the only piece of legislation to surface was a "stopgap" measure to provide, on a temporary basis, for payment of benefits pending appeal for individuals found ineligible for benefits. This was extended by legislation in October, 1983 (P.L. 97-118), and expired again in December. As 1983 came to a close, the authority for payments pending appeal had expired along with the 1980 provision allowing severely impaired SSI recipients who work to receive a special payment.

See statements by Senator Dole that chronicle the difficulties in developing legislation in *Congressional Record*, December 3, 1982, vol. 128, 140, pp. S13851–52 and *Congressional Record*, May 22, 1984, vol. 130, 68, pp. S6207–09.

15. Many of the key players in disability policy making, particularly in the Senate, had only recently been involved with the National Commission on Social Security Reform and the arduous task of shoring up the retirement system. Anything that worsened the financial condition of SSDI would worsen the condition of the combined cash benefits trust funds (retirement and disability), which were financially linked through interfund borrowing and a new provision for paying a reduced cost-of-living adjustment in the event of poor economic performance and low trust fund reserves.

interviews had been introduced in district offices and examiners were
being required to develop and consider medical evidence over at least
a twelve-month period. For those who believed the problems were
inherently administrative (poor case development, for example), these
steps reduced the need for legislation.

The more important factor contributing to legislative stalemate,
I would argue, was the absence of any good solutions, in the sense of
policies that would be broadly viewed as reasonable and cost-effective.
After all, what exactly was the problem? That was the real question.
What made the periodic review process so intractable was that it ex-
posed fundamental problems and long-standing inconsistencies in the
way disability was decided, whether for new applicants or those undergoing review. There were inconsistencies in the decisions made at
various levels of appeal as well as inconsistencies among the states and
among ALJs that were most clearly manifest when individuals, once
found eligible for benefits by reason of a severe disability, were subjected to a second eligibility determination. The probability of being
granted benefits differed depending on how far the individual proceeded through the appeals process; it differed over time; and it
differed from state to state, from ALJ to ALJ, and from court to
court. This had been true for years.[16] Since the problem was partly
one of quality control, partly one of substantive differences in the
standards and procedures governing decision makers at different levels of appeal, and partly one of changing standards and procedures
(including changing adjudicative climate), it was almost impossible to
glean from the gloomy statistics—either the termination rates or the
rates of reversal on appeal—any useful information about the performance or misperformance of SSA, its fifty-four subordinate agen-

16. For an indication of the extent to which these issues were not new, see
U.S. House of Representatives 1974, 1975, the 1975 Ways and Means Committee study
cited in Lando and Krute 1978, 9, and U.S. Congress 1979.

In Rhode Island, for example, 41 percent of people who filed for benefits in fiscal
year 1982 were granted benefits, while in New York, 22 percent were granted benefits.
In South Dakota, 77 percent of periodic reviews resulted in a continuation of benefits;
in New Mexico, the proportion was 43 percent (U.S. Congress 1983, 28–31).

According to a General Accounting Office study in 1976, cited in Burkhauser and
Haveman 1982, there was complete agreement among states on how and why to decide
a sample of cases only about a third of the time.

cies, and its corps of ALJs, or about ways to improve that performance.[17]

If the process was inadequate, involving poor case development
or insufficient individualization and face-to-face contact, the same
problem plagued the decisions made on the million or so people who
walked into local social security offices each year in quest of SSDI. If
the initial evaluation of mentally impaired claimants or people with
pain or multiple impairments was particularly difficult or error-prone,
so it would be when those same types of cases were reviewed. The
critical point is that the periodic reviews poured hundreds of thousands of people already on the rolls, already having established some
disability, into a decision process that was seriously flawed.

Absent any clear-cut remedies, the problem came to be framed
by political participants and the press in such a way as to suggest
seemingly insurmountable rifts over the nature of entitlement programs and the obligations of the government. People became divided
over the issue of whether an individual had (or should have) the
obligation to establish a continuing claim to benefits under a government program, or whether the government had the obligation, once
having granted benefits, to establish ineligibility in order to deny benefits. Likewise, people divided over the issue of whether a person,
once granted benefits and thus deemed by the government to be
eligible for benefits, could or should ever be told by that same government that they were not eligible for benefits. Put in a different
way, people divided over the issue of whether or not individuals with
identical circumstances should be treated differently depending upon

17. Social security ALJs historically reversed a high proportion of cases appealed to them—close to one out of two since the early to mid-1970s—and, depending
on the ALJ, the proportion of decisions reversed could range from less than 10 percent
to over 90 percent (U.S. Congress 1982, 58–74; U.S. Department of Health and Human
Services 1982, 9). A study conducted by the Department of Health and Human Services
examined the disparity between state agency and ALJ decisions. The study found
significant differences in decisions even when the same standards were applied to the
same cases. Factors cited include: face-to-face contact between claimant and decision
maker first provided at ALJ hearing (prior to legislation in 1983); new evidence added
to a file as it moved through the appeals process; different standards and procedures
used by state agencies and ALJs (including in the evaluation of evidence); and legal
representation at the ALJ hearing. See U.S. Department of Health and Human Services
1982.

whether they were, or were not yet, in benefit status. Conflicts that were basically philosophical, or perceived to be so—the resolution of which had such far-reaching implications for federal spending and the welfare of the disabled—were not readily resolved.

LAWMAKING OUTSIDE CONGRESS

What changed, then? In the absence of federal legislation, Congress found that disability policy was indeed being made—but outside Congress. On July 22, 1983, the state of New York went out of compliance with federal law and refused to process periodic reviews. Within three months, the states of Maryland, Virginia, Alabama, North Carolina, West Virginia, New Jersey, and Pennsylvania followed suit, and by the spring of 1984, fewer than half of all states were processing reviews normally. Some nine states had imposed moratoria or self-styled eligibility criteria; another eighteen states were operating under court-ordered eligibility criteria or subject to moratoria pending implementation of court orders (SSA data; Pear 1983). On April 13, 1984, Secretary Heckler announced a temporary nationwide moratorium on all periodic reviews.

On February 22, 1984, in a separate but related development, the U.S. Court of Appeals for the Ninth Circuit ruled against the secretary in a class action affecting 40,000 people, finding that benefits could not be terminated without demonstration of substantial improvement in medical condition or clear error in the original decision (Lopez et al. v. Heckler; SSA data; Pear 1984). Henceforth, an eligibility determination could not be made *as if* the individual were newly applying for benefits. Similar decisions had already been rendered in class actions filed in five district courts around the nation. By the spring of 1984, pending class actions dealing with medical improvement numbered twenty-eight, and the affected population ranged up to 230,000 people—potentially everyone terminated from the rolls since March 1981 who had not yet found their way back onto the rolls via appeal.

On the eve of the Social Security Disability Benefits Reform Act of 1984 (P.L. 98–460), the government—including the legislative branch, the judicial branch, the executive branch, and even the states—was at war with itself over the SSDI program. The power of

Congress to legislate was being challenged, the inequities among beneficiaries were becoming acute, and SSDI spending was increasing again. By 1984, federal legislation was necessary to *limit* the drain on the trust funds.

THE DISABILITY BENEFITS REFORM ACT OF 1984

The Social Security Disability Benefits Reform Act of 1984 had three clear goals: (1) to provide an explicit standard of review for beneficiaries under which improvement in condition rather than current condition would be the test for eligibility, (2) to improve the accuracy and nationwide uniformity of decisions, and (3) to return disability policy making to federal legislators.[18] In an important sense, the legislation was corrective or remedial rather than reform oriented.

The 1984 amendments evolved from two separate pieces of legislation: H.R. 2987 in the House and S. 476 in the Senate. H.R. 2987, introduced by Representative Shannon in May 1983, was a bill fashioned largely by a coalition of disability advocacy groups, including the Association for Retarded Citizens and the American Psychiatric Association. (The bill was nearly identical to a draft bill circulated by the Coalition of National Organizations Concerned with Protecting Benefits for Disabled Persons, dated April 14, 1983.) The emphasis of the bill was on expanding benefit eligibility, securing protections for people on the rolls, and, to the extent possible, allowing the generally liberalizing actions of the courts to influence disability policy. Beneficiaries would generally have been ensured continuing benefit status unless the government could establish significant medical improvement, regardless of education, vocational training, and other activities influencing work ability. To deal with the appeals process, H.R. 2987 would have eliminated reconsideration, and provided for personal appearances at the initial stage of determination. To deal with the situation in the courts, the bill would have required the

---

18. As reflected in U.S. Congress 1984, and statements by Senators Dole and Long in *Congressional Record*, May 22, 1984, vol. 130, 37, pp. S6207–12, and Representatives Pickle, Rostenkowski, and Conable in *Congressional Record*, March 27, 1984, vol. 130, 68, pp. H1958–60.

secretary of the Department of Health and Human Services to apply the decisions of a U.S. court of appeals as agency policy to all individuals within the states of that circuit. In addition, subjective evidence of pain (such as statements by friends or family as to intensity) would have been made a basis for a finding of disability. No additional financing would have been provided.

The bill was guided through the Subcommittee on Social Security and the Ways and Means Committee by subcommittee chairman Pickle. Emerging from the full committee in October as H.R. 4170, the bill retained the same general approach, although the details had been refined considerably to reduce expected costs. In particular, the medical improvement standard was redefined to ensure that beneficiaries who regained work ability for certain nonmedical reasons could be removed from the rolls. Also, the changes in the appeals process were restricted to apply only to review cases, and the statutory provision on pain was dropped. Retaining substantial support from the advocacy groups, the bill (renumbered H.R. 3755) was passed by the House the following March by a vote of 410-1 (*Congressional Record*, March 27, 1984).

On the Senate side, S. 476, introduced by Senators Cohen and Levin early in 1983 and subsequently modified, was similar in most important respects to the legislation progressing through the House. It underwent significant revision, however, when taken up by the Finance Committee in the spring of 1984. Under the leadership of Chairman Dole and with the active participation of Senator Long, the ranking minority member, the Finance Committee rejected the proposal to mandate circuit-wide compliance with court orders,[19] and added three significant new items: (1) a statutory provision on the evaluation of pain requiring objective medical evidence, (2) a financing provision calling for a reduction in the social security cost-of-living adjustment if necessary to protect SSDI reserves against unforeseen cost increases, and (3) a provision to ensure federalization of state operations in cases of sustained noncompliance with federal law. Also, the medical improvement standard was substantially revamped to en-

---

19. The Committee believed the issue had importance for the relation between the legislature and the judiciary that went well beyond the administration of the SSDI program, and noted that the issue might be constitutional at base, to be settled by the Supreme Court. See Committee on Finance 1984, 21.

sure that "legal and procedural hurdles" did not prevent the removal from the rolls of those people who could work (Committee on Finance 1984, 10). Reflecting the extent to which views differed between the House and Senate, the Finance Committee bill received unanimous support in committee and was approved in the Senate by a vote of 96-0 (*Congressional Record*, May 22, 1984).

Reaching a conference agreement, which consumed the better part of seven weeks, was predictably difficult. There were significant differences in the House and Senate bills; the administration generally supported the modifications made by the Finance Committee, while the coalition of advocacy groups (and now the American Association of Retired Persons) strongly opposed them; there were substantial differences in cost; and both bills had substantial support in the house from which they emerged. The final agreement, reached just days before the 98th Congress was scheduled to adjourn for the year, carried the indelible print of both houses. The House position generally prevailed on the construction of the medical improvement standard; the Senate position prevailed on the issues of pain and state compliance. In addition, the House provisions requiring compliance with court decisions and the elimination of reconsideration were dropped as was the Senate financing provision.

The major provisions of the 1984 amendments can be briefly summarized (U.S. House of Representatives 1984; Social Security Administration 1984).

1. *Eligibility (SSDI and SSI):*

   a. Standard for Determining Continuing Disability—Once on the rolls, beneficiaries may be found ineligible for benefits only if there is substantial evidence that the individual has medically improved or: (1) the individual has been a beneficiary of vocational therapy or advances in medical or vocational therapy or technology, (2) the individual's impairment is not as disabling as previously believed, or (3) the original decision was erroneous.[20] Ability to perform substantial

---

20. Benefits may also be terminated in cases of fraud, current work activity, or failure to cooperate or to follow prescribed treatment. The new standard is effective for all determinations made after the date of enactment and, among those made earlier, for individuals with cases pending administrative or judicial review or who were covered by a certified class action suit as of September 19, 1984.

gainful activity, the criterion applied to new applicants, is thus a necessary but not sufficient criterion for determining eligibility for beneficiaries undergoing review.

b. Standard for Evaluating Pain—In determination of disability (for applicants and beneficiaries), pain may not be found disabling without medical signs and findings, established by medically acceptable clinical or laboratory techniques, which show the existence of a medical impairment that could reasonably be expected to produce such pain. Subjective evidence of pain cannot be the basis of a finding of disability. (Codifies SSA policy; sunsets January 1, 1987.)

c. Evaluation of Multiple Impairments—In determination of medical severity of impairment, the combined effect of all of the individual's impairments must be considered even if no one impairment is severe.

2. *Payments Pending Appeal:* Reauthorized until January 1, 1988.

3. *Rulemaking:* The secretary must issue, by regulation, standards for determining disability which shall apply uniformly to all levels of determination, review, and adjudication. For the first time, such regulations would by law be subject to the public notice and comment rulemaking provisions of the Administrative Procedure Act.

4. *The Determination and Appeals Process:* Authorizes demonstration projects in which the opportunity for personal appearance is provided prior to a finding of ineligibility. In a portion of these projects, evidentiary hearings at reconsideration (mandated by legislation in 1983) would be eliminated.

No changes were made in the appeals process.

5. *Development and Evaluation of Evidence:* Medical evidence must generally be obtained from the individual's treating physician prior to evaluating evidence obtained from a consultative examination purchased by the government and, in the case of disabilities based on mental impairments, a psychologist or psychiatrist must generally make the medical and vocational assessment. In the case of beneficiaries undergoing review, a complete medical history of at least the preceding twelve months must be developed and all evidence in the file must be considered (codifies SSA policy).

6. *State Compliance with Federal Law:* The secretary is required to federalize disability determinations in any state found to be substantially out of compliance with federal law, regulations, and guidelines. Such action must be taken within six months of making a finding of noncompliance. (Sunsets December 31, 1987.)

7. *Work Incentives/Rehabilitation:* No new provisions. Next social security advisory council is directed to study and report on effectiveness of vocational rehabilitation, alternative approaches to work evaluation, and the possibility of predicting successful rehabilitation.

Section 1619, special payments for the severely impaired who work, is reauthorized through June 30, 1987.

Official cost estimates for the legislation ranged from $1.5 billion to $5.5 billion for the years 1984 to 1989.[21] No provisions were included for financing the changes.

Policy Making and the Economist

It is tempting to conclude that policy makers threw caution to the winds in the recent legislation, ignoring if not reversing earlier reforms that had been based on sound economic reasoning. Return-to-work issues, an important part of the economics literature on SSDI and dominant in the development of the 1980 legislation, were all but forgotten in 1984 as attention turned to guaranteeing "benefit rights" to those on the rolls. The idea that disability is fundamentally related to work ability and affected by individual choice seemed lost in the shuffle as advocacy groups, bolstered by the actions of the courts, clamored for a standard of review based on medical condition alone. Policy makers were faced with a crisis in disability which in many respects was a crisis in administration and adjudication. Issues relating to the federal-state form of administration, the multilevel appeals process, the method of establishing agency policy, and the procedures for gathering and evaluating medical evidence were among those in the foreground.

---

21. These estimates were made by the Congressional Budget Office and the Social Security Administration, respectively, and were developed using quite different methodologies.

To infer, however, that the issues being grappled with by Congress in 1984 were not fundamentally economic in nature, as they were in 1980, is to have an overly narrow view of the economics of disability and of what economists have to offer in the development of public policy. The task facing policy makers has been to design a reasonable group "insurance policy"—one that provides protection against major losses resulting from a common risk at a price the group is willing to pay—and to meet the terms of the "contract." This has not been an easy task given that the insured event cannot be accurately measured, the probabilities of occurrence, duration, and economic losses resulting from the event are affected by individual actions in ways that are extremely costly to monitor, and supply is politically determined by multiple organizational units, each with its own and often conflicting goals. In short, Congress has been grappling with a set of problems that are fundamentally economic in nature, akin to those faced by private insurers but exacerbated by the difficulty of nationwide, public supply.

To date, the research on the economics of disability and the SSDI program has generally focused on work incentives and the labor supply decision of severely impaired persons. This is one important aspect of the insurance problem.[22] Efforts to apply the insurance paradigm in a more comprehensive way—where the insurance problem (or the design of contract) is broadly conceived to involve not only the specification of eligibility criteria, premiums, and payment levels but also the entire governing structure established for determining eligibility, resolving disputes, and generally regulating the ongoing relationship between the "insured" and the "insurer"— are in their infancy. Such efforts constitute a promising line of research that is part of an emerging positive theory of insurance.[23]

---

22. See, for instance, Marvel 1982, Parsons 1980a, 1984b, M. Berkowitz et al. 1982, Leonard 1979, Hambor 1975, and Lando et al. 1979. In M. Berkowitz et al. 1982, the authors note that conventional studies of disability income policy, by focusing on questions of adequacy, have failed to address incentives, and suggest how they might be improved.

Other economic research on SSDI has centered on the related issue of the effectiveness of vocational rehabilitation and on multiple program overlap.

23. The insurance paradigm has inherent value for both researchers and policy makers in that it recognizes the interests of citizens in worker-taxpayer status and in

The next section highlights some of the unique problems inherent in attempting to insure against income loss due to disability and thus clarifies the basis for some of the age-old policy issues surrounding SSDI. The value of the insurance paradigm as an analytical framework for the economics of disability insurance may then be better appreciated.

SSDI FROM AN INSURANCE PERSPECTIVE

To appreciate the unique characteristics of "disability" and the problems that must be reconciled in any attempt to insure against the risk of income loss due to disability, it is useful to begin by considering a hypothetical situation. For illustrative purposes, suppose "disability" is a discrete event, the presence or absence of which can be costlessly verified and the occurrence of which results in the elimination of all earnings potential for a period of known duration. Moreover, suppose that the probability of an individual becoming disabled is known, and that this probability may vary across individuals and, for a given individual, may vary over time and across occupations. In short, let there be no information problems that would complicate and/or erode the value of the insurance contract.

In this setting, the design of an efficient insurance contract is straightforward. It is the one that maximizes the expected utility of policyholders, subject to a constraint that the insurer break even.[24]

---

disabled-benefit-receiving status and, by focusing on contract design, links issues of administration and enforcement with issues of incentives and benefit adequacy. It is, at once, a way of organizing the existing literature on the economics of disability and of framing questions for future research. See, for instance, Marvel 1982, Parsons 1984, Mashaw 1983, and Mashaw et al. 1978. Only Parsons develops a model explicitly from the insurance perspective; however, the other work could be easily translated into that perspective. See also W. G. Johnson 1979, which attempts to incorporate some of the issues raised here. Not addressed are those dimensions of the insurance problem related to imperfect state verification and administration and adjudication.

See Mayers and Smith 1982 and Joskow 1984 for analyses of other insurance types.

24. For an excellent introduction to the analysis of choice under uncertainty and the demand for insurance, see Hirshleifer and Riley 1979. This formulation assumes that the government, if it acts as insurer, behaves in a risk-neutral manner and operates the program on a self-financing basis. With private provision, firms are assumed to be able to diversify their risks sufficiently so that they behave in a risk-neutral manner with competition among insurers leading to zero expected profits.

Under such a contract, each individual would be provided full coverage against his or her actual loss, which in this case would equal the present value of foregone earnings during the period of disability, and all risk would be shifted to the insurer.[25] Moreover, each individual would be charged a total premium equal to his or her expected loss, with premiums differing according to risk characteristics (i.e., probabilities of disability) and losses (i.e., earnings potential). Premiums would reflect differences in probabilities of disability due to, say, age, health, and occupation, whereas benefit levels would reflect differences in foregone income arising from differences in, say, the number of years remaining until retirement, current and future earnings, and job skills and training. With everything else constant, the "worst risks"—those with the highest expected losses—would be charged the highest premiums, and those with the largest losses of foregone earnings would receive the highest benefits. In this setting, the competitive process—one in which profit-motivated firms compete to provide insurance, and buyers freely choose among suppliers on the basis of terms of contract—would be expected to generate an efficient insurance contract.

If this were an accurate characterization of the nature and state of knowledge about disability, none of the difficult problems typically faced by real-world insurers would arise. There would be no problem of determining initial eligibility, nor would there be a need to monitor the continuing eligibility of claimants. There would be no moral hazard problem since individuals would directly bear the expected costs and benefits of their own actions (in the sense that an individual's choice of a riskier job, for example, would increase his or her premiums). Also, there would be no adverse selection problem since everyone would be charged his or her own expected loss.

To this point, though, we have effectively ignored everything that makes "disability" a uniquely different event to insure than, say, loss of life or loss of property due to fire. In turn, we have described

---

25. This statement ignores premium loadings for selling and administrative expenses. If these costs are significant, the optimal policy will involve something less than full coverage as policyholders would prefer, *ex ante*, to accept some of the risk in exchange for lower total premiums. It is assumed throughout that health care costs are separately covered under another policy.

the general features of a policy which look most unlike those embodied in the SSDI program. Neither fact suggests, however, that the insurance paradigm (or any particular feature of the present structure of SSDI) should be abandoned; instead, what is suggested is the need for a more careful analysis of the characteristics of disability that must be handled in the formulation of a viable disability insurance policy, whether publicly or privately supplied. Without this deeper understanding of the intrinsic problems of disability insurance, the questions of how to improve SSDI cannot be reasonably addressed.

There are three unique and salient features of disability that reveal the dimensions of the insurance problem.

1. *The event against which individuals are attempting to insure is extremely difficult to measure, meaning that it is costly to determine whether the insured contingency has occurred.* Unlike loss of life or property, the event of "disability" is generally neither well-defined nor easily identified.[26] The definition of disability contained in section 223(d) of the social security act, which is not unlike that contained in private policies, is illustrative. It states that disability is the inability to engage in any substantial gainful activity by reason of a physical or mental impairment that is expected to end in death or to last at least twelve months.[27] Evidently, there are two distinct yet contingent elements of disability: physical or mental impairment (physiological, anatomical, or psychological loss or abnormality verifiable by clinical or laboratory diagnostic techniques), and complete inability to work, with the former event being of such severity that when combined with other factors it induces the latter. Income loss is contingent upon disability, which, in turn, is contingent upon impairment.

Several problems present themselves. First, disability is not directly observable but must be inferred from other circumstances or events such as severity of impairment, loss of employment, and absence of

---

26. The arguments presented here pertaining to the nature of disability draw on the insights of Nagi 1979, M. Berkowitz et al. 1976, Mashaw 1979, and Mashaw 1983. On the theoretical importance of state verification, see Spence and Zeckhauser.

27. The definition in most recently issued private policies mirrors this definition for disabilities lasting longer than some initial period, say a year, during which time an occupational definition applies. See Health Insurance Association of America 1982.

job skills. The measurement of disability is thus no better than our ability to observe and measure these associated events. In the case of verifying underlying impairment, for example, there are some cases, such as a broken or amputated arm, where impairment can be carefully identified and its severity measured at relatively low cost. In other cases, such as those involving certain mental impairments or pain, limits on medical or scientific knowledge may simply preclude accurate identification and measurement of severity and duration.[28] The accuracy and cost-effectiveness of determinations as to impairment and disability are thus vitally determined by the cost of applying known clinical and diagnostic procedures and the extent of scientific and medical knowledge, both of which can change rapidly.

Second, and no less problematic, the link between severity of impairment and ability to work is weak, except in the case of very severe impairments, such as paralysis, or quite nonsevere impairments, such as a broken finger. This is simply another way of saying that ability to work with any given impairment is a function of a variety of things—age, education, and work experience, along with a myriad of other medical, vocational, and motivational factors—and that the importance of these things varies with different impairments and different individuals. Any particular impairment (let alone combination of impairments) will be associated with different degrees of disability in different people and in the same individual over time. People with widely different impairments may be afflicted with identical degrees of disability.

Evidently, limits on knowledge and technology may make it difficult to determine precisely even the nature and severity of an individual's impairment, let alone how that influences his or her ability to work over time. A problem of formulating a standard of disability that reasonably captures the differences in condition (see Mashaw 1983) is then superimposed on a problem of diagnosis and evaluation of condition. This is complicated by the fact that while the severity of

---

28. In such cases, evaluation may have to rely on symptoms rather than clinical signs and findings; impairment and disability may not be separable, having to be inferred from the same behavioral manifestations; and there may be no well-established criterion for consistent classification, even on the basis of symptoms. See Nagi 1979.

most impairments can be represented on a continuum, as can the individual's quality or quantity of education or job skills, disability is frequently used as an all-or-none concept to mean the transition from ability to inability to work.

An important implication of these measurement and verification problems is that error is part and parcel of any disability determination process. Error, in turn, introduces a source of risk into the insurance contract itself—the risk that an individual who is actually disabled will be found ineligible for benefits (referred to as a type I error), or, conversely, that an individual who is able to work will be found eligible for benefits (referred to as a type II error).[29] This is troubling, of course, since the demand for insurance is predicated on risk reduction.

The control of error through, say, alternative standards, evaluation techniques, or incentive structures, and the correction of error through administrative review or an appellate process, pose challenging economic problems. The reason is that a reduction in one type of error, for example erroneous denials, generally comes at the expense of the other type, in this case more erroneous allowances. The relative cost of the two errors must therefore be explicitly addressed. The best that can be achieved, given imperfect information about who is disabled, is to devise a disability determination process that balances the costs of erroneous allowances and erroneous denials from the perspective of policyholders who are not yet disabled. By so doing, the costs of contract risk can be just offset, at the margin, by the savings from denying benefits to unintended claimants, and total error costs can be minimized.[30] Reductions in both types of errors, which would have the effect of simultaneously reducing contract risk and cost, must

---

29. See Mashaw 1983, Mashaw et al. 1978, Parsons 1984b, and Marvel 1982 on the economic implications of error; see Nagi 1979 on the nature and sources of error. On the potential for accuracy, Mashaw draws the conclusion: "the accuracy of decisions—whether persons granted benefits are in fact disabled—is virtually impossible to evaluate in a substantial portion of disability determinations." See Mashaw 1979, 160.

30. See, in particular, Parsons 1984b, which explicitly models the implications of imperfect state verification for the optimal level of benefits and screening rigor. This perspective on the design of an optimal contract is similar to that adopted by Buchanan and Tullock (1962) in their analysis of constitutional design.

generally await the use or development of new standards or evaluation techniques rather than the tightening or loosening of existing techniques (this assumes, of course, the efficient use of existing standards and procedures).

The design of an efficient disability determination and appeals process is an integral part of the economics of disability.

2. *The insured individual can affect both the probability of incurring a loss and the amount of the loss, and it is extremely costly to observe and monitor the individual's risk prevention and loss reduction activities.* In the case of disability, actions taken by the individual both prior to and after the onset of impairment can affect the probability of becoming disabled and the resulting loss (in terms of duration and foregone income). These actions include choice of: occupation (for example, is it physically demanding, dangerous, or high pressure?); personal safety (are seat belts worn?); medical attention, both pre-impairment preventive and remedial care and postimpairment care, where timing and quality are both critical; and education and vocational training, both pre- and postimpairment (does the individual have diversified job skills?).

Since actions designed to reduce expected losses are generally costly, the mere presence of insurance—which shields policyholders from part or all of their losses—reduces the incentive to engage in activities that would reduce the risk of incurring the insured event or the losses that would result. (On moral hazard, see Arrow 1963, Pauly 1974, and Spence and Zeckhauser 1971.) The potential for moral hazard is thus significant, and optimal contract design may dictate that some of the benefits of risk sharing be sacrificed by providing less than full coverage in order to provide proper incentives for risk prevention and loss reduction. This problem is familiar from other insurance contexts where deductibles and coinsurance are used.

As a general matter, if risk prevention and loss reduction activities could be costlessly observed and related to the probability of disability or the amount of loss, moral hazard would not necessarily create any problem. Indeed, it need not even arise. The efficient contract would simply make the payment of benefits contingent on a certain set of actions. (For example, if a particular physical therapy program were known to lead to recovery from a particular impairment, then payment of disability benefits could be made contingent upon participation in that program.) If enforced, such "forcing terms" motivate the insured population to invest in the optimal amount of loss prevention activity prior to the onset of disability, and to invest in the optimal amount of rehabilitation activity after disability. By eliminating the potential for moral hazard, these restrictions on contract terms can reduce program costs and increase the welfare of policyholders.[31]

More typically, there will be circumstances in which the activities of the insured population are costly to monitor or have uncertain effects that cannot be usefully incorporated into contract terms. In these cases, individuals will not bear the full expected costs and benefits of their actions. Too little effort will be devoted to risk prevention and loss reduction, and, as a consequence, program costs will be higher than they otherwise would be. The fundamental economic problem, then, is to balance, through contract design, the additional benefits of more complete risk sharing against the loss of incentives for efficient risk prevention and loss reduction.

As this discussion should highlight, the moral hazard problem in disability is pervasive and affects many margins of individual choice, ranging from choice of occupation to quality of medical care. Providing appropriate incentives to work in the presence of a severe impairment—the focus of the labor supply literature[32]—is to address but one example of moral hazard.

3. *Since the causes of disability are only imperfectly understood and not easily measured, classification of the insured population according to risk probabilities is costly and imperfect.* If, because classification according to probability of disability is costly, premiums do not closely reflect differences in expected losses, then adverse selection can be a significant problem.

---

31. Recognizing that insurers must, in order to break even, set premiums based on the *anticipated* actions of insured workers, insured workers have an incentive to negotiate for or accept policy terms that restrict coverage or allow for monitoring of their actions. If these actions can only be measured through a "noisy signal," then contract terms incorporating this signal will introduce additional risk into the contract. Again, this risk must be considered in contract design. For an analysis of imperfect monitors and the implications for contract design, see Harris and Raviv 1978.

32. Actually, the literature is more narrowly focused on the adverse effects of SSDI on the labor supply decision rather than on how SSDI might be restructured to mitigate those adverse effects.

Given any particular premium, low-risk people will tend not to buy insurance unless required to do so, and only the people who, from the perspective of the insurer, are the worst risks, will buy insurance. The complex set of cross-subsidies that results will tend to subsidize high-risk individuals and impose costs on low-risk individuals. In at least some of the latter cases, these costs will be sufficient to offset the gains from risk sharing. As in the case of moral hazard, premiums for those who participate in the program must be higher than they otherwise would be to reflect the now higher average risk.[33]

Compulsory participation, characteristic of a public program like SSDI, can avoid the consequence of adverse selection involving partial participation, but it is unlikely to do so without reducing the welfare of some low risk individuals.

As the above discussion should highlight, insurance against income loss due to disability can be expected to be a difficult and complex product to provide, whether publicly or privately. All of the standard problems of insurance—moral hazard, adverse selection, measurement of loss, and accuracy of claims—are present and must somehow be controlled through the terms of the "contract."

PROBLEMS IN DECENTRALIZED SUPPLY

In addition to problems dealing with the nature of the product being supplied, there are also problems inherent in the way we have chosen to supply disability insurance. Incentive and control problems run throughout the provider side of the program, affecting the actions of the primary "insurer" as well as intermediary providers of claims-related services—Congress, federal administrators, ALJs, state governors and disability examiners, and physicians and vocational rehabilitation counselors. Running a cost-effective program dictates that incentives be carefully structured so that the diverse interests of all these parties are reconciled, and reconciled in a manner that minimizes the costs involved in providing the insurance product.[34]

---

33. For a theoretical model of the implications of adverse selection for market equilibrium, see Rothschild and Stiglitz 1976.

34. In the literature on the agent principal relations, "agency costs" involve the cost of monitoring the agent's behavior, the costs of bonding and restricting his or

To illustrate this problem, let us consider the incentive structure facing the states and federal administrators and the recent failure of states to comply with federal disability rules. A clearer case of an inadequately controlled agent-principal relation would be hard to find. The states administer the SSDI program for the federal government on a voluntary basis and do so with full federal reimbursement. All employees hired and all expenses incurred by the states are thus paid for with federal funds (presently, about $600 million annually).

What if a governor decides that his or her state will not abide by federal rules and that eligibility reviews will be stopped or a more lenient standard will be used for determining eligibility? In such a situation, fewer citizens and potential voters are turned away, and fewer poor citizens must be supported by state welfare coffers. The costs of erroneous allowances are thus shifted to the federal government to be shared by all taxpayers, rather than internalized and borne by state residents. As the law is structured, the costs of all state decisions, whether correct or incorrect, prompt or delayed, are borne by the federal government.

What are the constraints on such actions? Under the law before 1984, a secretary of the Department of Health and Human Services desiring to halt such actions by federalizing operations faced a series of procedural hurdles in a process that could not be realistically completed in less than a couple of years. And what are the incentives of federal administrators to move aggressively to federalize disability operations in a state? Federalization involves going into a state, laying off workers, hiring replacement workers on a higher pay scale, and insisting that beneficiaries (often with visibly severe impairments) be removed from the rolls. Any net savings would accrue to the trust funds, and only after significant up-front costs had been incurred. Given that the process would be, by law, protracted, and given that there would be costs associated with taking such an action, the incentives are strong to at least wait and see—wait and see if the state might

---

her actions, and the reduction in the overall value of the relationship due to unresolved agency problems (in the context of disability, excessive benefit costs and taxes resulting from erroneous allowances or sacrificed welfare resulting from erroneous denials). For an introduction to the agent-principal problem, see Jensen and Meckling 1976, and for implications for decentralized decision making, see Kaplan 1982, chapter 13.

voluntarily come back into compliance or if Congress might alter the law.

These are standard "agency" problems that arise whenever decision-making authority and hence discretion must be delegated to individuals or groups with potentially conflicting interests and goals. A divergence between the interests of individuals or subgroups and the overall organizational goals arises and, like any other problem, erodes the value of the contract unless proper incentives are provided, either through direct monitoring and control of actions or else through a careful structuring of payoffs.

It was a recognition of incentive problems on the provider side that prompted the Senate Finance Committee in 1984 to approve the provision putting a strict timetable in the law for federalization of disability operations in cases of sustained noncompliance by states. Considerably more remains to be done if nationwide accuracy is to be ensured—and direct financial incentives (penalties for noncompliance, for example, or a pro rata sharing of administrative costs) would seem to hold real promise.

PROBLEMS IN PUBLIC SUPPLY

If the problems described to this point were the only ones faced in trying to formulate a socially valuable (and financially viable) disability insurance program, Congress would, much like a private insurer, have its hands full. The conditions and circumstances of the disabled, which are difficult to assess, are always changing, as are the technologies for evaluating and responding to those conditions. The actions of policyholders and providers affect the value of the insurance contract, just as the details of the contract affect the actions of policyholders and providers. Making matters more intractable, the federal courts are taking an increasingly active role in disability policy making, rendering decisions that undermine financing by raising program costs and making them unpredictable.[35]

---

35. On the role played by the courts over the years in the provision of private insurance, see Faulkner 1960, 101–105, 529–37, Hunter and Phillips 1932, 48–70, Angell 1963, 199–206, Huebner and Black 1982, 197–98; and on public insurance see E. Berkowitz and McQuaid 1978, Soule 1984, and additional views by Senator Long in U.S. Congress 1984.

But the task facing Congress is even bigger. In the private sector, competition provides strong incentives to resolve the various problems described to this point.[36] As prospective policyholders move their business (or prospective owners move their capital), inferior contracts and/or producers suffer losses; superior contracts and/or producers are rewarded. An important by-product of this process is that valuable information is provided on how consumers value different contracts or services relative to their cost of production and on new ways to handle the insurance problem. This fosters experimentation and innovation in contract design, which are so critical for dealing with a complex and changing phenomenon like disability.

In the public sector, by contrast, with supply organized around a single producer serving the entire nation, neither the efficient production, acquisition, nor use of information is fostered. How does one know, for instance, whether some new evaluation technique is cost-effective, or whether costs (program or total economic) would rise or fall if partial benefits were paid to disabled beneficiaries who go back to work, or whether pain is an insurable risk? How does one know whether society values an expansion of the system more than that expansion will cost? Even if one knew, who in government has the incentive, the responsibility, *and* the capacity to acquire information, develop new ideas, and reflect them in operating policy?

SSDI is applicable to over 100 million workers, and hundreds of thousands of persons are involved somehow in the provision of benefits to four million people. Ideas must generally be tried the cumbersome way, by experimenting with a law or regulation that applies to all of these people. In our political system, moreover, changes in the law must generally pass muster before, if not be actively sought by, the most intensely interested or affected parties—often those whose employment or livelihood depends on the continuation and growth of the program, rather than those who are merely interested in having insurance provided at minimum cost. (See Leonard and Zeckhauser 1983, 148–51.)

When all is said and done, the ability of SSDI to respond flexibly

---

36. On private incentives to resolve the insurance problem, see Mayers and Smith 1982. Leonard and Zeckhauser (1983) more fully develop the theme that the political process may be incongruous with efficient supply of social insurance.

to changes in knowledge and to new opportunities—whether in the area of prevention, diagnosis, evaluation, treatment and training, benefit schedules, eligibility, or administration—is inherently limited. The pressures to expand the system are ever-present.

In short, given that the fundamental problem of insuring against disability is an *informational* problem, the supply of SSDI is organized in a particularly difficult way, with public production and nationwide, compulsory participation. Public supply not only inhibits the production and use of relevant information but also eliminates the market test as a way of evaluating alternative contract designs. (For a general statement on this issue, see Hayek 1945.)

IMPLICATIONS

A look at SSDI from an insurance perspective suggests that the program is plagued by a set of problems stemming principally from imperfect measurement of disability, imperfect knowledge about prevention and cure, and imperfect political institutions through which supply is organized. These are not new problems, nor are they easily reconciled.

A relatively negative conclusion might be drawn from all of this. Short of truly radical reform of SSDI—which would involve altering the event against which society seeks to insure (for example, insuring against physical or mental loss only), or which would remove the government from the business of producing, as opposed to financing, insurance—there may be no way around these problems. Stated another way, we may simply lack the knowledge, the technology, and the political wherewithal to provide social insurance against income loss due to disability in a way that is immune to the rollercoaster ups and downs of financial despair and beneficiary despair that have characterized SSDI in the past decade. Efforts to tighten administration, as in the 1980 legislation and the regulatory initiatives of the late 1970s, are undoubtedly effective at reducing erroneous allowances and program costs, but not without denying benefits to some disabled people who belong on the rolls. Efforts to loosen administration, as in more recent regulatory initiatives and the 1984 legislation, are undoubtedly effective at ensuring eligibility for more disabled people, but not without granting or continuing benefits to some people who can work and thus increasing program costs. Both actions induce error, and both tend to set in motion political dynamics that undermine the attainment and perceived legitimacy of the original goals.

While there is a good bit of truth in this gloomy picture, a careful analysis of SSDI from the insurance perspective would likely suggest that there are still great strides to be made by narrowing the swings in the system and generally improving the welfare of the people served by the program. After all, what value is there in an insurance program if the terms of the "contract" are not knowable in advance? Too much contract risk—either in terms of the premiums that will be charged or the benefits that will be paid—destroys the value of insurance.

A social insurance program attempting to retain public support must have a structure of benefits and eligibility that can be perpetuated, and this, in turn, necessitates that costs be reasonably predictable and that the program be administered in a way that enforces, rather than undermines, the terms of the contract. The value of SSDI may be improved therefore by modest reforms designed to *control* (as distinct from tighten) the system and ensure that eligibility is determined under a common set of rules established by the federal government. Changes consistent with this objective would be those that made outcomes more predictable and more replicable, such as by bolstering state compliance through sanctions or other financial incentives, or by providing more explicit standards of disability in the law. Introducing performance measures and standards where they do not now exist would be another way of achieving this objective, serving to channel the actions of individuals and groups with divergent interests and, at the same time, to provide information that is critical for revising processes. Taking steps to convert the ALJ hearing from a de novo review of an individual's case to an appellate review of a prior agency decision, for example, could provide valuable information on the performance of state examiners and ALJs. Other areas pertaining to the adjudication of claims and the process by which disputes are resolved that warrant consideration include the number of levels of appeal, the applicability of court decisions to yet unlitigated cases, and the desirability of a special disability court.[37] Legislative changes designed to control administration and eligibility, and thereby reduce uncertainty, carry potential benefits for all participants in SSDI.

It is interesting to note that from this perspective, the 1980 and the 1984 legislation may have more in common than meets the eye. Both pieces of legislation attempted to deal with an erosion in the value of SSDI, which in 1980 stemmed from rising and unpredictable costs and in 1984 from uncertainty of payoff. Both pieces of legislation attempted to control administration, enforcement, and eligibility. (The medical improvement standard was no small part of this effort.) Considerably more needs to be done in this area, however, as evidenced by the swing in the program that helped bring us the legislation in 1984, and the swing in the opposite direction that is taking place right now.

But there is more to be learned by thinking about and analyzing SSDI from an insurance perspective than is suggested by these quite limited options. As highlighted in the last section, inherent in the nature of disability and in the nature of insurance is a problem of incentives, and how to properly structure those incentives. In regard to SSDI, the incentive effects of concern range from pre-impairment incentives affecting occupational choice to postimpairment incentives affecting return to work, and from the incentives affecting the various individuals (including doctors, lawyers, psychiatrists and psychologists, vocational rehabilitation counselors, and physical therapists) and units of government involved in the disability determination process to those affecting individuals and units of government involved in the appeals process. Each set of incentives warrants careful scrutiny to

---

37. A denied disability claim proceeds through three levels of administrative review before reaching a federal court. Once in court, the case may be handled as an individual suit or as part of a class action. The court, in turn, in handing down a decision to, say, grant benefits, can affect agency policy for a group ranging from one to thousands of people, and each court can, of course, hand down a decision which embodies a different interpretation of the law. The cost of litigating SSDI claims and the enormous commitment of resources to the disability appeals process, stemming from inefficiencies in the determination and appeals process, were of particular interest to the President's Private Sector Survey on Cost Control.

ensure that it is structured efficiently and that actions are channeled in a way that advances the overall goals of the SSDI system.

To date, legislation has dealt, to a greater or lesser degree, with the work incentive problem for those on the rolls. Beginning in 1960 with the introduction of special SSI payments to those who work despite severe impairment, such legislative actions have been designed to reduce the financial barriers to return to work. To a lesser degree, legislation such as the tighter cap on family benefits, introduced in 1980, has tried to deal with the work incentive problem for the *potentially* disabled, those who are working despite severe impairments. The combination of declining labor force participation and a growing recognition of the importance of labor market participation by the disabled to the well-being of all Americans suggests that work incentives—broadly construed to include incentives for training, education, therapy, and return to work—will be an increasingly important public policy issue in the years ahead.

Where there is a general paucity of legislation and public debate is on the question of how the existence and shape of SSDI affect the size of the potentially disabled population, as distinct from the beneficiary population. Ensuring that the potentially disabled—those with severe enough impairments to be found eligible for benefits and who are nevertheless working—stay at work and do not drop out of the labor force just because of the availability of SSDI is only part of the problem of controlling SSDI, and it is the part generally addressed in the economics literature on work incentives. The other part of the problem is ensuring that the nature of the system does not inadvertently add to the size of the potentially disabled population. This would be the natural by-product of failing to provide appropriate incentives for preventing disability, or, more accurately, those things associated with disability—illness, accident, disease, limited or nondiversifiable job skills, and limited labor market options. In this regard, the grading of premiums according to risk characteristics (such as smoker/nonsmoker) and the grading of benefit rates or duration according to recovery characteristics are worthy of investigation. The importance of prevention as an area of future public policy concern is highlighted by the fact that there are already forces at work to increase the potentially disabled population, namely the aging of the population and the trend toward higher retirement ages under federal programs such as social security.[38]

Ultimately, the goal of efforts to manage and control SSDI, or to control the adverse effects of SSDI on the choices made by workers and beneficiaries, is to reduce the aggregate cost of disability and thereby improve the well-being of society.

CONCLUSIONS

In this paper, I argue that to properly understand recent legislative developments in SSDI and to appreciate the difficult public policy issues that are likely to lie ahead, it is fruitful to look at SSDI from an insurance perspective. What exactly is the system insuring against, how is supply organized, and in what ways does the system influence the choices people make, whether as workers, beneficiaries, public suppliers, or providers of claims-related services? By focusing on efficient "contract design," the insurance perspective links issues of incentives and benefit adequacy with often neglected issues of administration and enforcement. It recognizes the common interest of the working and disabled populations in spreading the risk associated with income loss due to disability and minimizing the aggregate cost of disability.

Some policy makers have been reluctant to view SSDI as an insurance program, where incentives are seen to be a critical aspect of the affordability and desirability of the public program. This, no doubt, is a reflection of the system's historical development. As originally conceived, SSDI was fashioned as an "early retirement" program. Benefits were made available only to workers aged 50 and older who became permanently and totally disabled, and were calculated in precisely the same way as retirement benefits—based on past earnings in covered employment averaged over a certain number of years.

---

38. It is interesting to note that the Social Security Amendments of 1983 (sec. 201 of P.L. 98-21) mandate a study by the Department of Health and Human Services on the impact of increasing the retirement age on those people who, because they are in physically demanding jobs or poor health, cannot extend their work lives. The issue of concern is whether the SSDI program can or should accommodate this population.

Because of the age limitation and the strict definition of disability in the original law, the eligible disabled population was not unlike the elderly population, with an extremely low probability of returning to work once having quit or lost work.

But a lot has changed in the past thirty years, not only our ability to diagnose, evaluate, and treat impairments once thought totally or permanently disabling, but also—with the help of economists and other researchers—the way we think about "disability." In addition, the beneficiary population being served by SSDI has changed a great deal. A program once serving a quarter of a million disabled workers aged 50 and older is now serving almost four million Americans of all ages, including disabled workers and their families. Some 25 to 30 percent of those disabled workers are under 50 years of age. Prevention of illness or accident, and recovery, rehabilitation, and work now carry more potential benefits—and their absence carries higher costs—than ever before.

The time is right for both researchers and policy makers to take a fresh and critical look at the SSDI program from an insurance perspective. The challenge facing researchers is to develop a consistent overall framework for analyzing disability and the disability insurance program that translates into a coherent set of policy options that addresses the problems faced by policy makers. The challenge facing policy makers is to provide an affordable, enforceable, and valuable insurance product for the nation's workers and disabled persons.

3 · LABOR SUPPLY INCENTIVES AND DISINCENTIVES FOR DISABLED PERSONS

Jonathan S. Leonard

If one accepts the desirability of a federal program such as Social Security Disability Insurance (SSDI) that provides income to disabled persons, there are still a number of difficult questions to be faced concerning the design of such a program. Chief among these in recent debates has been the trade-off between equity and efficiency. Equity considerations may call for the state to provide some income to disabled persons who become poor so that they may keep what is left of body and soul together. It is, however, generally not possible to perfectly differentiate those who cannot work from those who can. Indeed, whether out of desperation or out of choice, some impaired individuals work while others with the same medical diagnosis do not.

The crux of the matter is that disability is not simply a medically defined condition, but depends rather on an array of psychological, sociological, and economic factors. A person who perceives himself or herself as disabled may thereby become disabled. A person who is perceived by others as disabled may thereby be disabled. And a person who finds greater economic returns to disability than to work may not struggle so hard to work. This need not be a question of fraud or dissembling, but merely of adapting to the given incentives. This paper will focus on estimates of how people have adapted their

I thank John Bound for his comments.

work and labor force decisions to the incentives embodied in the social security disability system.

The efficiency considerations come into play at two levels. As income is provided for disabled persons, some who would have worked will no longer do so, and in some cases the people taking advantage of disability income will not truly be disabled. Providing disability income to the able-bodied is not only an inefficient waste of resources, it also undermines the legitimacy of the program. While this case is clear-cut, the second is more difficult. Since disability is not a medically defined yes-or-no state, but rather a continuum that depends on the economy and society as much as on the individual, a generous policy might expand the definition of disability and extend benefits to a greater proportion of the population. As it did so, however, we would find a decreasing proportion of people working, and so less income produced that could be redistributed. Hence we are faced with the trade-off between equity and efficiency, which at base must always remain a value judgment. All that an economist can hope to do is provide those responsible for policy with some idea of the magnitude of the trade-off. As the SSDI program is liberalized in terms of eligibility and benefits, what do we expect to happen to the beneficiary rolls and to labor force participation?

There have now been a few studies on this question, and they agree on the direction, but not the magnitude, of the effect. It is safe to say that we have not developed as full an understanding or consensus on this question as on the related labor supply questions of the effect of the minimum wage, of unions, of social security retirement pensions, of income and payroll taxes, or of various other welfare programs. The studies have, however, been of considerable use in drawing attention to the labor supply effects of SSDI, pointing out the link between the growth of SSDI beneficiary rolls and the decline of labor force participation rates, and in establishing some estimates of the range within which the true labor supply effect of social security disability is likely to fall.

Before delving into details, we should recognize that the question itself presents a formidable technical challenge. There are essentially three methods of trying to determine the labor supply effects of SSDI, which differ according to the nature of the data used—time-series, cross-section, and longitudinal (a pooled time-series of cross-sectional observations). We shall consider each in turn.

Consider the case in which the simple conception of disability apparently embodied in early SSDI legislation is true: disability is exogenous and the disabled cannot work. Also, make the extreme assumption of perfect screening: those who can work cannot receive SSDI. In a time-series analysis, we would expect to find no relation between SSDI benefits per beneficiary and the number of beneficiaries, nor between the number of SSDI beneficiaries and labor force nonparticipants. Under the assumptions that disabled persons cannot work and the able cannot receive SSDI benefits, there can be no labor supply effect. Disabled persons cannot work, so their labor supply is zero. The SSDI program cannot reduce this. At the other end, the able-bodied cannot receive SSDI benefits, so changes in SSDI benefit levels cannot affect the beneficiary or labor force status of those able to work. These assumptions are simple and may appear naive, but they appear to have had a strong influence on policy until recent years. More important, they are in principle testable. In contrast to the more highly refined econometric tests based on cross-section and longitudinal data, the tests based on time-series are more directly accessible and do not impose as much structure on the data.

The problem faced by those who would claim that SSDI has no labor supply effects is to explain away figure 3.1 (and the associated data series in table 3.1), reproduced from Parsons (1984a). This is the simplest sort of analysis because it does not begin to control for the other possible factors that may affect both SSDI beneficiary rates and labor force participation rates. Correlation does not prove causation, but since 1957 the labor force participation rate of 45- to 54-year-old males appears to fall as the proportion of these men on SSDI beneficiary rolls rises. If all SSDI beneficiaries could not work, we would expect no relationship between the likelihood of participating in the labor force and the levels and availability of SSDI benefits. Moreover, we know that SSDI beneficiaries, according to regulation, must be out of the labor force, so the rise in SSDI beneficiaries could by itself explain much of the decline in labor force participation rates. While other factors may explain other parts of the decline in labor force participation rates, no one has shown the dominance of such factors. The labor force nonparticipants report negligible liquidation of pri-

FIGURE 3.1
Nonparticipation in the Labor Force
and Social Security Disability Recipiency,
Males 45–54, 1947–82.

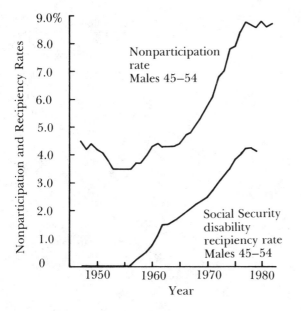

Source: Reproduced from Parsons 1984a.

vate assets, and receive little financial support from relatives. It is
difficult, then, to point to one other factor that has played as large a
role as SSDI benefits in explaining the decline of labor force participation among prime-age males.

REVIEW OF PAST STUDIES

TIME-SERIES STUDIES

A number of studies have pursued this type of time-series analysis,
some also controlling for other variables. Among the first was that of
Gastwirth (1972), who points to the connection noted above between

TABLE 3.1

Data Series for Figure 3.1

Year	Labor Force Nonparticipation Rate of Males 45–54 (%)	Social Security Disability Rate of Males 45–54 (%)[a]
1947	4.5	.00
1948	4.2	.00
1949	4.4	.00
1950	4.2	.00
1951	4.1	.00
1952	3.8	.00
1953	3.5	.00
1954	3.5	.00
1955	3.5	.00
1956	3.5	.00
1957	3.7	.23
1958	3.7	.36
1959	4.0	.51
1960	4.3	.76
1961	4.4	1.13
1962	4.3	1.54
1963	4.3	1.54
1964	4.3	1.63
1965	4.4	1.79
1966	4.7	1.96
1967	4.8	2.11
1968	5.1	2.25
1969	5.4	2.37
1970	5.8	2.51
1971	6.1	2.75
1972	6.8	3.03
1973	7.0	3.27
1974	7.8	3.50
1975	7.9	3.84
1976	8.4	4.03
1977	8.8	4.23
1978	8.7	4.25
1979	8.6	4.17
1980	8.8	n.a.
1981	8.6	n.a.
1982	8.7	n.a.

Source: Reproduced from Parsons 1984a.

[a]The ratio of male disability recipients 45–54 years of age to the number of males 45–54 years of age.

the mysterious drop in the labor force participation rate of prime-age males and the increase in the proportion of men receiving disability benefits. As possible explanations of the increase in beneficiaries, he suggests (but does not test) the change in the disability laws that allowed people under age 50 to receive benefits, the 1965 amendment that changed the definition of disability from "permanent" to "expected to last 12 months," and increasing awareness of the program's existence. Using additional information on the labor force participation of disabled persons who received no public assistance, Gastwirth considers that, at most, 78.3 percent of newly eligible beneficiaries would have previously been in the labor force. Using Nagi and Hadley's (1972) estimate that 45 percent of applicants for disability benefits have a high work motivation, Gastwirth assumes that at least 55 percent of newly eligible beneficiaries would previously have been in the labor force. After roughly bounding the labor supply effect in this manner, Gastwirth concludes that "about half of the observed decline in male participation rates during the 1960s may have resulted from changes in the disability laws."

Gastwirth's upper bound is questioned by Swisher (1973), who argues that among the severely disabled, 4 percent of the beneficiaries and 44 percent of the nonbeneficiaries were in the labor force, so at most 40 percent of severely disabled new beneficiaries were likely to have previously been in the labor force. The difference between these two estimates may be taken as an indicator of the importance of disability definition and screening in affecting the labor supply effect of SSDI.

The connection between SSDI and labor force nonparticipation is reinforced by Siskind (1975). Using simple cross-tabulations, he shows that increases over time in SSDI eligibility could help explain both the absolute decline in participation and the differentially more severe decline among black men.

These early studies simply compare increases in SSDI beneficiary rolls with declines in labor force participation. The importance of economic factors in this relationship is examined more explicitly by Hambor (1975). In the context of economic decision making, one expects an increase in SSDI applicants when there is a decline in alternative economic opportunities. This could explain Siskind's observation of a higher application rate among blacks, as well as Hambor's finding that the applicant rate increases when the unemployment rate increases. It is important to note that if all SSDI applicants were out of the labor force in any case, there would be no reason to expect them to respond at all to unemployment rates. Yet when the difficulty of finding a job increases, applications for SSDI also increase.

I estimate the separate effects of macroeconomic cyclical fluctuations and of SSDI program characteristics on SSDI beneficiary levels and on labor force participation (Leonard 1979). In time-series regressions of labor force participation rates on SSDI beneficiary rates and cyclical indicators, labor force participation rates fall by 1.4 to 1.9 percentage points for each 1-percentage-point increase in the beneficiary rate (the ratio of social security disability beneficiaries to population), even controlling for the business cycle effect.

In a separate set of time-series regressions of labor force participation rates on average SSDI benefit levels, average earnings, and trend and business cycle indicators, I find that a $100 increase in average real monthly SSDI benefits reduces nonwhite male participation rates by 4 percentage points and white male participation rates by 3 percentage points, controlling for cycle and trend (Leonard 1979).

It seems then that the fruitful question to ask is not whether the SSDI program has affected labor supply, but rather how great a reduction in labor supply the SSDI program has caused. The best estimates of this come from econometric analyses of cross-section data on individuals, but the best are not without flaws.

To develop an appreciation for the challenge faced by those who would estimate the labor supply effect of SSDI in cross-section data, consider the following prototypical model:

$$LFP_i = f(W_i, NW_i, x_i) \tag{3.1}$$

where

W_i = the expected income if the ith individual is in the labor force,

NW_i = the expected income if the individual is out of the labor force, including expected SSDI benefits, and

x_i = a vector of other individual characteristics.

The essential problem in estimating such a function is that by definition W_i is unobservable for labor force nonparticipants and NW_i is unobservable for labor force participants. In other words, any sample at a point in time is composed of participants for whom we observe W_i, but not NW_i, and nonparticipants for whom we observe NW_i but not W_i. Yet theory tells us that the participation decision will depend in part on W_i relative to NW_i. The econometric problem, then, is to develop adequate controls for W_i and for NW_i when they are not directly observed.

Economists discuss the labor supply issue in terms of elasticities. The elasticity of labor supply with respect to wages is the proportionate change in labor supply divided by the proportionate change in wages. Responses greater than one are termed elastic, and those less than one, inelastic.

PARSONS

The estimates of the labor supply effect of SSDI that have perhaps drawn the most attention are those of Donald Parsons (1980a). Parsons assumes that an individual chooses to be out of the labor force if the expected utility of being in is less than that of being out. Labor force participation equations are estimated as a function of SSDI benefits, welfare benefits, wages, a mortality index, age, and unemployment.

Parsons's estimates are based on a subsample of 3,219 men from the National Longitudinal Surveys (NLS) who were 45 to 59 years old in 1966. There are a number of points that deserve attention concerning both the characteristics of this sample and the specification of the model. Wages for 1966 are used as a proxy for expected labor force earnings in explaining labor force participation during a survey week in 1969. Individuals without a reported 1966 wage are presumably eliminated from the sample, so, as Parsons notes, individuals with long-term labor force absences will be under-represented. These are likely to include the most severely disabled who in turn might be less responsive to economic forces. If so, this will tend to bias upwards Parsons's estimate of responsiveness. However, most of the empirical evidence suggests more disabled persons are also more responsive to potential SSDI benefits. Also among the long-term nonparticipants will be long-term SSDI beneficiaries, whose behavior may differ from more recent beneficiaries, given changes in the rigor of program screening. Parsons also notes that the use of prior wage rates is a misspecification since expected labor force earnings are the appropriate variable in his model. In particular, for those whose health declined since 1966 (the 1969 disabled persons most likely to be in the sample), the 1966 wage will overestimate the real wage expected in 1969. Considering the chances that such a person becomes unemployed, earnings will be further overestimated. For those disabled people who are more likely to be out of the labor force, Parsons will report a wage that is too high. This by itself will lead to an underestimate of the response to expected earnings, but is partially controlled for by Parsons's mortality index.

A crucial problem faced by all studies of disability is constructing a measure of health and disability. It is possible that a prime-age male might seek to justify being out of the labor force by exaggerating ill health or disability. In a clever approach to this problem, Parsons uses a variable that is presumably not subject to such self-serving distortion: death. Mortality from 1969 to 1976 is used as a proxy for 1969 health status. However, as I earlier show (Leonard 1976), there is substantial attrition in the NLS sample for reasons other than death, but which may be correlated with health. Presumably, individuals who disappeared from the NLS sample after 1969, but were not reported to have died, are included in Parsons's 1969 sample with a mortality index of zero, which will bias toward zero the coefficient on the mortality index.

Parsons estimates probit equations for labor force participation as a function of the replacement ratio and other variables. The chief variable of interest is the replacement ratio, the ratio of monthly potential social security benefits to the 1966 hourly wage rate. The measurement problems surrounding potential SSDI benefits can be severe, although much of this is due to the limitations inherent in the NLS data rather than to Parsons's handling of the data. First, one would like to know what income is expected conditional on being out of the labor force, but SSDI and welfare benefits, even together with the mortality index, can only proxy for this expected income. Second, because of data limitations, Parsons constructs his measure of SSDI benefits by using 1966 hourly wages as a measure of average monthly earnings. However, average monthly earnings actually depend on much more than hourly wages during one year. The actual benefit computation formula is quite complex. SSDI benefits depend on family structure as well as on average monthly benefits. Since these other factors are not taken into account, Parsons's SSDI benefits measure can only differ from his wage measure by nonlinearity in the SSDI benefit schedule. The consequence, as Parsons notes, is that his wage and SSDI benefit levels are highly correlated, forcing him to enter these variables in ratio form, but this ratio is purely a function of the wage and of the progressivity of the benefit schedule.

The schedule is progressive; benefits do not increase as rapidly as wages. So the replacement ratio, as measured by Parsons, should fall with wages. Parsons's result may then be interpreted as saying that low-wage men are more likely to drop out of the labor force, and this is more likely in a case of ill health. Since there is, as near as I can tell, no variation in Parsons's replacement ratio conditional on a given wage, hypotheses concerning the effect of the replacement ratio cannot be differentiated from those concerning the wage. Again, part of this problem is unavoidable in the NLS data set since it does not include an earnings history that could be used to construct a better measure of average monthly earnings, and so of benefits.

John Bound (1985) reports a replication of Parsons's specification using a sample of *nonapplicants* from the 1972 Social Security Survey of Disabled and Non-Disabled Adults. Although some of these people may have dropped out of the labor force in anticipation of applying for SSDI benefits, it is unlikely that a majority would do so. In other words, since the sample is restricted to people who have not applied for SSDI, it is unlikely that much of their nonparticipation in the labor force could be explained by the SSDI program benefits. Yet Bound finds a 0.88 elasticity of labor force nonparticipation with respect to the replacement ratio among the sample of nonapplicants. This raises the strong suspicion that the constrained replacement ratio is picking up the effect of other welfare programs or of low wages.

Parsons's main finding is that the elasticity of nonparticipation with respect to the replacement ratio is 0.63, and that it varies greatly with the mortality index. Importantly, these cross-section estimates can in turn explain much of the decline in the labor force participation rates of 45- to 54-year-old men, and differences between the decline in labor force participation of blacks and whites.

HAVEMAN AND WOLFE

In contrast to the large labor supply elasticity estimated by Parsons, Leonard, Halpern and Hausman (to be discussed later) and others,

Haveman and Wolfe (1984a) and Haveman, Wolfe, and Warlick (1984) estimate a relatively inelastic labor supply response to SSDI benefits.

Haveman and Wolfe's criticism of Parsons embodies two points. First, Parsons's results are not robust to different specifications estimated in a different sample. Neither expected disability transfers nor expected wages are measured precisely, among other problems. Second, even if one still accepts a positive correlation between expected benefits and becoming a beneficiary (which Haveman and Wolfe's results cast doubt on), correlation does not prove causation. Other factors, which Haveman and Wolfe do not test, such as work-related injuries, spouses' earnings, eligibility standards, and private pensions, may have changed over time to affect labor supply and/or beneficiary rates.

Haveman and Wolfe's estimates are based on a 741-person subsample of 45- to 62-year-old men in the 1978 Michigan Panel Study of Income Dynamics (PSID). At this stage it becomes important whether one is asking what determines labor force withdrawal or what determines SSDI application or beneficiary status. Haveman and Wolfe seem to focus on the first question. This is important because it means they do not attempt to estimate the responsiveness of SSDI applications to SSDI benefits, but rather they estimate the labor force participation response to nonwork income flows. As they note, done correctly this would be an onerous task given the multiplicity and complexity of programs providing welfare and disability income, each with its own eligibility regulations and benefit calculations. Rather than attempt the difficult task of estimating separate responses to each welfare or disability program, Haveman and Wolfe estimate a single grouped response to a set of disability-related transfers including SSDI, Supplemental Security Income (SSI), veterans' disability benefits, other disability pensions, and for disabled persons a share of other welfare and help from relatives. The cost of this procedure is that having lumped these disability transfers together, one cannot untangle their respective roles in explaining the results. In particular, these estimates do not tell us directly how people respond to the SSDI program.

Haveman and Wolfe's econometric model follows Lee (1979); it assumes that the errors in the income flow equations are uncorrelated either with each other or with the participation equation error.

In addition, as Haveman, Wolfe, and Warlick note (1984, 90), for this model to be identified, some variable that determines labor market earnings or disability transfers must be excluded from the direct determinants of labor force participation. While desirable in theory, this may not be obtainable in practice. As is typical of such models, identification is achieved either by the seemingly arbitrary exclusion of variables from some equations, or by functional form.

The first step in Haveman and Wolfe's method is to estimate a probit equation of labor force participation that is not a function of expected incomes in and out of the labor force. Most of the variables in this equation are insignificant. Those people claiming severe long-term disability who are aged 59 to 62, Protestant, unmarried, and veterans are significantly less likely to be in the labor force. This equation is then used to correct for sample selection, following Heckman (1976), in both earnings and disability income equations. In both cases these selectivity correction variables turn out to be insignificantly different from zero. One potential advantage of using the PSID is the possibility of using past earnings or wages in estimating potential earnings, but Haveman and Wolfe do not use this information.

The final step is the estimation, again, of a probit equation for labor force participation, this time as a function of the imputed expected income flows. These results are reproduced in table 3.2 from Haveman and Wolfe. Haveman and Wolfe find an elasticity of labor force participation with respect to disability income that ranges from −.0205 in a replication of Parsons's specification down to −.0056 with the addition of dependent benefits, additional controls, selectivity corrections, and eligibility adjustments. Haveman, Wolfe, and Warlick (1984) find an extremely nonlinear response with much larger elasticities among the more disabled persons and those with lower earnings. Note that the calculation of elasticities is not always transparent. This is a very useful result in that it cautions against the use of simple linear models to capture widely varying behavior and gives us some feel for the wide range of estimated responses that can be found in a single specification in a single sample. In particular, given the highly nonlinear response, it is clear that the elasticity calculated at sample means (the result usually reported) need bear little relationship to the mean elasticity in the sample, or the mean elasticity of individuals on the margin of some hypothetical policy change.

TABLE 3.2
Probit Estimates of
the Labor Force Participation
of Men Aged 48 to 62

	Parsons (1)	H-W Replication (2)	Column 2 Specification with Split Replacement Rate (3)	Column 2 plus Inclusion of Dependent Benefits and Additional Controls[d] (4)	Column 2 plus Selectivity Correction (5)	Column 3 with Eligibility Adjustment (6)	Column 3 plus Selectivity Correction Eligibility Adjustment, and Additional Controls (7)
Constant	5.626	6.094	5.954	6.137	5.673	5.889	5.83
	(10.94)[a]	(4.97)	(4.42)	(4.79)	(5.53)	(4.68)	(5.20)
Price variables							
SSB/W	−.00542	−.00626	—	—	−.0032	—	—
	(−2.48)	(−1.59)			(−.85)		
SSBD/W	—	—	—	−.0017	—	—	—
				(−.43)			
SSB	—	—	−.0007	—	—	—	—
			(−.41)				
PSSB	—	—	—	—	—	−.0024	−.0012
						(−.87)	(−.48)
W	—	—	.022	—	—	.022	−.019
			(.57)			(.78)	(−.67)
WEL/W	−.00278	.00260	—	.020	.0014	—	—
	(−1.97)	(1.72)		(1.28)	(1.13)		

WEL	—	—	.0003 (.87)	—	—	.0004 (1.00)	-.0001 (-.31)
UR	-.835 (-3.13)	-.457 (-.73)	-.498 (-.79)	-.364 (-.31)	-.178 (-.31)	-.524 (-.83)	-.1858 (-.01)
Demographic variables							
Age	-.0639 (-7.15)	-.0683 (-3.09)	-.0700 (-3.18)	-.0700 (-3.03)	-.0643 (-3.47)	-.073 (-3.25)	-.0701 (-3.51)
Disability status[b]	-.944 (-8.21)	-2.008 (-9.88)	-2.017 (-9.89)	-2.080 (-13.78)	-2.331 (-13.46)	-1.621 (-3.32)	-2.54 (-4.99)
Elasticity of labor force participation with respect to social security benefits	-.030[c]	-.0205	-.0147	-.0069	-.0177	-.0067	-.0056
-2 × log likelihood ratio	1,301	143.6	141.0	141.5	264.0	141.6	272.0
N	3,219	741	741	741	796	741	796

Source: Reproduced from Haveman and Wolfe 1984a.

Notes: Data for 1969 in Parsons; for 1977 in H-W estimates.

[a] Asymptotic normal test statistic reported in parentheses.

[b] The constructed subsequent mortality index for Parsons; index of extent of reported disability for H-W.

[c] Parsons reports an elasticity of nonparticipation of .63, which is equal to the participation elasticity of -.030.

[d] The additional control variables added are: (1) a dummy variable where not married, no children = 1; (2) a dummy variable where married, no children = 1; (3) other household income; and (4) a dummy where long-term occupation is manager or professional = 1. The coefficients and t-values for these variables in the col. 3 specification are, respectively, -3.46 (-1.07); -.96 (-0.46); -.032 (-1.76); .151 (0.05). These coefficients and asymptotic t-values remain stable throughout the remaining runs reported.

An example from Haveman and Wolfe (1984b, 60) will help illustrate the importance of this point. They report that the elasticity of labor force participation with respect to expected disability transfer income is −.0005 in their simple model or −.0003 in their extended model. This appears to be, as they say, insubstantial at best. But the simulation results produced by Haveman and Wolfe (1984b, 61, table 5), using the very same estimates, dispel this notion. They report that a 20 percent change in expected disability income would elicit a 1.04 percent increase in the disability recipiency rate. This is an elasticity of 0.58. (See Bound 1985 for related arguments.) This is larger than the elasticity estimated by me (Leonard 1979), and only slightly less than Parsons's (1980a) own estimate of 0.63.

As Haveman and Wolfe's simulations clearly demonstrate, point estimates of an elasticity may be very misleading when dealing with a nonlinear response. In particular, those people with low earnings, in poor health, and older, are more responsive to expected disability benefit levels.

LEONARD

I have written two works on this topic. The first (1976) uses the same data set as Parsons—from the NLS—and finds that 30 percent of the variance in weeks out of the labor force in 1965 among men can be explained by variation in disability benefits, conditional on self-reported health, age, and family characteristics. This study also demonstrates (p. 89) the importance of sample attrition bias in the NLS (and presumably in similar longitudinal samples as well). Only 15 percent of men who disappear from the NLS sample between 1965 and 1971 are known to have died by 1971. The remainder of those persons who disappear from the sample tends to include more disability beneficiaries, more long-term nonparticipants, and more physically impaired men than does the full 1965 cross-section. In other words, where disability shows its strongest effect, and where labor force participation is lowest, the sample is truncated, biasing toward zero the estimated impact of health on labor force participation on longitudinal samples. If these sample dropouts are also among the most responsive to SSDI benefits—which is open to question—the estimated responsiveness to benefit levels will also be biased toward zero.

This early study is also of some use because it discards a number of other potential explanations of the decline in male—particularly black male—labor force participation rates. The first set of these may be termed dislocation models. First, single men typically have lower labor force participation rates than do married men. But at least between 1940 and 1970 there has been if anything a reduction in the proportion of black men over the age of 45 who are single (p. 14). A second dislocation argument for blacks is that the decline in agricultural employment could reduce reported labor force participation rates. However, the movement off the farms had been largely completed by 1960, whereas declines in labor force participation continued well beyond 1960 (p. 23). A third more general dislocation argument is that poor labor force participation among 50-year-olds today is the tail end of poor attachment among 30-year-olds twenty years ago. The empirical evidence, however, does not support this argument. The recent declines are a phenomenon affecting many age groups, and have not been explained by changes in marital status, structural unemployment, or some past decline in participation.

A second set of explanations uses family utility models to argue that the decline in husbands' labor force participation is merely the expected income effect from an exogenous increase in wives' labor force participation. However, marital status and wives' earnings have only a small and insignificant effect on male labor force participation. Moreover, the premise of the argument, that wives' labor force participation has increased, turns out to be true only for 45- to 54-year-old nonwhite women between 1965 and 1974.

By examining and discarding a number of competing explanations for the decline in male labor force participation rates, this early study sets the stage for a more refined analysis of the impact of the SSDI program on the labor force participation of prime-age males. In a subsequent study (Leonard 1979), I first calculate an upper bound on the possible labor supply effect. If all 45- to 54-year-old male SSDI beneficiaries had otherwise been in the labor force, then at most 66 percent of the 8.9 percentage point decline in nonwhite participation and 90 percent of the 3.7 percentage point decline in white participation from 1957 to 1975 could be attributed directly to the SSDI program. These may not, in fact, be true upper bounds since, as Parsons points out, with a high and uncertain probability of rejection among applicants, one might expect more than one labor force drop-out for each resulting SSDI beneficiary.

Using a sample of 1,685 men aged 45 to 54 drawn from the 1972 Social Security Survey of Health and Work Characteristics merged with social security beneficiary records and earnings histories, I estimate the labor supply effects of the SSDI program. Note that this sample over-represents disabled persons, so an elasticity calculated at the sample mean from a nonlinear specification may be an overestimate. This model is as follows:

$$SSDK = F(SSD, W, X) + e \qquad (3.2)$$
$$W = Zb + u \qquad (3.3)$$

where:
$SSDK$ = probability of being an SSDI beneficiary
SSD = expected SSDI benefits
W = expected labor market income
Z, X = vectors of individual background characteristics, and
u, e = error terms.

The major econometric problem is that a large proportion of the sample, the SSDI beneficiaries in particular, are out of the labor force and have no observable current wage. One might want to impute wages to this group, using a wage equation estimated for the subsample with observable wages, and correcting for sample selection bias following Heckman (1976). This method requires estimating the probability of observing a positive wage, but in this application this is nearly equivalent to estimating the probability of not being an SSDI beneficiary, which is what we are after in the first place. This approach, which does not arise in the original Heckman application because the probability of having an observable wage is not taken explicitly as a function of the expected wage, would require maximum-likelihood estimation of a nonlinear simultaneous system.

Note that to the extent that expected social security disability benefits are correlated with other expected disability or welfare benefits in a manner not controlled for by other exogenous variables, the estimated response here may be biased.

Since I am willing to leave the coefficient on W in the beneficiary equation unidentified, I can avoid the simultaneity problem. As in indirect least squares, I replace W by $Zb + u$ as in equation 3.4:

$$SSDK = F(SSD, Zb + u, X) + e. \qquad (3.4)$$

Note that the estimated coefficient on an element of Z, say Z_i, that is also an element of the vector X, will be the sum of the coefficient on the corresponding X_i in equation 3.2 plus the product of the coefficient on W in equation 3.2 times the coefficient on Z_i in equation 3.3.

Expected SSDI benefits are estimated as the product of de jure benefits, given eligibility and the probability of being eligible for benefits. Using a sample of recent applicants and assuming no sample selection bias, equation 3.3 estimates the probability of eligibility as a function of health and background characteristics. If applicants were more eligible than nonapplicants in ways not controlled for in our eligibility equation, then the estimated coefficient on SSDI would be biased toward zero in equation 3.3 because of overestimation of expected SSDI benefits among nonapplicants.

The data set includes the respondents' claimed knowledge of a social security program that pays disability benefits. We can take this knowledge as either endogenous or exogenous. If we impute positive SSDI benefits even to those who claim to be ignorant of the program, then equation 3.3 can be thought of in two ways. Either we have made the restrictive assumption that everyone knows about the program, or we are estimating the joint probability of knowing about and applying for the program. Alternatively, if positive expected benefits are imputed only to those who know of the program, then knowledge of the program is taken as exogenous, and we have a classical control group with which to test the effect of SSDI benefits on labor force participation.

Past wage is used to help infer current expected wage. The data set includes the social security earnings record, which reports annual earnings up to the maximum amount that is subject to social security taxes. I select the most recent set of positive past annual earnings and correct for quarter worked and inflation. The specification includes a binary independent variable set to one if the past wage was at the taxable ceiling, to correct for the truncation of this variable. To correct for health and disability status, I include a set of twenty-seven binary independent variables for specific health conditions.

I find that the social security disability program has had a large and significant effect in reducing labor supply. The elasticity of labor supply in response to expected SSDI benefits is found to be 0.35 in the results discussed below. Estimation of the model supports the hypothesis that labor force participation falls because more men become SSDI beneficiaries when expected SSDI benefits rise relative to wage income.

The key variable, SSDI benefits, is imputed in two steps. De jure benefits are calculated as a deterministic function of past wage history and number of dependents. The correlation between the calculation of de jure benefits and actual benefits received by beneficiaries is 0.81, since exact data on the date of disability determination are unavailable. To impute expected SSDI benefits, the calculated de jure benefits are multiplied by the probability of being eligible, which is estimated using a sample of recent applicants. This process is subject to criticism since the errors in the eligibility and beneficiary equations may be correlated. More than the usual degree of caution must be exercised in interpreting the coefficient on this variable—it measures the response not to dollar benefits but rather to expected benefits. Since eligibility and recipiency are positively correlated, the estimated coefficient on expected benefits may be positive even if, conditional on eligibility, dollar benefits have no true effect on being a recipient. An alternative approach would enter dollar benefits separately. On the other hand, eligibility is primarily a function of self-reported health, which should clearly influence the application and screening decisions.

Eligibility for SSDI benefits is determined by state agencies in a subjective process that takes account of age, education, occupation, and the degree of disability. Legally, total disability expected to last at least one year is the prerequisite. Ninety percent of the recipients in the sample report themselves totally disabled, as do 68 percent of the nonrecipients who are out of the labor force. For a sample of 45- to 54-year-old men who applied for SSDI between 1966 and 1972, health condition is obviously a prime determinant of eligibility. Another major factor is having established disability insurance coverage by having worked the required number of quarters in social security covered employment. So far, the provisions of the law seem to be borne out in actual practice. According to the law, race should not affect eligibility. That being nonwhite significantly decreases eligibility is either evidence of sample selection bias or measurement error, or else reflects the de facto application of the law.

I find that a $180 increase in yearly benefits will increase the proportion of SSDI beneficiaries in the population by 1 percentage point. This is equivalent to an elasticity of 0.35, a substantial response among men who are usually considered incapable of working. This specification can be interpreted as estimating the joint probability of knowing about and applying for SSDI benefits, and may underestimate the true response, since positive expected benefits are imputed to those who claim to be ignorant of the program. The same 1 percentage point increase in the proportion of beneficiaries is produced by a $105 increase in mean yearly benefits when the sample is limited to those who claim to know of the SSDI program. This corresponds to an elasticity of 0.44. This estimate is unbiased if knowledge of the program is taken to be exogenous. Spreading knowledge of the SSDI program is taken to be exogenous. It does not by itself seem to be a sufficient explanation for the growth in the beneficiary rolls. Even when the sample is limited to those who know of the program, those with higher expected benefits are more likely to be beneficiaries.

Similarly, the more one expects to be able to earn, the less likely one is to be a beneficiary. As past wage reaches the ceiling on social security taxable earnings, the probability of being a beneficiary approximates zero. The elasticity of beneficiary status with respect to having wages that surpass the ceiling is − 19.4. Below the ceiling, the probability of becoming a beneficiary drops by 1 percentage point with a 12 percent increase in the level of past monthly wages. The sharply decreased probability of becoming a beneficiary when past wages are at or above the ceiling may reflect the fact that a disabled white-collar worker can often continue working while an identically disabled blue-collar worker cannot, due to the physical demands of the job. The negative coefficient on years of schooling is taken as further evidence of the same effect.

The color of one's skin makes little difference. A higher proportion of black than white males are in the SSDI program, because blacks face poorer job opportunities and are in poorer health. If the economic position of blacks comes into line with that of whites, we expect equal proportions of blacks and whites to be beneficiaries.

These results indicate that the growth in the proportion of SSDI beneficiaries among prime-age males has been due to the liberalization of eligibility requirements, and to the increase in benefit levels relative to potential earnings. Declining job opportunities seem to be a plausible explanation for the program's accelerating growth during the 1970s, but not for the 1960s. It is possible that medical advances now allow many who would have died to live on, though disabled in some cases. However, given the increases in real income and real per capita health expenditures, it seems implausible to attribute the increasing proportion of beneficiaries in a given age group to deteriorating health. This question merits further research.

Do these estimated cross-section responses correspond to the observed changes over time? Half of the increase in the proportion of SSDI beneficiaries can be accounted for by applying the cross-section coefficients to time-series data. This in turn can explain about half of the decline in the labor force participation rate (LFPR), using previously described time-series regressions. Between 1957 and 1975, the average monthly benefit of new 45- to 54-year-old beneficiaries rose from $94 to $148 in real 1972 dollars. The real average monthly earnings of production workers increased from $374 to $437 during the same period. The percentage of all male workers with annual earnings below the taxable ceiling fell from 41.3 to 23.8. Over this period there have been seven jumps in the ceiling, so the annual percentage above the ceiling has not dropped smoothly. Changes in other variables have been negligible. For example, the percentage of persons who were married with spouse present inched up from 83.9 to 84.3.

Multiplying the changes over time in wages and benefits by the estimated coefficients implies a 1.8 percentage point increase in beneficiaries, more than half of the historical 3.5 percentage point increase for men of both races.

Over time, increases in beneficiaries have been matched more than one for one by decreases in labor force participants. Since a 1.8 percentage point increase in beneficiaries was calculated, applying cross-section coefficients to time-series changes, and since participation was estimated to drop by more than one point when the percentage of SSDI beneficiaries increased by one point, these results imply at least a 1.8 percentage point decrease in labor force participation. The actual decline from 1957 to 1975 was 4.2 points for men of all races, so I conclude that the growth of expected benefits relative to potential earnings can explain nearly half of the puzzling decline in LFPR.

While all econometric work is subject to criticism, and others have since estimated both considerably larger and smaller effects, the basic result that the growth of the SSDI program has caused a significant part of the decline in LFPR remains strong, in my judgment, even if one discards all of the cross-section evidence and simply focuses on the time series. The proportion of beneficiaries and of labor force nonparticipants have both increased. We know that beneficiaries must be nonparticipants, and we have no other compelling explanation of the increase in nonparticipants.

I also note (Leonard 1979) that the phenomenon of a falling LFPR in response to a disability insurance program does not appear to be unique to the United States. In Canada, the LFPR of 45- to 54-year-old men fell 2.3 percentage points between 1972 and 1979 (Statistics Canada 1972–1979), following the inclusion of disability insurance in the Canada and Quebec pension plans in 1970. Perhaps the most outstanding example of this sort is in the Netherlands, where disability insurance has reached crisis proportions. By 1977, 23 percent of all insured 50- to 54-year-olds, 31 percent of the 55- to 59-year-olds, and 42 percent of the 60- to 64-year-olds were beneficiaries of the Disability Security Act (Emanuel 1979, 10). (See also Burkhauser, chapter 10 in this volume.) Social insurance programs for disability seem to have reduced the LFPR among prime-age males in the Netherlands and Canada, as well as in the United States.

Other explanations of the decline in LFPR in the United States do not appear to be consistent with the data. In cross-section regressions, veteran status increases the probability of being out of the labor force, but the percentage of veterans among 45- to 54-year-olds has been declining since the 1960s as the bulk of World War II veterans passed through this age group. It should also be noted that both government employees' disability and private disability insurance programs reported unusual growth during the 1970s, contributing to the decline in LFPR.

The SSDI program has acted as an escape hatch out of the labor force for disabled men. The more generous the benefits and the poorer the labor market conditions, the more attractive the escape hatch. Reducing unemployment, improving rehabilitation efforts among partially disabled persons, and extending social security hospital in-

surance and supplemental medical insurance to disabled persons in
the labor force would all be humane ways of helping these men to
continue productive lives.

SLADE

Evidence of a strong work disincentive for older men under the SSDI
program has also been found by Slade (1984). Using a sample of men
aged 58 to 63 from the 1969 longitudinal Retirement History Survey,
Slade estimates the elasticity of nonparticipation with respect to potential SSDI benefits to be 0.81, and an even larger 0.90 when the
sample is limited to those with self-reported health limitations. For
nonparticipants, wages were imputed from a wage equation using a
sample selection correction. Potential SSDI benefits were calculated
using an earnings history. The replacement ratio—the ratio of potential benefits to potential earnings—has a negative and significant
coefficient in probit equations for labor force participation. Slade's
estimated elasticity of nonparticipation with respect to the replacement ratio is 0.81, larger than Leonard's (1979) and Haveman and
Wolfe's (1984a) and Parsons's 0.63 (1980a), but lower than Parsons's
1.80 (1980b). Surprisingly, Slade also finds that the interaction effect
of SSDI benefits with self-reported health is small. Slade has imputed
high potential SSDI benefits to the perfectly healthy who are in the
labor force and who presumably can expect to receive little if any
actual SSDI benefits, which would tend to bias his estimated response
toward zero, making the substantial positive response he finds even
more remarkable. Since his data set includes an earnings history, the
collinearity problem should be reduced, but estimates are only presented in the constrained replacement ratio form.

REJECTED APPLICANTS

An original approach to the question of the labor supply effects of
SSDI is to ask what happens to rejected applicants. The studies on
this issue report *average* behavior, and so are not directly comparable
to the previously discussed estimates of *marginal* behavior. Lando,
Farley, and Brown (1982) report that 32 percent of applicants were
rejected in 1980 for lack of insured status, and another 46.1 percent

failed medical screening. Both rates had risen since 1970. Both types of rejections offer insights into the screening efficiency and labor supply effects of SSDI.

In an early study, Treitel (1976) used internal Social Security Administration records, of a type unavailable to outside researchers, to follow male applicants initially denied benefits in 1967. Of the rejected applicants, 39.7 percent did not work at all in the four subsequent years, while 24.1 percent worked for twelve or more of the sixteen quarters. By 1973, 13.8 percent of these men had died, and 16.1 percent had reached retirement age. On the other hand, 36.2 percent reported social security earnings the previous year.

In preliminary work, John Bound (1985) has pursued this line of analysis, using the 1972 Survey of Disabled and Non-Disabled Adults and the 1978 Survey of Disability and Work. Bound limits his sample to men between the ages of 25 and 61 who had sufficient earnings history to qualify for SSDI. The rejections should then be on medical grounds, and the rejected applicants are presumed to be in relatively good health compared to beneficiaries. Despite the fact that to qualify for SSDI most applicants must have a history of working, Bound reports that only about half of the rejected applicants were working at the time of the surveys, and only two-thirds worked at some time during the previous year. Earnings for those who did work were on average less than half those of the able-bodied. Nearly all rejected applicants suffered a drop in real earnings, averaging about a third for those with any positive earnings at all.

These important findings paint a different picture of the labor supply effect of SSDI, one that should cause us to hesitate before accepting the results of more methodologically complex studies. If the screening process rejected only those who could work, we would expect the proportion of rejected applicants working to be similar to that of comparable nonapplicants. The inference drawn from estimates of large labor supply effects is that screening is imperfect. Many type I errors are made, with applicants called disabled even though they can work. The inference drawn from the experience of rejected applicants is that many type II errors are also made, with applicants called nondisabled even though they cannot work. Neither finding need contradict the other, and both indicate the difficulties of screening entry into the SSDI program.

In 1978, 4.25 percent of men between the ages of 45 and 54 were on SSDI, and Bound finds that 41 percent of rejected applicants in that age range were in the labor force. Bound then connects the type I and type II errors by arguing that medically rejected applicants are likely to be in better health than beneficiaries, so at most 41 percent of beneficiaries would be expected to work in the absence of SSDI. If we use Bound's estimate, the SSDI program can account for 1.75 percent of the 45- to 54-year-old men who would not otherwise have been out of the labor force, which is much below other estimates.

This type of calculation depends, of course, on the assumption that program stringency has not changed greatly over time. It will tend to underestimate labor supply effects if program stringency has increased over time. In this case, beneficiaries from earlier applicant vintages might be more capable of work than later rejected applicants. This approach also leaves as a puzzle why beneficiary rolls have been increasing and labor force participation rates falling. Perhaps information about the program has been spreading, or the stigma of applying has been reduced, so we have been approaching the steady-state beneficiary rate without any change in the underlying true disability rate.

OTHER STUDIES

Two early studies report a substantial impact of ill health on earnings and labor force participation. Both Luft (1975) and Scheffler and Iden (1974) find this result, but do not connect it directly with disability benefit programs. Treitel (1979a) notes the curious fact that the recovery rate among SSDI recipients has not increased even though the average age has declined. Holding health, occupation, and other background variables constant, he finds in a logit regression that high ratios of benefits to predisability earnings significantly reduce the probability of recovery, and argues that the SSDI program appears to function as an early retirement program for older middle-aged persons with severe medical impairments.

RISK AVERSION

The importance of uncertainty in influencing application for SSDI benefits has also been stressed in recent preliminary work by Halpern and Hausman (1984). They note that while the program has grown, it is still selective, with only 26 percent receiving SSDI benefits in 1972 among the 7.7 million adults between the ages of 20 and 64 who claimed they were either unable to work at all or unable to work regularly. Some disabled persons are not eligible for benefits, and others may be deterred because they expect their application for benefits to be rejected. According to Lando, Farley, and Brown (1982), the Social Security Amendments of 1977 may have played a role in reducing the number of applicants accepted, which in turn may have been instrumental in reducing the number of applicants. Disabled worker awards reached a peak in 1975 and subsequently fell. The decrease in total awards since 1975 has been brought about by lower acceptance rates at both the initial application and reconsideration stages, and has been accompanied by increasing appeals through the administrative law judge system. For example, initial allowances as a percentage of initial determinations fell from 51 percent in 1966 to 39.9 percent in 1975 to 21.9 percent in 1980 (Lando, Farley, and Brown 1982, 7).

An increasing number of people whose initial applications were rejected have appealed these decisions, so that by 1980, 35.7 percent of all successful applicants achieved their awards after initial rejection (Lando, Farley, and Brown 1982, 7). There are two important points here. First, even with a stable policy it would be quite difficult for a marginally disabled individual to predict with great accuracy his or her chances of receiving SSDI benefits were he or she to apply. Given the multistage nature of the determination and appeals process and the paucity of detailed information on the characteristics of those accepted or rejected at each stage, it is no easy task for an econometrician to estimate these probabilities. Second, policy has not been stable, and this has complicated the estimation problem; there is uncertainty about which regime is currently in force. Both forms of uncertainty are likely to affect potential applicants. This is particularly true when it is costly to apply, as it would be under the regulation that applicants be out of the labor force for five months (and then typically wait three months for an initial determination).

A more stringent determination program does appear to have reduced applications. As the initial allowance rate has fallen, the number of applications per 100,000 insured workers has fallen from a peak of 1,656 in 1974 to 1,173 in 1981 (Lando, Farley, and Brown

1982, 5). Halpern and Hausman extend the typical binary choice model of disability beneficiary status to include risk aversion on the part of potential applicants facing uncertainties of the determination process. This allows them to separate out two determinants of applications that were typically mixed together in previous studies: the level of benefits relative to wages, and the expected probability of being allowed onto the beneficiary rolls. Their study also differentiates the application decision from the determination process. Halpern and Hausman find that "the probability of acceptance has a significant, but not a particularly large, effect on the probability of application. Potential applicants seem more sensitive to the benefit level than to the probability of acceptance" (p. 6). In particular, their cross-section estimates of a 0.16 elasticity of applicants with respect to probability of acceptance is enough to account for most of the fall in applications between 1975 and 1981. On the other hand, they find a far stronger elasticity of applications with respect to benefits—equal to one; in other words, a 20 percent decline in benefits per beneficiary leads to a 20 percent decline in applications. The end result of a highly refined model embodying advanced econometric techniques to allow for risk aversion and uncertainty is that "the applications decision is a good deal more sensitive to benefit levels than to the probability of acceptance" (p. 41). While these are preliminary results from an ongoing study, and so are subject to revision, they do show evidence of a substantial labor supply response to changes in SSDI benefits.

Halpern and Hausman also echo an important methodological problem pointed out by Leonard (1979). A difficult problem that has yet to be fully resolved, it is that "the appropriate probit equation to correct for any sample selection bias (in the wage equation) is a reduced form equation for the probability of applying for SSDI. This equation, however, is a reduced form of the structural utility model which is estimated so that efficient estimation would require simultaneous estimation of the entire wage and utility model" (p. 30). It is worth noting that such a simultaneous estimation has apparently not yet been attempted.

The SSDI program is administered at the state level, but is federally funded; this leaves the states considerable discretion, and also questionable incentive to police entry into the program or to review the current disability status of beneficiaries, except for what is explicitly mandated or budgeted for by the federal government. There is significant and substantial variation across states in the SSDI application and beneficiary rates (Bound 1977; Lando 1979), part of which is correlated with cross-state variation in unemployment rates, sex, and race.

Marvel (1982) finds that the variation in applicant rates across states can be explained not only by variation in health status, but also by variation in SSDI benefit and income levels. Marvel also reports mixed evidence of the effect of program stringency on applicant rates. The denial rate has an insignificant impact on application rates in 1976 and 1977 cross-sections. However, once Marvel accounts for unobserved state-specific variables by taking first differences, the denial rate has a significant and substantial effect. In other words, the states that increased denial rates the most also experienced the greatest decline in application rates. Marvel concludes that "an important subset of potential SSDI beneficiaries reach a decision whether or not to apply for benefit states based on their economic circumstances and the probability of being certified as incapable of working" (p. 411), and suggests that benefits might be scaled "both with respect to severity of impairment and actual labor market earnings" (p. 412) to reduce the likelihood of attracting questionable applicants.

Parsons (1984b) rigorously models the SSDI screening process, which may be thought of in terms of Bayesian decision making and reducing type I and type II errors. Extending Marvel's analysis of cross-state variation, Parsons estimates that the elasticity of application rates with respect to the denial rate is -0.15 in the first year and -0.39 cumulatively after two years. In other words, a 10 percent increase in denial rates produces a 4 percent decrease in application rates after two years. Potential applicants respond not only to benefit levels but also to the stringency of the screening program. Parsons reaches the important conclusion that imperfect screening is costly to both the donor and the disabled person. Transfers intended for severely disabled persons are diverted to others when screening is imperfect, and aggregate expenditures on disabled persons may well be limited by inefficient screening—another version of Okun's leaky bucket. Parsons's conclusion is an important one for policy: "The recent controversy over the attempt to periodically re-examine those disability recipients most likely to have recovered work capability suggests that political limitations as well as economic and technological ones exist on the screening decision. Nonetheless it seems apparent that the combination of these limitations has had profound negative effects on the efficiency and level of social insurance for the disabled" (p. 39).

WHAT WE HAVE LEARNED

METHODOLOGICAL: HUMILITY BEFORE THE UNOBSERVABLE

For all their other differences, all the economic models of the labor force participation decision agree that the expected incomes in and out of the labor force are, in theory, important variables. In practice, the studies differ mostly on how these expected incomes are imputed. The central unavoidable problem is that we can observe neither the wages of those who are out of the labor force nor the SSDI benefits and other nonlabor income of those who are in the labor force. We can make noble attempts to estimate what a labor force participant would earn were he or she to enter the labor force, and what income a worker would receive were he or she to drop out of the labor force, but by their very nature such estimates extrapolate beyond what is observed and so are subject to more than the usual level of error. One may easily have reservations about the details of any particular technique, but it is worth recognizing that differences among the estimates are in large part a measure of the difficulty of the problem.

SUBSTANTIVE

All of the studies agree that disability transfer programs lead to some reduction in labor supply. Disability is then not a purely medically determined condition, but one that is conditioned by economic and other factors. A more generous disability transfer program will tend to draw some people out of the labor force. The most compelling evidence of the labor supply effect of the SSDI program is perhaps also the simplest: for each older male added to the beneficiary rolls over the last twenty-five years, roughly two men have dropped out of the labor force. More complicated studies of the elasticity of labor

TABLE 3.3

Labor Supply Effects
of Social Security Disability
on Males

Study	Data Set	Sample Size	Sample Analyzed	Results	
Parsons (1980a)	National Longi- tudinal Survey	3,219	Age 48–62 years in 1969	Elasticity of labor force nonparticipation	.63
Haveman and Wolfe (1984)	Panel Study of Income Dynamics	741	Age 45–62 years in 1978	Elasticity of labor force nonparticipation	.06–.21
Slade (1984)	Longitudinal Retirement History Survey	5,403	Age 58–63 years in 1969	Elasticity of labor force nonparticipation	.81
Leonard (1979)	Social Security Survey of Health and Work Conditions	1,685	Age 45–54 years in 1972	Elasticity of beneficiary status	.35

force nonparticipation with respect to SSDI benefits have produced
a wide range of estimates, summarized in table 3.3, which are comparable to the labor supply effects of other sources of nonlabor income
(see Danzinger, Haveman, and Plotnick 1981). The elasticity of nonparticipation with respect to the replacement rate has been estimated
by Parsons to be from 1.80 (1966) to 0.63 (1969). At the 8.8 percent
nonparticipation rate observed for 45- to 54-year-old men in 1977,
Haveman and Wolfe's (1984a) estimates of the elasticity of nonparticipation with respect to disability transfers range from 0.21 to 0.06.
Leonard's (1979) estimate of the elasticity of SSDI beneficiary status
with respect to SSDI benefits is 0.35. Efforts by Halpern and Hausman
(1984) to split this response up indicate that people have been more
responsive to the dollar amount of benefits than to the probability of
a successful application, although Marvel's and Parsons's tests across
states suggest that increased stringency in screening has reduced applicant rates.

SUGGESTIONS FOR FUTURE RESEARCH

Most of the recent studies of the labor market effects of the SSDI program have focused on 45- to 54-year-old men. While some of the most interesting behavior has occurred among this group, we know relatively little about the response of women or of younger men.

The studies discussed above focus on the decision to apply for SSDI benefits, or the decision to drop out of the labor force. The cost of an SSDI program depends not only on the number of beneficiaries but also on their duration on the rolls (keeping in mind the transfer of the older disabled persons to retirement rolls). Until recently, departure from SSDI and re-employment were rare, but little research has been done on the duration of beneficiary status. A natural analogy is to the hazard-rate models of unemployment insurance duration, in particular to a model with beneficiary duration determined by the competing risks of death and recovery (see Katz 1985).

The SSDI program itself provides a variety of benefits. The separate effects of the medical insurance component are likely to differ in important ways from those of the "cash" component, and merit further study.

The SSDI program is only one of a number of disability transfer programs. We know relatively little about the direct effects of such related programs as veterans and federal disability, state temporary disability, and private disability insurance, or about the interactions of these disability programs with workers' compensation, welfare, rehabilitation programs, affirmative action for disabled persons, or work redesign programs. Some of these other programs are discussed in other papers in this series, but the interconnections are not yet well understood. The administration of SSDI merits further research, in particular the incentives created for appeal during the adjudication process.

At a crude level, the policy options are to change benefit formulas or to change program eligibility and screening. Most of the research to date has focused on replacement rates. Most of the recent policy initiatives and political controversy have concerned the screening process. While benefit schedules could be adjusted to minimize the disincentive to work, the issue of replacement rates would probably be of little importance if the screening process could be improved to keep out undeserving beneficiaries and keep in the deserving.

4 · SOME LESSONS FROM THE WORKERS' COMPENSATION PROGRAM

John D. Worrall and Richard J. Butler

Introduced in 1911, workers' compensation (WC) is our oldest social insurance program. It is mandatory in forty-seven states and virtually so in the other three. The program has much in common with the unemployment insurance (UI) and Social Security Disability Insurance (SSDI) programs, but it differs from them in many important aspects. WC was paying benefits almost thirty years before the Old Age, Survivors, and Disability Insurance (OASDI), and over forty years before SSDI. Unemployment insurance did not appear until twenty-five years after WC (E. Berkowitz and M. Berkowitz 1984, 1985).

There is much that the WC system can teach us about U. S. disability policy. The program has survived for three quarters of a century and, despite serious political challenges, changing technology, and the introduction of a host of disability programs, it has thrived. The public policy issues confronting the SSDI program are similar to those that WC has dealt with, and continues to deal with, today. The litigious state of the SSDI program provides but one example of a public policy problem common to both programs.

The WC program must make disability determinations. Claim-

We thank the National Council on Compensation Insurance and the U.S. Department of Education for research support, and David Appel for helpful comments. Remaining errors are our own. The views expressed in this paper are not necessarily those of the National Council on Compensation Insurance or the U.S. Department of Education.

ants can be determined to be temporarily, or permanently partially, or totally disabled. Such determinations are made on different bases in the various states. The measurement of the degree of impairment or work disability, as well as its work relatedness, can result in dispute and litigation. The SSDI program, on the other hand, has a dichotomous disability determination: totally disabled (and hence a beneficiary if other requirements of the law are met), or not eligible for benefits. Again, the disability determination process has resulted in an SSDI program that has become increasingly litigious.

There are incentives for the principal actors in the WC system to litigate claims. The nominal costs of administering the WC system are higher than those of SSDI. Part of the reason for this lies in the nature of the WC program and its attempt to grapple with the difficult problem of permanent partial disability determination. The social security program has no such partial disability system. The disability determination process in WC is compounded by the requirement that the disability or impairment arise out of or in the course of employment. For the overwhelming number of cases, it is not difficult to establish whether an *injury* arose out of or in the course of employment, but for certain classes of claims such as occupational disease and "cumulative trauma," this requirement can be problematic.

The attribution of causality is crucial in answering questions as to who benefits and who pays. This can be seen from many perspectives. Consider a claimant who suffers an asbestosis-related disease. Is the claim to be made against a workers' compensation insurance carrier, or as an action against an asbestos manufacturer? Although the insurance carrier could be the same in both instances, they are frequently different. The amounts of money involved in any potential award are different, as are the level of the attorneys' fees in any settlement. Similarly, suppose a claimant is permanently and totally disabled and chooses not to file a workers' compensation claim, or is found, erroneously, to have a disability that did not arise out of or in the course of employment. That claimant could draw benefits under the SSDI program with the cost burden of disability shifted from the private to the federal "insurance" system. There will be incentives to file claims where they have the highest expected value. Some of these claims will be fraudulent.

The WC system is a true insurance program. Although it is a

state-mandated program, it is financed, in the main, through the private sector. The program is subject to the classic problems of adverse selection and moral hazard. The program administration and structure vary across the states. Self-insurance is permitted in some states, and can be contracted by individual firms or by groups. In twelve states, the state competes with private insurance companies and insures employers' WC risk. In six states, the state has established monopoly state funds and does not permit competition from private insurance carriers. In the states where competition is permitted, it is fierce. Workers' compensation insurance is big business. Over two million families may receive a WC indemnity benefit in a single year.[1] The current annual cost of WC insurance programs is nearly $25 billion a year. With over five hundred firms selling WC insurance, the 1982 combined market shares of the top four and eight sellers were only 24.4 and 38.4 percent, respectively.

Workers' compensation programs are the largest source of indemnity benefit payments to workers between the ages of 16 and 64 who are expected to be disabled for six months or more. WC payments are larger than veterans' payments to the same population and are fully one-third as large as transfer payments to that population under the Social Security Administration's (SSA) old age survivors disability and health insurance programs (OASDHI). Similarly, the WC medical payments made to or in behalf of the long-term disabled are one-third as large as those made under Medicare for the same target group (see Berkowitz and Hill, chapter 1 of this volume).

Almost six million people are injured on the job each year, of which 4.5 million require medical treatment only. The remainder receive indemnity benefits, and about 325,000 of those suffer permanent disability as defined in the WC laws. Some of these injured persons are added to the stock of all those with a work disability who attribute their disability status to a job accident or injury (Worrall and Appel 1985, 16). As of 1978, there were nearly two million people who attributed a work disability to such job-related injuries or occu-

---

1. In a recent cross-section, we found 1.7 million families receiving benefits in the month before interview. As most of the temporary total disability cases are of less than six weeks duration, we would observe only a fraction of these indemnity beneficiaries in a cross-section.

pational disease (Worrall and Field 1981; Worrall 1980). Many of these workers have had their lives disrupted, suffered serious trauma, and had their standard of living reduced. Their families, and society at large, have been affected by their disabilities. Five or six thousand workers die in job accidents each year, and although we cannot determine the exact number, others die of long-latency occupational diseases. Where do these workers, or their families, turn for help when they experience the trauma of job injury? If the system is operating as planned, they turn to the WC program.

Workers' compensation benefits consist of virtually unlimited medical cost coverage, as well as an indemnity benefit for workers whose injuries result in lost work time. In all states, indemnity benefits are paid after an injured worker has completed a "waiting period." This waiting period ranges from one to seven days, and is either three or seven in most states. If the injury is serious enough that the worker experiences a nonwork spell that extends through a "retroactive date," benefits are paid for the waiting period. Hence, lost work time cases that are for short duration do not receive indemnity benefits for the waiting period. Although our concern in this paper is with the more serious claims, the short duration claims are interesting in that there is clearly an incentive for claimants to extend the duration of their nonwork spells—first, beyond the waiting period to qualify for indemnity benefits, and second, beyond the retroactive period to partially replace wages lost during the waiting period.

Workers who suffer more serious job injuries or occupational diseases are also eligible for vocational rehabilitation services. Presumably, these services will restore such workers to the labor market. However, it is not clear that the financial incentives inherent in the WC system do not impede the successful use of vocational rehabilitation services. As with the SSDI program, successful vocational rehabilitation can mean the cessation of indemnity benefit payments (the SSDI payment is not an indemnity payment). Many of the longer duration temporary total disability claims become permanent partial disability claims. If the injured worker could receive timely and prompt vocational rehabilitation services, the duration of some of these claims might be reduced. However, consider the case of a claim that is litigated as to the extent of the permanent partial impairment. A worker has the possibility of accepting vocational (and medical) rehabilitation services, with concomitant speedy return to work. If the worker *perceives* that a more rapid return to work will result in a smaller permanent partial disability award, there is incentive to forego or underutilize such services. Similarly, consider the case of workers whose after-tax indemnity benefit replaces 100 percent of lost wages. Such workers can choose to accept vocational rehabilitation services and return to work, or forego such services, extending their nonwork spells at no financial cost to themselves. SSDI beneficiaries considering VR services have had to face similar incentive issues, and in addition, before the Disability Amendments of 1980 (P.L. 92–265), they risked losing their medical coverage for a period of time if they returned to the labor market and suffered a relapse. We should expect to see SSDI beneficiaries who have low percentages of their predisability wages replaced by SSDI benefits using vocational rehabilitation services as a vehicle for exit from the SSDI rolls.[2]

As this brief introduction indicates, there are a host of incentive issues in the WC system that are present in the other social insurance programs. Evidence has recently begun to accumulate that the level of indemnity benefits affects both claim frequency and the duration of claims. As with SSDI and UI, the number of claimants is not independent of benefit levels. We strive to set benefit levels that are adequate to protect injured workers and their families, but we must accept the possibility that the benefit levels we choose may affect the risk-bearing behavior of employees and the provision of safety by employers.

Workers' compensation, like UI and unlike SSDI, is experience-rated.[3] Very small firms have a nominal premium price that reflects the expected accident and claims experience of all firms in the same line of business. This beginning price, called the manual rate, can be adjusted downward in response to competition. These adjustments take many forms, with the payment of dividends to policyholders and price deviations on the part of insurers being two of the more common. Approximately 85 percent of firms in the U. S. economy are

---

2. This is what M. Berkowitz et al. (1982) find in their examination of the SSDI beneficiary rehabilitation program.

3. See National Council on Compensation Insurance 1981 for an excellent introduction to experience rating in WC. We are simplifying considerably in our discussion of the topic.

manually rated only, but these firms employ less than 15 percent of those who work. The remaining 15 percent of firms, employing 85 percent of those employed, are experience-rated. The degree of experience rating varies directly with the size of the firm. The largest firms that are perfectly experience-rated are referred to as self-rated.

The beginning nominal premium of the self-rated firms, which can be and is adjusted by market forces, reflects only their own actual (and hence expected) experience. Firms in between these two extreme cases have their manual rate modified based upon a weighted average of their actual and expected loss (i.e., claims cost) experience. The weight, which is zero for the actual experience of manually rated firms, and one for self-rated firms, is a function of firm size. Three years of experience are used to calculate the modification factor used to adjust manual rates to reflect experience rating. As premiums vary with firm size, the safety incentive *may* vary by firm size as well.

In the next section of the paper, we present a brief sketch of a model of employee choice and firm profit maximization, and examine the implications of the model for employee benefit application (claim filing) and employer safety provision.[4] Then we consider the source of the available evidence of the effect of benefit levels on these two behaviors.

EVIDENCE ON EMPLOYEE AND FIRM INCENTIVE RESPONSE

Suppose we are in world A. In this world, employers and employees can bargain costlessly, and they both have full information. There is no government in this world, and no WC insurance. Labor markets in world A are perfectly competitive, with perfect factor mobility at zero cost. Workers in world A can derive income from two possible states, an injured state and a noninjured state, and they want to max-

---

4. The basic model is presented, either explicitly or implicitly, in Chelius 1977, Darling-Hammond and Kniesner 1980, Butler 1983, Butler and Worrall 1983, Ehrenberg 1984, and Ruser 1984. Oi (1973, 1974) provides an analysis of economics of safety, and Smith (1979) provides a review of the compensating differential literature. W. G. Johnson (1983) presents the labor supply model and finds little impact of WC benefits on the labor supply of permanently partially impaired workers in New York State.

imize their utility. They engage in choices over a set of firms offering various wage-income and probability-of-injury pairs. Workers in this world are risk averse, and have the same preferences. As a consequence, firms offering a higher probability of injury must offer a higher wage, a compensating differential to attract labor.

Firms in world A have different technologies. They can reduce the probability of injury, but only at an increasing cost of doing so. Firms are profit maximizers, providing for safety in such a way that the marginal benefit of safety provisions is equal to its marginal cost.

In world A, an optimal number of injuries takes place. As firms offer the profit-maximizing wage-injury probability pairs and workers select the utility-maximizing pair, a set of compensating wage differentials (for risk bearing) and injury rates result.

Now suppose we move to world B. Here we have introduced perfectly experience-rated WC insurance, but all else is identical to world A. World B employees would be indifferent between buying WC insurance themselves or having it provided via a payroll "tax." The optimal number of injuries would occur in world B, but the size of the compensating differentials required for risk bearing would be reduced. From the firms' perspective, the reduction in wages would be exactly offset by the cost of providing WC insurance; consequently, the firms' provision of safety would remain unchanged.

Finally, consider world C. In this world, the government mandates the provision of less than perfectly experience-rated WC insurance. Recall that approximately 85 percent of employers in the economy are manually rated, and some of the remaining 15 percent are less than perfectly experience-rated. The safety incentive is weakened for these firms. If the firms' reduction in wages induced by the introduction of less than perfect experience rating is greater than the firms' cost of providing such benefits, the marginal benefit of safety provision falls and the number of injuries could rise (Butler and Worrall 1983; Ehrenberg 1984; Ruser 1984). In world C, employee incentives for safety could dominate employer incentives, and the optimal number of injuries need not take place.

Obviously, the labor market is closer to the depiction in world C than in world A or B, but even world C is far from the reality of the U. S. labor market. Workers and employers cannot bargain costlessly. Workers and employers do not have perfect information about the probability of injury. Labor markets are not perfectly competitive (and some would argue that they do not even clear). Workers cannot sort themselves costlessly into different firms. We do not know that workers are paid fully compensating differentials for risk bearing. Violation of the assumptions given for the imaginary worlds above leads to real-world measurement problems we observe in WC insurance, as well as analogous problems with other disability programs. Consider the lack of fully compensating differentials as but one example.

We noted that in world C employee incentives could dominate and the optimal number of injuries need not take place (i.e., there could be "too many" injuries). Suppose, however, that with the introduction of perfect experience rating, the fall in wages, if any, was *less* than the cost of providing such benefits. Firms' safety provisions would no longer be unchanged (the world B case). Firms would have an incentive, through their increasing marginal costs of injury, to increase their level of safety provision.

Research has been conducted in an effort to determine if compensating differentials are paid for risk bearing. Smith (1979) reviews many of these studies, and Arnould and Nichols (1983), Butler (1983), Dorsey (1983), and Dorsey and Walzer (1983) provide recent examples of such studies that control for WC benefits. Each of the 1983 studies finds positive compensating differentials for risk bearing, and each finds a trade-off—as predicted by the model briefly discussed above—between WC benefits and wages. Dorsey had establishment data that enabled him to test for both compensating wage and compensating nonwage (fringe benefits) differentials. He finds both were paid. He also finds a one-to-one trade-off between WC costs and wages, which is also found by Dorsey and Walzer, using a different specification and data set. Butler, and Arnould and Nichols, find a less than one-to-one trade-off between WC benefits and wages, which is what one might expect given that the probability of injury is less than one. Both papers also find positive compensating differentials.

PROGRAM BENEFITS, INJURY RATE AND CLAIMS FREQUENCY, AND EXPERIENCE RATING

A number of economists have examined the relationship between benefit levels, waiting periods, retroactive periods, and claims frequency. The research has been done for cross-sections, time-series, and pooled cross-section time-series data, at the level of the establishment, industry (two- or three-digit Standard Industrial Classification [SIC]), or the state. Studies have been done within a single state and across states. Some of this literature is discussed by Worrall (1983), Ehrenberg (1984), and Worrall and Appel (1985). The principal, and virtually unanimous, finding of this research over different time periods and specifications, from both structural and reduced form equations, is that injury rates or claims frequency vary directly with WC benefits (Butler 1983; Butler and Worrall 1983; Chelius 1973, 1974, 1977, 1982, 1983; Ruser 1984; Worrall and Butler 1984; Worrall and Appel 1982). A brief review of several of these studies is instructive.

In Butler and Worrall (1983), we examine the frequency of temporary total and permanent partial disability claims over the period 1972–78. We choose that time frame because it followed immediately the *Report of the National Commission on State Workmen's Compensation Laws* (1972). This presidential commission report recommended substantial benefit increases be adopted by the state WC programs. Perhaps with an abhorrence of a potential federalization of the WC system, states implemented many of the commission's benefit recommendations.

Using the data from thirty-five states over the period under study, we estimate the parameters of a system of simultaneous equations, embedding an indemnity claims rate equation in the labor supply and demand system. We observe only those firms, in the aggregate, that insured through the private market, but we are able to correct for sample selection bias. We find that the average elasticity is 0.4 over the time period under study, i.e., for each 10 percent increase in real workers' compensation benefits, there is a 4 percent increase in the indemnity claims rate. *Real* benefit increases account for over half of the increase in temporary total and minor permanent partial disability claims, as well as one-third of the increase in serious permanent partial disability claims. We find this elasticity despite the fact that we control for the secular trend in injury rates and real benefits. We also find that workers are paid compensating differentials for risk bearing.

Ruser (1984) estimates the reduced-form parameters of an injury-rate equation. He includes wages and hours as right-hand-side variables, and, although his basic view of the problem is similar to ours, he decides not to instrument wages and hours. He estimates his parameters with generalized least squares. He pools cross-section time-series data from 1972 to 1979 on twenty-five three-digit SIC manufacturing industries over forty-one states. His injury-rate elasticity with respect to benefits is 0.35 for his preferred specification. Although his results are not strictly comparable to our own—he has only one benefit variable, and we have three, for example—they are in the same ballpark. More importantly, Ruser makes an explicit test of the impact of experience rating on the injury rate.

Reasoning that the degree of experience rating varies directly with firm size, Ruser maintains that the sign of an interaction variable for benefit and firm size in his reduced-form injury-rate regression should be negative if experience-rated firms have greater safety incentive than manually rated firms. His hypothesis is sustained. This finding is an important one that conflicts with a study by Chelius and Smith (1983) which finds no measurable impact of experience rating on firms' provision of safety.

Butler (1983) examines the injury-rate experience of fifteen industries within one state over a 32-year time span. He finds that a 10 percent increase in benefits leads to a 10 percent increase in injury rates (i.e., an elasticity of 1.0). The injury-rate response is stronger for more serious claims. We have updated this study (Worrall and Butler 1984), and find that the elasticities are actually greater than 1.0, being 1.7, 2.8, and 1.1 for permanent total, permanent partial, and temporary total disabilities, respectively. Butler (1983) also finds positive compensating differentials are paid for risk bearing. The size of the differential, $182 more in yearly wage income for each additional day of lost work time due to job injury, is substantially more than the daily wage over the sample period. This indicates that workers are being rewarded for both the pecuniary and nonpecuniary aspects of risk bearing, but, as Ehrenberg (1984) points out, it does not guarantee that differentials are fully compensating.

Chelius has done a series of studies of the injury-rate/benefit response. These have been cross-section and pooled cross-section time-series studies. We shall consider one of each. Chelius (1977) presents a cross-section study of relatively homogeneous industries in eighteen states. He estimates structural parameters for wage and injury-rate equations with two-stage least squares. He finds a positive, statistically significant relationship between workers' compensation benefits and injury rates, but he does not find positive compensating differentials. He does not report a benefit elasticity, nor does he report variable means; consequently, we are unable to compare his elasticity estimates with our own.

Chelius (1983) analyzes the injury-rate experience of two-digit SIC manufacturing industries over the 1972–78 time period in twenty-eight states. His pooled cross-section time-series result is that there is a statistically significant relationship between the percentage of income replaced by expected WC indemnity benefits and the industry's injury rate. He tests his hypothesis using as the dependent variable the ratio of the number of injuries per 100 full-time workers in a given industry, time period, and state to the number of injuries for like workers nationwide. His independent variables are the ratios of income replacements and waiting periods. No elasticities are reported.

Although the evidence is strong that there is either a reporting (claim filing) or true injury-rate response, or perhaps a combination of the two, as WC benefits rise, there is little evidence on the impact of benefit increases on an employer's safety incentive. As noted above, Ruser (1984) has found that the benefit/injury-rate response is weaker in large firms, i.e., larger (experience-rated) firms have a stronger safety incentive than smaller (manually rated) firms. However, Chelius and Smith (1983), using different data and specifications than those used by Ruser, are unable to find any experience rating effect.

Chelius and Smith assume that production technology *within* an industry is either homogeneous or varies randomly across states. They reason that the differences between the average injury rates of large experience-rated firms and small manually rated firms should vary with the state and industry WC benefit level. They do not, however, find such a relationship in their data.

Victor, Cohen, and Phelps (1982) and Victor (1983, 1985) have examined the employer's potential response to financial incentives. Victor develops a simulation model (e.g., 1985) based on the actual algorithm used to experience-rate firms in most states. He compares the safety incentive of experience-rated and self-insured firms. Using actual industry and state-specific examples, he demonstrates that the safety incentive arising from experience rating of "larger firms or small- and medium-size firms in more hazardous industries"

(p. 83) may be greater than for that of self-insured firms. Knowledge of the extent of the financial incentives provided to employers by the WC system is scant. Given the public policy implications, research in this area should be encouraged.

As with research on WC experience rating, studies of the duration of nonwork spells associated with job injuries are scant. Although there is rapidly expanding UI literature in these areas, we know of only three studies of hazard rate in the WC system, and these are limited to temporary total disability claims. In Worrall and Butler (1985) and Butler and Worrall (1985), we use individual claims data from a random sample of claimants for low back injury in the state of Illinois. The rates of transition from a disabled to a nondisabled state are modeled as a function of the wage, WC benefit, and other control variables. Although the sample was longitudinal, and some claims were monitored for three and a half years, not all of the low back claimants had completed their disability spells. In Worrall and Butler (1985), we use a proportional hazard model, and in Butler and Worrall (1985), we mix the scale parameter of a Weibull with an inverse generalized gamma (as a heterogeneity control). The principal finding of these studies is that the duration of disability varies directly with WC benefits and indirectly with the wage. The benefit elasticity is 0.2 when an explicit distribution of time is assumed (Butler and Worrall 1985). In Worrall et al. (1985), we pool micro data from twelve states to take advantage of state variation in benefits and wages.[5] The pooled state results are similar to the Illinois results. In the same study, we also use the Illinois sample to examine the benefit elasticities by age cohort, which range from 0.1 for low back claimants under 25 years of age to 0.4 for those who were 45 to 54 years old. The expected duration of a low back claim in the pooled state data ranges from twenty-three weeks for those under 25 years old to forty-two weeks for those who were 55 or older.

The duration of nonwork spells varies with the opportunity cost of time. The seriously injured worker, or SSDI beneficiary, may receive cash benefits from more than one source, although this possibility is seldom modeled explicitly.

---

5. Ehrenberg (1984) recommends this be done, as it has in the UI literature.

WORKERS' COMPENSATION AND RECEIPT OF MULTIPLE BENEFITS

During the period since World War II, we have witnessed an influx of women into the labor force, and a large increase in the number of families with multiple earners. As inflation has moved these families into higher tax brackets, the true replacement rates for workers' compensation insurance benefits may have been higher than the nominal replacement rates used in many research studies. This is because workers' compensation indemnity benefits are not taxed. Consequently, a nominal replacement rate of two-thirds of an individual injured worker's gross wage could result in a greater than two-thirds replacement of net family lost income.

During the 1960s and 1970s, we also witnessed an explosive growth in the size of disability income programs. To the extent that workers' compensation recipients were also receiving income from other programs, their "full replacement rate," i.e., their average weekly benefit from all sources divided by their pre-injury weekly wage, could also have been higher than their nominal workers' compensation insurance replacement rate.

Most disability income programs have as two of their explicit goals the adequacy and equity of benefits. The benefits offered by these disability programs serve as an incentive for benefit recipients to continue on the program rolls, and also as an inducement to new entrants. Failure to consider this phenomenon can lead to underestimates of program costs. Similarly, the failure to consider the joint benefits offered by multiple programs could lead to biased estimates of the strength of the incentives or disincentives offered by the collective set of programs.

Respondents to the 1978 Social Security Survey of Disability and Work were asked whether, during the month preceding the interview, any member of their families had received benefits from workers' compensation, social security, Supplemental Security Income, veterans' benefits, public assistance, unemployment insurance, civil service, Aid to Families with Dependent Children, and other benefit programs. In addition, if the benefits were received because of a disability, respondents were asked to indicate whether they themselves, or their spouse, their children, or another relative were the benefit recipient.

There were 837, 997 families with disabled persons and 795,819 nondisabled survey respondents, each with at least one family member who received workers' compensation benefits in the month prior to the interview. (See table 4.1.) These 1,633,816 families represented not only families receiving benefits from recent workers' compensation insurance policies, but also families receiving benefits for job-

TABLE 4.1
Numbers of Families
Reporting Benefits, 1978

Benefits	Disabled Family[a]	Nondisabled Family
Workers' compensation alone	520,110	513,119
Workers' compensation and		
Social security (SS)	138,705	141,238
Supplemental security income (SSI)	4,924	6,200
Veterans benefits (VA)	15,627	5,798
Public assistance (PA)	3,395	—
Unemployment insurance (UI)	11,772	11,895
Civil service (CS)	4,244	—
Other benefits (O)	8,166	—
Aid to families with dependent children (AFDC)	—	42,180
Workers' compensation and		
SS and AFDC	255	—
SS and CS	719	—
SS and VA	12,058	35,981
SS and SSI	1,696	—
SS and O	5,709	—
SS and PA	8,496	—
SSI and AFDC	4,186	—
VA and O	35,291	—
Workers' compensation and		
SS, SSI, and AFDC	7,319	—
SS, VA, and O	453	—
SS, VA, and UI	4,504	—
SS, VA, and CS	453	—
SS, SSI, and PA	49,020	—
SS, UI, and CS	—	39,408
SS, VA, UI, AFDC, PA, and CS	442	—

Source: 1978 Social Security Administration Survey of Disability and Work.

[a]Respondent had a work disability.

related injuries and illnesses suffered in earlier years. The figure may also include families that the respondent characterized as receiving workers' compensation benefits which were actually benefits paid under the Federal Employees Compensation Act, or other programs (such as black lung benefits). Approximately 37 percent (600,587) of the families receiving workers' compensation benefits were also receiving benefits from one of the eight programs listed above.

Social security was the major program overlap with workers' compensation. Twenty-seven percent (446,909) of the families with a workers' compensation recipient also received a social security benefit. Again, the percentage did not vary with the disability status of the respondent.

Of the families receiving workers' compensation benefits with a disabled respondent, 22 percent received benefits from one other program, 8 percent from two other programs, and 7 percent from three or more additional programs. The comparable figures for families with a nondisabled respondent are: one additional program, 26 percent; two additional programs, 4 percent; and three or more additional programs, 5 percent. Families with a nondisabled recipient are slightly more likely, given receipt of overlapping benefits, to be receiving such benefits from one additional program only.

Not surprisingly, a family with a disabled respondent was five times more likely to receive workers' compensation benefits than a family with a nondisabled respondent.

One would expect that the percentage of families with overlapping benefits would be at least as great as the percentage of individuals with overlapping benefits. The survey results indicate that this is the case. (See table 4.2.) Sixteen percent of the respondents who received workers' compensation benefits in the month prior to the interview received benefits from additional programs. Although this individual benefit overlap is less than half that of the family overlap, it is startling to note that it is entirely accounted for by the multiple benefits received by disabled respondents. Of the 675,951 disabled respondents, 19.5 percent or 131,581 individuals, received multiple benefits. Ten percent received benefits from one additional program, and 6.5 percent from two other programs. Ten percent of the individuals who received workers' compensation benefits also received social security benefits.

TABLE 4.2

Numbers of Individuals
Reporting Benefits, 1978

Benefits	Disabled[a]		Nondisabled	
	Self	Spouse	Self	Spouse
Workers' compensation alone	544,370	15,546	166,477	123,596
Workers' compensation and				
Social security (SS)	60,329	16,686	—	35,436
Supplemental security income (SSI)	4,924	—	—	—
Veterans benefits (VA)	9,053	35,291	—	5,796
Public assistance (PA)	—	—	—	—
Unemployment insurance (UI)	—	—	—	—
Civil service (CS)	4,244	—	—	—
Other benefits (O)	—	—	—	—
Aid to families with dependent children (AFDC)	—	—	—	—
Workers' compensation and				
SS and AFDC	—	—	—	—
SS and CS	—	—	—	—
SS and VA	2,513	—	—	—
SS and SSI	899	6,908	—	—
SS and O	5,709	453	—	—
SS and PA	—	—	—	—
SSI and AFDC	—	—	—	—
VA and O	35,291	—	—	—
Workers' compensation and				
SS, SSI, and AFDC	—	—	—	—
SS, CS, and O	—	—	—	—
SS, VA, and O	453	—	—	—
SS, VA, and UI	—	—	—	—
SS, VA, and CS	—	—	—	—
SS, SSI, and PA	—	—	—	—
SS, UI, and CS	—	—	—	—
SS, VA, UI, AFDC, PA, and CS	—	—	—	—

Source: 1978 Social Security Administration Survey of Disability and Work.

[a]Respondent had a work disability. Spouse may or may not have had a work disability.

Although there was no benefit overlap reported by nondisabled respondents, they did report some overlapping benefit receipt by their spouses. Such respondents reported that 164,828 of their spouses received a workers' compensation benefit in the month preceding the interview and that 25 percent of these recipients received benefits from an additional program. Comparable figures for the spouses of disabled respondents indicate that 78,864 received workers' compensation benefits, and 75 percent of them received benefits from at least one additional program.

Disability is a flexible state. The evidence in some of the studies cited above indicates that claimants have some control over the classification of the severity of and duration of their nonwork spells associated with job injuries. Claimants respond to economic incentives. They may receive payments from multiple sources, and these affect their claim filing and risk-bearing behavior. The case is the same with other social insurance programs.

Permanent Partial Disability: Market Imperfections and Litigation

Permanent partial disability claims account for about 65 percent of the indemnity benefits paid under the state WC system, and yet they represent only 25 percent of the total claims. Permanent partial claims are quite troublesome because they may be classified or rated with respect to severity before an indemnity award is finalized. The rationale for compensating work injuries and occupational disease varies across the states.[6] Burton (1983) notes that there are two basic rationales offered for permanent partial compensation—impairment or disability. Examples of impairment would include the loss of a finger, or the loss of strength in a muscle. Impairments are measured after maximum medical improvement. Impairments may lead to functional limitations. For example, the loss of strength in a muscle may lead to

---

6. See Berkowitz, Burton, and Vroman (1979) for a thorough discussion of permanent partial disability, or Berkowitz and Burton (1985) for their most recent treatment of the topic. Burton and Vroman (1979) discuss the various rationales in their report for the Interdepartmental Workers' Compensation Task Force.

an inability to lift. This functional limitation, in turn, may lead to a work disability.[7] Disability is defined as an inability to perform one's normal social role. When normal social role is defined as "work," some people will have a degree of flexibility in deciding whether to adopt a disability status.

In imaginary world B we described a lottery for injuries. Suppose a worker knows the exact probability that he or she will be injured in any job. Assume that the worker and firm enter into an optimal contract, and the worker is subsequently injured. If the worker and firm (or agents acting on their behalf) could observe the degree of impairment and work disability exactly, with zero monitoring cost, there would be a problem neither with the classification of permanent partial claims, nor with their litigation.[8] However, when we introduce uncertainty, lack of perfect information, insurers' incentives and the possibility of profit, monitoring costs, conflicting medical testimony, injured and angry workers, regulators, political power blocs, alternate recovery mechanisms, and a workers' compensation bar (to name a few), we have the workers' compensation system.

Burton (1983) provides a taxonomy of the ways that states actually, rather than theoretically, make permanent partial benefit determinations. He lists five bases for benefits: impairment, disaggregated functional limitation, aggregated functional limitation, loss of earning capacity, and actual loss of earnings. States may list a specific impairment, or they may make an award for the loss of use (functional limitation) associated with the impairment. Most states have "scheduled" injuries. These are lists of specific injuries together with benefits and maximum durations for payment. States also provide for the compensation of "nonscheduled" cases. These cases can be rated on the basis of a "whole man." What percentage of a whole person is lost as a result of the work injury? The loss may be defined in terms of functional limitation or impairment. Alternatively, nonscheduled cases are rated in some states on the basis of *potential* loss of earnings. The determination of either the percentage of a whole person or the percentage of potential loss of earnings capacity is rife with the fertilizer to grow litigation.

---

7. See Nagi (1965, 1969) for the original development of these concepts.
8. We are obviously simplifying here.

The first four methods used to make permanent partial determinations are, generally, proxies for the work disability rationale for compensating injuries. The fifth method, actual loss of earnings, is a direct attempt to compensate for work disability. Severe impairments may not lead to work disability, and mild impairments may lead to severe work disability. Ten workers with identical impairments may have ten different degrees of work disability, ranging from none to totally work-disabled. Consider two people who both lose their eyes as the result of an injury at work. One may have twenty years of formal education, an extraordinary endowment, and be among the leading economists of his or her time. Another may have six years of schooling, a less than normal endowment, and be a 65-year-old former laborer who is totally disabled from work. These two cases represent extremes, but consider another case with two people who have the same set of observable pre-injury characteristics, who suffer the same job injury and subsequent impairment. There is a positive probability that the subsequent work disability of these two workers will differ. There is unobserved heterogeneity across workers, and it can be fixed or changing at constant or nonconstant rates over time.

The first four methods used to make permanent partial ratings require that such ratings be made before most of the person's work life takes place.[9] Hence, one young injured worker may receive a permanent partial award that replaces a small fraction of lost wages over time, and another may receive an award that replaces many times his or her actual wage loss. Berkowitz, Burton, and Vroman (1979) select a sample of permanent partial claimants who were injured in 1968, and stratify the sample on the basis of age, sex, body part injured, severity of injury, and jurisdiction. They use earnings data supplied by SSA to compare the earnings streams of injured cohorts and comparison cohorts, and find wide disparities in the percentage of earnings replaced. They also find that earnings losses vary directly with the permanent partial rating; that earnings losses are greater for the cohort of controverted claims; and that the probability of controversion increases with the permanent partial rating.

The fifth method used to make permanent partial ratings, ac-

---

9. The age distribution at the time of job injury is skewed, with those injured far more likely to be younger workers.

tual earnings loss, does not require that disability ratings be made in advance of the actual time flow of work disability. Only three states have adopted wage loss systems, and these are not without flaws.[10] As with the potential earnings method described above, the injured workers' subsequent earnings stream in the absence of work injury cannot, by definition, be observed. Consequently, assumptions must be made about that time path, such as that the injured worker's real wage would have grown at the compound rate of productivity growth, or at the mean rate of a similar cohort's growth. The assumed time path of wages can be used to compute an earnings loss, if any, by subtracting out the worker's actual earnings. Only a percentage of earnings loss is replaced, and that percentage is subject to a minimum wage loss requirement (say, at least 15 percent) to receive any benefits to replace lost wages. The minimum is designed, in part, to accommodate transitory changes in wages. Claims compensated under an actual loss of earnings method should not be classified as permanent partial disabilities, because there may be a period of earnings loss followed by a continuous period of no earnings loss (no work disability). Among the potential criticisms of this system of compensating permanent partial disabilities is that there may be a period of no earnings loss (not necessarily a short period), followed by a period of earnings loss. It may be difficult to demonstrate that such interrupted earnings spells are the result of job injuries that occurred in previous years. Another criticism is that workers who suffer severe impairments that affect other aspects of their lives may receive no compensation under wage loss statutes. This is as much a criticism of the work disability rationale for compensating occupational injuries as it is of wage loss systems for compensating permanent partial impairments.

The time flow of benefit payments and the method used to compensate permanent partial injuries can have different incentive effects. Benefits can be paid on a periodic basis (weekly, monthly) with resulting worker income and substitution effects if the periodic payment is contingent upon labor market behavior, as it is in pure

---

10. Florida and Louisiana have wage loss systems, and New York compensates some of its claims with a wage loss system. Arizona, Michigan, and Pennsylvania have wage loss laws, but do not compensate the bulk of their claims on the basis of actual earnings losses. Burton (1983) describes the criteria of the wage loss programs.

wage loss states. Benefits can also be paid in a lump sum. Lump sum benefits are generally not conditioned directly on subsequent labor market behavior, and they generate income effects only.

The practice of "lump-summing" cases is known by various names in different states (washouts, redemptions, and compromise and release settlements, for example). In a world with full information and heterogeneous time preferences, noncoercive optimal lump summing could take place. But the Florida and Louisiana wage loss laws, for example, make it extremely difficult to receive lump sum benefits. This impediment was probably designed for at least three reasons: to limit the incentive to attorneys to be involved in the WC system (attorneys take a percentage of lump sum payments at the time of award in contested cases); to protect injured workers' interests (workers do not know the future with perfect certainty); and to minimize the error associated with the measurement of the impact of injury on earnings loss. It is not clear that the first two of these necessarily maximize utility from the perspective of injured workers, or that the potential work disincentives of the third do not offset measurement gains. However, the evidence that we do have from the state of Florida indicates that the introduction of a pure wage loss system with strict controls on lump-summing will greatly reduce the amount of litigation in the system. The wage loss system in Florida went into effect in 1979; it may be that as experience with the new law matures, those most interested in litigation will find ways to increase it.

The WC system was introduced with the expectation that workers would relinquish their right to tort action in the case of occupational injury or disease in return for certain and swift payment of WC benefits. It was believed that the abandonment of a liability system and adoption of the "no fault" WC system would eliminate litigation. Under the liability system, payment for job injury was neither certain nor swift. Under the WC system, litigation has not disappeared. Given the divergences from our previously described world B, this should not be surprising. One might hypothesize that anything that increases monitoring cost, or the expected benefit of a claim, might lead to more litigated claims. For example, suppose the list of conditions that are eligible for benefits is expanded to include "stress" cases that result in work disability. One might postulate that the total number of genuine, fraudulent, and litigated claims would all increase.[11] Similarly, suppose that the probability of winning a case that was controverted, as well as the costs of such controversion, were held constant, and that benefits were doubled. The expectation is that more claims would be litigated. The introduction of any uncertainty or gray areas in the determination of disability will lead to litigation. These lessons are evident in the WC system, and have become so in the SSDI program.

The amounts of money at stake in controversion are greater in more serious cases. A random sample of WC claims arising from April 1979 to April 1982 (table 4.3) can be used to demonstrate this point.

Although the percentage of controverted claims varies across states, from a low of 27 per 1,000 in Wisconsin to a high of 277 per 1,000 in Michigan, in all four states the percentage of controversion varies directly with the seriousness of the claim. Within the permanent partial claim class, the probability that a claim will be controverted approaches one for more serious injuries to certain body parts (see Vroman 1978 or Berkowitz, Burton, and Vroman 1979). This is what one would expect to find given a probability of successfully litigating a claim and the appropriate cost conditions. However, the cost conditions could overwhelm the seriousness of claim rule. Consider a state where the costs of settling small "nuisance" permanent partial claims (including induced claims) of certain classes (e.g., cumulative trauma) are less than the costs of litigating such claims. One might expect to see a flood of such claims, for example from older workers as "retirement supplements." More serious claims for work injury resulting from cumulative trauma would be more likely to be controverted because of the lack of certainty surrounding the relationship between the current alleged limitation and past repeated wear and tear associated with job task performance. Heart cases can be especially difficult. Was a worker's death, or severe functional limitation as a result of a heart condition, due to job performance or to disease (or smoking) that was unrelated to the job? A worker might suffer a work-related stroke at home and never associate this event with his or her job. Another worker might suffer a stroke on the job and file a WC

---

11. See, for example, Staten and Umbeck's studies (1982, 1983) of the Federal Employment Compensation Act (FECA) claims of air traffic controllers.

TABLE 4.3

Controversions by
Claim Type,
Selected States, 1979–82

State	Temporary Total (%)	Permanent Partial (%)	Permanent Total (%)	Death (%)
Connecticut (5.0)[a]	2.9	8.2	9.5	28.5
Illinois (14.8)	5.3	24.1	27.7	51.8
Michigan (27.7)	22.1	40.6	48.4	63.5
Wisconsin (2.7)	1.9	7.3	10.0	25.0

Source: National Council on Compensation Insurance, detailed claim call data.

[a]Percentage of all claims that are litigated.

claim when the event would have occurred irrespective of his or her working at that particular job.

Where uncertainty as to causality, probability of successful litigation, and disability rating exists, so does the opportunity for signaling (see Spence 1974). It is not clear that in such circumstances workers will not overutilize medical services, which are provided to them on an individual basis at virtually zero price, to support determinations of more serious injury. Similarly, employers (or their agents) may resort to controversion to demonstrate that they will not tolerate fraudulent or excessively generous awards (or, in some cases, even fair ones). Workers may seek to controvert their claims to signal that theirs are "different" from others.[12] Finally, the efficient use of vocational rehabilitation services may be distorted.

VOCATIONAL REHABILITATION AND WORKERS' COMPENSATION

Virtually all WC statutes provide for vocational rehabilitation benefits,[13] and eighteen states have special funds to help finance the provision of vocational rehabilitation services. These funds are financed

---

12. Berkowitz, Burton, and Vroman (1979) find that the *pre-injury* earnings of workers whose claims were controverted were lower for the two years immediately before the year of injury than the earnings of those who did not seek to controvert their claims.

13. As of January 1, 1983, only three states did not have specific provisions for the rehabilitation of disabled workers.

by a variety of means, including: a tax on compensation paid by insurers and self-insurers; a premium tax on insurers and self-insurers; payments from a second injury fund; appropriations from state general funds, which in turn may be financed by these methods; and assessments in death claims with no dependents involved. The SSDI program has a beneficiary rehabilitation program that is financed through the trust fund. Beneficiaries receive VR services from the federal-state vocational rehabilitation program. Larson and Burton (1985) provide a description of various WC special funds, as well as statistics on their use by the states. The U.S. Chamber of Commerce (*Analysis of Workers' Compensation Laws*) publishes an *Annual* that provides information on the rehabilitation aspects of WC statutes, as well as on other program parameters.

The goal of vocational rehabilitation services is to restore an injured worker to employment, preferably with the pre-injury employer. Over half of the states have WC vocational rehabilitation sections, but only a quarter provide rehabilitation services directly to injured workers (U.S. Department of Labor 1983). The remainder simply refer injured workers for vocational rehabilitation services, with some WC rehabilitation sections monitoring the claimants' progress.

As of January 1, 1983, most states paid a maintenance allowance to injured workers undergoing vocational rehabilitation. The allowance varied considerably across states, being a flat $10 a week in Mississippi, for example, but in New Hampshire consisting of "board, lodging, travel, books and basic materials *in addition to compensation*" (U.S. Chamber of Commerce 1983, 24–25). The maintenance allowance is generally limited to a specific time period, which can be quite short.[14] From the employee side, we can visualize the decision to participate in vocational rehabilitation and the extent of participation as utility-maximizing decisions (see Crawford and Killingsworth 1984).

From the employer side, we can visualize the provision of such services as a profit-maximizing activity. Note that the incentives of an individual firm to supply VR services under WC and those of the government to supply such services under SSDI can differ. Experience rating encourages the firm to assist "impaired but able" workers

---

14. Iowa provided for thirteen weeks with the possibility of a thirteen-week extension (U.S. Chamber of Commerce 1983, 24).

to return to work. As with the employee claims rate and employer provision of safety, the employee incentives to participate and the extent of participation may differ in intensity from the desire of employers to offer (or coerce employees to accept) such services.

Consider the underlying theoretical model of choice implied in the duration-of-disability studies discussed earlier. The higher the reservation wage (WC benefit), the less painful it is for an injured worker to delay or forgo return to employment. However, to the extent that employers pay these benefits, they have an incentive to encourage injured workers to return to work. This is most apparent in the case of self-insured and experience-rated firms, as these firms may have to pay for a temporary (or permanent) replacement for the injured worker in addition to paying the injured worker's WC benefits. Similarly, the incentives for early rehabilitation intervention and speedy return to work will be negative for the employee and positive for the employer in those situations where the determination of the disability rating or size of the WC award is, or is perceived to be, a function of the utilization of vocational rehabilitation.

In those cases that are litigated, the incentives for rehabilitation can be negative for all parties. For example, claimants may want to present themselves as being severely disabled in order to maximize the size of their awards and the strength of their bargaining position in any lump sum settlement discussion.[15] The employer may be hoping to win the litigated case and forego any costs, or settle for a lump sum at as low a price as possible. In some states employees who accept lump sum settlements forfeit the right to future services, including vocational rehabilitation, provided by the WC system. They may, however, receive such services from the federal-state vocational rehabilitation program if they have a substantial barrier to employment and the potential for re-employment with VR services, and if they meet other program requirements.

An employee's decision to undergo a VR treatment program can be a function of his or her time preference. Consider a utility-of-income maximizer who suffers real, but vocationally remediable, wage loss. Suppose the wage loss is only partially replaced by WC indemnity

---

15. The claimant's attorney may handle all these discussions with little input from the client.

benefits, which are uncertain. The employee must decide to undergo rehabilitation now or delay receipt of such services, when delay in seeking remediation can lead to permanent deterioration of market skills, and the date of a lump sum settlement is subject to negotiation. The employee trades a presumably higher lump sum settlement for a lower net earnings stream beginning at the time vocational rehabilitation treatment is completed.

Recent empirical evidence indicates that vocational rehabilitation services are used by a small percentage of WC claimants, but that they are more likely to be used the longer a disability spell lasts within a claim class, or the more severe a claim (National Council on Compensation Insurance 1984). The National Council on Compensation Insurance (NCCI) examined a random sample of claim reports filed in 1982 in thirteen states. Two-thirds of the claims (971,361) were closed, and the remainder (507,133) were still open. The NCCI sample has as many as four reports on some claims. Reports are made at 6, 18, 30, and 42 months, if claims are still open.

Only 1.55 percent of claimants (23,000 of nearly 1,500,000) used VR services. The percentages of closed and open claims utilizing VR services were 0.41 percent and 3.75 percent, respectively (NCCI 1984, 10). Claims that closed between the 30th and 42d month of a WC spell (closed at the 4th report) were more likely to have utilized VR services, with 4 and 5 percent of temporary total and permanent partial claimants, respectively, using such services. The percentage was higher yet for cases still open at 42 months (4th report) with 14 and 13 percent of temporary total and permanent partial claimants utilizing VR services, respectively, but the absolute number of claims open at 4th report was small.

The cases of claimants using VR services, either open or closed, are far more costly than those that do not use VR services. Closed claims that utilized VR services had average incurred indemnity benefits three to five times higher than those that did not. Claims that were still open were at least twice as expensive as closed claims at comparable time stages. Claimants who utilized VR services, and who were on WC spells that were incomplete, had average incurred indemnity benefits twice as large as those who did not receive VR services (NCCI 1984, 14). A claim still open at 30 months (3d report), which had received VR services, had incurred average indemnity benefits of nearly $50,000 and incurred average VR costs of an additional $4,400 (NCCI 1984, 11).

Several findings of the NCCI study stand out. The first is that long-duration temporary total claims are about as likely to use VR services as permanent partial claims. The second is that the claims of those using VR services are far more expensive than the claims of those who do not. The third is that not many permanent partial disability claimants use VR services. We have used NCCI total incidence rates for all benefit types and incidence rates for each benefit type to compute the estimated number of permanent partial claims in the NCCI sample and the number of permanent partial claimants who utilized VR services. We estimate that only 3.3 percent of all permanent partial claimants (8,150 of 244,000) used VR services. VR intervention may be doing a magnificent job with the clients it is reaching, but it is not reaching many.

The Compendium on Workmens' Compensation lists "restoration of earning capacity and return to productive employment" (1973, 25) as one of the two most important objectives of the WC system, the other being income replacement. Most injured workers do have those two goals met, but a sizable number of permanent partial claimants do not. Many of these end up out of the labor force, drawing SSDI or other benefits. Some continue to receive WC indemnity benefits, but many have received a lump sum settlement and are left to their own devices.

The WC statutes offer incentives to injured workers to accept VR services. One incentive is the maintenance benefits received while utilizing VR services. Another is the requirement that injured workers must accept VR services, which is the case in about three-quarters of the state statutes. The mandatory acceptance requirement is accompanied by either a reduction in or nonpayment of benefits for those who refuse such services. The SSDI program has such a requirement, which until recently was largely ignored. Its enforcement in WC does not seem to be widespread. Even if workers are coerced into accepting such services, they can accept them half-heartedly or not utilize them efficiently.

The structure of the WC program mitigates against the efficient use of VR services. The income replacement goal and the labor market restoration goal are in conflict. The use of litigation may impede the delivery of VR services, and lump-summing practices in many states exclude injured workers from continued receipt of service. Workers may not have good information about the efficacy of rehabilitation services, or they may simply feel that the benefit of undergoing a VR treatment plan is exceeded by its cost. SSDI beneficiaries and WC permanent partial claimants are not breaking down doors to demand rehabilitation services. More frequently, they are getting in the attorney line to attempt to maximize the value of their claims.

CONCLUSIONS

People respond to incentives. If social insurance benefits increase, applications for beneficiary status will increase. The evidence from the WC program indicates that applications (claim filing), and perhaps risk bearing and injuries, are quite sensitive to changes in the level of benefits. Not only is claim frequency responsive to benefit levels, but what evidence there is indicates that the duration of nonwork spells associated with the receipt of WC indemnity benefits is a function of the level of those benefits. These findings are in harmony with what we observe for the SSDI program. Although research has not been conducted on the impact of the "full" replacement rate on employee behavior, it is worth noting that a significant number of families and individuals receiving a WC indemnity benefit also receive benefits from other programs.

Evidence on the method of financing the WC program, with emphasis on experience rating and its impact on employer incentives, is sketchy at best. It seems clear that if, as we believe, experience rating does encourage employers' provision of safety, the claim-filing and/ or risk-bearing incentive of employees is much stronger. There is evidence that there is a one-to-one trade-off between WC costs and wages, and a reduction in the size of compensating differentials with WC benefit increases.

The disability determination process is a particularly difficult one. The rationale for such determination, as well as the actual method used, varies across states. The amount of indemnity benefit awarded is a function of this rating. As the rating process is not a perfectly objective one, with determinations known with certainty, *ex ante*, by employees and employers, there may be efforts by both sides to affect the outcome of the rating process. These efforts may include litigation, failure to efficiently utilize VR services, and excessive use of the medical care system.

The introduction of additional uncertainty into the WC system, an increase in the expected value of a claim (via benefit increases or rising probability of successful litigation), or increasing monitoring costs will increase the likelihood of litigation. Some cases are particularly problematic—permanent partials in general, and heart disease, cumulative injury, and occupational disease cases in particular.

The fashion in which benefits are paid can affect the quantity of litigation and labor market behavior. Lump-summing produces income effects only, and periodic payments conditioned on labor market activity may produce both income and substitution effects. Lump-summing may offer greater incentive for attorneys to counsel their clients to contest claims, although this is not necessarily the case. The evidence from Florida, a wage loss state, indicates that litigation decreased dramatically with the virtual end of lump-summing in that state.

The structure of the WC program may mitigate against the use of VR services. One of the primary goals of the program is restoration to the labor market. This goal is generally being met, but few WC beneficiaries are using VR services. The nature of the disability determination process may be such that people postpone or forgo VR services in an effort to maximize their indemnity award. This failure to utilize VR services early in the postinjury process can result in fewer people returning to the labor market. In some states, the process of ending services completely, with the awarding of lump sum benefits, limits injured workers' rehabilitation options.

The incentive issues are similar in the WC system and other social insurance programs. However, the WC program is a true insurance program. It is state-mandated, but financed through the private sector. It does not suffer from the welfare schizophrenia of pay-as-you-go public quasi-insurance programs. It provides indemnity payments to two million people a year, and medical benefits for over twice that number. The key actors in the system, employees and employers, and their agents—attorneys and insurers—pursue their own self-interest. They pursue their self-interest with a set of incentives that the economic and political markets have provided. Should these incentives change, so will the actors' behaviors.

5 · WORKERS' COMPENSATION AND EMPLOYMENT: AN INDUSTRY ANALYSIS

James Lambrinos and David Appel

An oft-neglected yet significant aspect of the social insurance program in this country is workers' compensation insurance. Designed to provide medical care and indemnity payments to injured workers, it covers more employees and pays more in benefits than many more widely studied programs. One need only reflect on the extensive analysis devoted to the unemployment insurance system, which is roughly equal in size to workers' compensation, to appreciate the lack of attention to this very important program.

It is only in recent years that economists and policy makers have begun to address the myriad of equity and efficiency issues surrounding the operation of the workers' compensation system. In that time there has been a great deal of emphasis on the incentive effects of the benefit delivery system, but less attention has been paid to the impacts on the employer and on the cost of the system. And while there have been several studies of the effect of workers' compensation on wages, fringe benefits, and compensating wage differentials, there has never, to our knowledge, been a formal analysis of the incidence of these costs, nor has there been a study of the employment effects of the workers' compensation program.

We thank Richard Butler and John D. Worrall for helpful comments, and David Durbin for very capable research assistance. The usual disclaimer applies.

This paper attempts to fill a small part of that void, by estimating the employment impact of differential workers' compensation costs by jurisdiction and industry. Under a set of fairly restrictive assumptions, we compute the upper-bound estimates of the employment effects of the workers' compensation program in eleven industries across thirty-eight states. These estimates reflect the assumption that employers absorb the full cost of the workers' compensation coverage and shift those costs forward to consumers in the form of increased product prices. The first section of the paper describes workers' compensation rate making, and is followed by discussions of the theoretical model, the data base, and the results. We conclude with a discussion of the policy implications of the analysis.

WORKERS' COMPENSATION PRICING

Workers' compensation insurance provides for full medical coverage and partial wage replacement for injury or illness arising "out of and in the course of " employment. The system arose in the early decades of the twentieth century as part of a well-known quid pro quo in which employees relinquished their rights to tort actions against their employers in exchange for swift and certain settlement of their claims for industrial accidents.

While conceptually quite straightforward, the pricing of workers' compensation insurance is technically a rather more complicated matter. As might be expected, different types of employment have differing expected costs of illness and injury. Therefore, in order to meet the typical statutory requirement that prices be neither "excessive, inadequate nor unfairly discriminatory," rates must vary by type of employment. Furthermore, as the regulation of benefit levels and pricing is jurisdictionally a state matter, the prices are computed for each state independently. A very brief description of the pricing procedure follows.[1]

---

1. A complete description of the pricing program can be found in *The Pricing of Workers Compensation Insurance* (National Council on Compensation Insurance 1981).

Broadly speaking, workers' compensation premiums must cover the expected losses and expenses allocable to policies written while the rates are in effect. Both equity and efficiency demand that this hold true in the aggregate (i.e., at the statewide level), and at the level of the insured individual as well. The failure to adhere to this can create unintended interjurisdictional, interindustry, and interfirm cross-subsidization, or a combination of these, which can have far-reaching and adverse effects. Thus, the pricing procedure is three-tiered: initially the average statewide price level is computed, followed by adjustments for individual industries or classes of employment and finally by adjustments for individual firms.

The first step in the process is the assessment of the adequacy of rates at the state level. Total premium volume at current rates is compared to total projected loss and expense costs to determine the overall premium level change for the state. That total change is then distributed to the approximately six hundred individual classification codes in two stages. First, each classification is assigned to one of three industry groups—manufacturing, construction, and all other. The premium change is initially distributed to these three groups, and then ultimately to the individual class codes within each group. The resulting prices are known as "manual rates."

The manual rates thus determined represent the average loss and expense cost per unit of exposure (i.e., per \$100 of payroll) within each of the classifications. These rates can vary substantially across classes of employment; for example, the maximum rate will routinely exceed the minimum by a factor of 100, and in the extreme can exceed the minimum by factors up to 1,000. (Expressed as a percentage, the price structure can encompass rates from 0.1 to 100 percent of payroll.) Thus the employment impact could range from negligible to quite substantial.

After the manual rate is established, individual firm prices may be further adjusted through the application of a number of mandatory and voluntary programs. The most significant of these are mandatory. One, premium discounts, reduces rates for larger insured firms to reflect fixed costs in the insurance production process and economies of scale in the servicing of larger risks. The other, experience rating, modifies an insured firm's price depending on its own loss experience relative to the classwide average. Both programs (as well as other, voluntary ones) are designed to tie an individual firm's price more closely to the costs it generates.[2]

THEORETICAL MODEL

Although workers' compensation premiums are paid by employers, the program will have an impact on both employers and employees. Under certain conditions employers will bear the entire burden: if the supply of labor is perfectly elastic and employees view the workers' compensation cost as a general payroll tax, then employers bear the full cost. On the other hand, if labor supply is less than perfectly elastic, or if employees treat expected benefits as a form of nonwage compensation, then employees can bear some or all of the costs.

Shifting of the cost of workers' compensation is particularly important in determining the program's employment effect, and warrants a detailed investigation of its own. Dorsey (1983) has found a dollar-for-dollar trade-off between total compensation (wages and fringe benefits) and workers' compensation costs, while Butler (1983) has found a less than one-to-one trade-off between wages and workers' compensation benefits. In addition, Arnould and Nichols (1983) and Worrall and Borba (1985) have found reductions in compensating wage differentials associated with workers' compensation coverage.[3]

These studies, when taken together, suggest that employees will bear at least some of the burden of the workers' compensation cost. In a world of perfect information, homogeneous preferences, and actuarially fair prices, this would come as no surprise; workers' compensation prices would reflect the real cost of providing benefits contingent on work injury, and employees would be willing to purchase such coverage either independently or through the wage bargaining process. Of course, in a world of imperfect information and heterogeneous preferences, the same results may not obtain.

---

2. These programs are not insignificant in their cost impact. Premium discounts can be as high as 12.5 percent, while experience modifications can range from 80 percent discount to 400 percent surcharge.

3. On the other hand, Hamermesh (1979), in examining the incidence of the payroll tax, finds roughly two-thirds of the burden borne by employers.

The equation presented below computes the change in the demand for labor assuming that employers treat the entire workers' compensation premium as an increase in the cost of labor. This will be equal to the employment effect if labor supply is perfectly elastic, and is the upper bound if supply is less than perfectly elastic. Assuming both product and labor markets are competitive, production functions are constant returns to scale, and firms are in long-run equilibrium (i.e., operating at minimum long-run average cost), the change in the demand for labor can be shown to be composed of output and substitution effects as follows:[4]

$$\dot{L} = [\epsilon\, S_L - (1 - S_L)\sigma]\dot{w}.$$

That is, the percentage change in the demand for labor ($\dot{L}$) is dependent on four factors: labor's share of output (S_L); the commodity price elasticity of demand (ϵ); the elasticity of substitution (σ); and the percentage change in wages ($\dot{w}$). Since employers are assumed to bear all the workers' compensation costs, the percentage change in wages is equal to the workers' compensation premium. Consequently, the employment effects in an industry can be found by obtaining the workers' compensation premium rate, the share of labor in value added, and estimates of the elasticity of substitution and price elasticity of demand.

DATA

To determine the impact of workers' compensation premiums on employment within an industry, estimates of S_L, σ, ϵ, and $\dot{w}$ must be available for each of the industries. Furthermore, the data for each of these variables must be available for roughly the same time period. The data-collection phase of the project was complicated by the fact that workers' compensation rates are not calculated for industrial categories that conform to the U.S. Department of Commerce's Standard Industrial Classifications (SIC). Rather than defining plants by the primary product being produced, plants are classified by the primary type of labor employed. Since all of the other data were available

---

4. A complete derivation of the model is available from the authors upon request.

by SIC codes, a mapping from the workers' compensation classification codes to the SIC codes was necessary.

Table 5.1 lists the eleven industrial classifications that provided reasonable mappings. These eleven industries, representing nine two-digit major industry groups, employed over 2.4 million workers in 1980.

The data on labor share in value added in 1980 were taken from the *Annual Survey of Manufacturers* (U.S. Dept. of Commerce 1983). This variable ranged from a low of 12.4 percent for petroleum refining to a high of 78.6 percent in stationery products. Overall the mean was 39.3 percent with a standard deviation of 19.9 percent.

Estimates of the price elasticity of demand were obtained for ten of the industries from studies by Braithwait (1977, 1980) in which demand functions are estimated for fifty-three commodities. Three different demand models were chosen—the linear expenditure system, the generalized linear expenditure system, and the indirect ad-

TABLE 5.1

Eleven Standard
Industrial Classifications
and Comparable
Workers' Compensation Classifications

Standard Industrial Classification	Code	Workers' Compensation Classification	Code
Food and kindred products	20	Food and tobacco[a]	Schedule 5
Distilled liquor, except brandy	2085	Spiritous liquors mfg.	2130
Wood household furniture	2511	Furniture mfg. wood	2883
Stationery, tablets, and related products	2648	Stationery mfg.	4251
Inner tubes	3011	Rubber tire mfg.	4420
Instruments	3931	Musical instrument mfg.	3383
Footwear, except rubber	314	Boot or shoe mfg.	2660
Tobacco products	21	Tobacco	Group 057
Motor vehicles and car bodies	3711	Automobile mfg. or assembly	3808
Petroleum refining	2911	Oil refining—petroleum	4740
Jewelry	3911	Jewelry mfg.	3383

[a]Tobacco was removed from this category.

dilog. Elasticities did not vary a great deal depending upon which demand model was chosen. The elasticities employed in this study represent those obtained with the generalized linear expenditure system. Since Braithwait does not treat musical instruments as one of his fifty-three commodities, an additional source was needed. Houthakker and Taylor's (1966) study of consumer demand provided this estimate.

Estimates of the elasticity of substitution were available for eight of the industries, from a study by Ferguson (1965) that computes elasticities for nineteen different industries. Those estimates range from 0.24 in food to 1.30 in petroleum, with 80 percent falling between 0.75 and 1.25. The three industry groups in this study for which no estimates were available were assigned an elasticity of one.

Data on workers' compensation rates are calculated separately for each state by classification code. Since benefit levels vary considerably by state, the premium rates across states also show a large amount of variation. Aggregating across the thirty-eight states contained in the National Council on Compensation Insurance data sets, we obtain estimates of the "national" average. Table 5.2 presents all the data for S_L, σ, ϵ, and $\dot{w}$, and the data for each of the states are contained in table 5.3.

RESULTS

Table 5.2 also contains the complete set of results using the data on workers' compensation rates aggregated across all of the states contained in table 5.3. Given that increased labor costs are shifted forward, the workers' compensation rate and the share of labor in value added will determine the change in prices, which range from a 0.22 percent increase in tobacco to a 2.91 percent increase in stationery products. Since nine of the eleven industries have price elasticities that are in the inelastic range, the output effects are smaller than the price effects in all but two of the industries. The mean output effect is 0.67 percent, with a low of 0.00 percent in the tobacco industry and a high of 2.27 percent in musical instruments.

In addition to the scale effect, there is also a substitution effect which will reduce optimal employment levels. The mean percentage

TABLE 5.2

Labor Share in Value Added (S_L), Price Elasticities of Demand (ϵ), Elasticities of Substitution (σ), Workers' Compensation Rates ($\dot{w}$), and the Effect on Labor Demand

Industry	ϵ	S_L	σ	$\dot{w}$	Substitution Effect	Output Effect	$\dot{L}$
Food	−0.35	.308	0.24	5.0	−0.83	−0.54	−1.37
Liquor	−0.38	.137	1.00	6.4	−5.52	−0.33	−5.86
Tobacco	−0.01	.170	1.18	1.3	−1.27	−0.002	−1.28
Furniture	−0.83	.506	1.12	4.0	−2.21	−1.68	−3.89
Stationery	−0.04	.786	1.02	3.7	−0.81	−0.12	−0.92
Petroleum	−0.27	.124	1.30	2.8	−3.19	−0.09	−3.28
Tires	−0.44	.425	0.76	4.6	−2.01	−0.86	−2.87
Footwear	−0.68	.438	1.00	2.1	−1.18	−0.63	−1.81
Motor	−0.31	.500	0.24	4.2	−0.50	−0.65	−1.16
Jewelry	−0.17	.404	1.00	2.5	−1.49	−0.17	−1.66
Musical instruments	−1.27	.525	0.76	3.4	−1.23	−2.27	−3.49
Average				3.64	−1.84	−0.67	−2.51

decrease in employment due to substitution is 1.84 percent, ranging from 0.81 percent for stationery products to 5.52 percent for liquor products. Thus the impact of workers' compensation is greater on employment than on either prices or output. For example, for the food and kindred products industry, a reduction of 1.37 percent in the total employment of roughly 1.5 million suggests that employment would increase by 21,000 if the cost of labor were to decrease by the workers' compensation rate.

Since the workers' compensation rate is determined on the basis of injury experience and costs, it is interesting to compare the decrease in employment for each industry with its corresponding rate. Intuitively, one might expect the employment effects to be directly proportional to the rates, with the impacts greater in the more hazardous industries. While there is, generally, a positive relationship, the employment effect is not a monotonically increasing function of $\dot{w}$, due to the effects of variations in S_L and ϵ across industries. Naturally, the employment effect is directly proportional to the workers' compensation rate, *ceteris paribus*.

Figure 5.1 contains a plot of employment effects ($\dot{L}$) and the workers' compensation rate ($\dot{w}$). Since the workers' compensation rate plays an important role in determining the employment effect, there is a generally positive trend indicated by the graph. Examining the plot carefully, we find that in a pairwise comparison of two industries, a higher $\dot{w}$ does not always lead to a greater $\dot{L}$. Of the fifty-five pairs of industries, ten of these lead to an inverse relationship between the employment effect and the workers' compensation rate. For example, the workers' compensation rate in stationery products is 3.7 percent, which is nearly one-third greater than the rate for the petroleum industry (2.8), yet the employment effects are -0.81 percent in the former and -3.28 percent for the latter. This produces the counterintuitive result of increasing employment, in relative terms, in the more hazardous of the two industries. To isolate the industries in which there is an inverse relationship between $\dot{w}$ and $\dot{L}$, we calculated the covariation terms between $\dot{w}$ and $\dot{L}$ which equal $(\dot{w} - \bar{\dot{w}}) \times (\dot{L} - \bar{\dot{L}})$. The sign of the covariation term reveals that of the eleven industries, three of these produced negative covariation terms. Both stationery products and motor vehicles had greater than average workers' compensation rates and lower than average employment effects. Mus-

FIGURE 5.1
Plot of Employment Effects (L̇)
on Workers' Compensation Rates (ẇ)

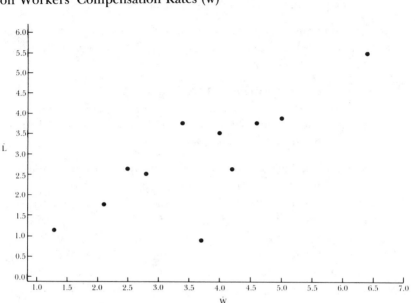

ical instruments, on the other hand, had a negative covariation term by virtue of a lower than average workers' compensation rate and a greater than average employment effect. Table 5.3 reports the sign of the covariation terms for each of the industries by state.

CONCLUSION

The model utilized in this research allows us to estimate the price, output, and employment effects of workers' compensation rates in eleven industries across thirty-eight states. The most notable findings are:

1.   Price increases associated with higher labor costs range from 0.22 to 2.92 percent, with a mean increase of 1.43 percent.

2.   Output effects are generally small, given that demand is inelastic in all but two of the industries. The reductions in output range from 0.00 to 2.27 percent, with a mean of 0.67 percent.

3.   The employment impact is the sum of the substitution and output effects. The mean decrease in employment is 2.51 percent, ranging from 0.81 to 5.52 percent.

4.   The correlation between workers' compensation rates and employment effects is positive and significant, and the covariation terms are generally positive, indicating that the more hazardous industries have larger reductions in employment.

If policy makers are interested in minimizing workplace injury and illness, it is desirable for the employment effects to be greatest in the more hazardous occupations. To that extent, our analysis suggests that the system is functioning well. However, certain anomalies do exist. Insofar as L is also dependent on S_L, σ, and ϵ, the employment effects are not a monotonically increasing function of the workers' compensation rate. The negative covariation terms indicate the instances where higher than average rates are associated with lower than average employment effects, and vice-versa. In these cases, there is a tendency to shift employment into more hazardous industries.

Note, however, that our results are dependent on several rather restrictive assumptions—in particular the assumption that employers bear the full burden of the workers' compensation cost, and pass it forward to consumers in the form of increased product prices. An alternative hypothesis, for which chapter 4 provides some empirical evidence, is that employees absorb that burden, either partially or fully, in the form of reduced wages and fringe benefits. In this case, the employment effect will, *ceteris paribus*, be smaller than those found above.

TABLE 5.3
Workers' Compensation Rates, Employment Effects, and Covariation Signs by State, for Eleven Industries (by SIC Code)

State	20	2085	2511	2648	3011	3931	314	21	3711	2911	3911
Alabama											
Compensation rate	3.2	11.0	4.7	1.9	3.4	1.9	1.2	1.3	3.6	1.5	1.9
Employment effect	.88	10.07	4.57	.47	2.12	1.95	1.03	1.28	.99	1.75	1.26
Covariation sign	+	+	+	+	−	+	+	+	−	+	+
Alaska											
Compensation rate	12.5		8.3			4.4				4.8	3.0
Employment effect	3.42		8.08			4.52				5.63	1.99
Covariation sign	+		+			+				+	−
Arizona											
Compensation rate	8.8		10.8	6.0	9.2	4.4	2.8		9.9	8.1	2.8
Employment effect	2.41		10.51	1.50	5.74	4.52	2.41		2.72	9.50	1.86
Covariation sign	+		+	+	+	+	+		+	+	+
Arkansas											
Compensation rate	6.0	8.6	7.1	3.5	10.1	3.9	2.7		6.6	2.3	2.0
Employment effect	1.64	7.87	6.91	0.87	6.30	4.01	2.32		1.82	2.70	1.33
Covariation sign	+	+	+	+	+	−	+		+	+	+
Colorado											
Compensation rate	5.1	6.5	5.8	3.1	4.3	2.8	2.4		4.4	3.2	2.0

TABLE 5.3 continued

State	20	2085	2511	2648	3011	3931	314	21	3711	2911	3911
Employment effect	1.40	5.95	5.64	0.77	2.68	2.88	2.06		1.21	3.75	1.38
Covariation sign	+	+	+	+	+	−	+		−	+	+
Connecticut											
Compensation rate	5.7	12.0	8.6	4.1	6.4	3.6	3.4	4.6	5.0	5.2	3.9
Employment effect	1.56	10.98	8.37	1.02	3.99	3.70	2.92	4.51	1.38	6.10	2.59
Covariation sign	−	+	+	+	+	+	+	+	+	−	+
District of Columbia											
Compensation rate	12.3		13.3			6.9					5.6
Employment effect	3.37		12.94			7.09					3.72
Covariation sign	+		+			+					+
Florida											
Compensation rate	8.8	8.6	8.3	7.7	6.3	6.7	3.9	3.1	7.3	6.4	2.3
Employment effect	2.41	7.87	8.08	1.92	3.93	6.89	3.35	3.04	2.01	7.50	1.53
Covariation sign	+	+	+	−	+	+	+	+	−	+	+
Georgia											
Compensation rate	4.6	5.9	6.7	3.2	3.4	4.7	3.0	1.7	4.7	4.7	1.3
Employment effect	1.26	5.40	6.52	0.80	2.12	4.83	2.58	1.67	1.29	5.51	0.86
Covariation sign	+	+	+	+	+	+	+	+	−	+	+
Hawaii											
Compensation rate	7.8	15.4	8.9	5.9	16.3	4.9	3.3			6.6	3.1
Employment effect	2.14	14.09	8.66	1.47	10.17	5.04	2.84			7.74	2.06

Covariation sign	+	+	+	+	+	+	+	+		+	+
Idaho											
Compensation rate	5.4	5.9	7.3		3.6	2.4	1.7		4.2	2.2	2.0
Employment effect	1.48	5.40	7.10		2.25	2.47	1.46		1.16	2.58	1.33
Covariation sign	+	+	+		+	+	+		–	+	+
Illinois											
Compensation rate	5.1	8.6	7.9	5.3	6.0	4.2	2.2	3.2	5.6	3.6	2.6
Employment effect	1.40	7.87	7.69	1.32	3.74	4.32	1.89	3.14	1.54	4.22	1.73
Covariation sign	+	+	+	+	+	–	+	+	–	+	+
Indiana											
Compensation rate	1.9	3.3	2.9	1.3	2.0	1.1	0.7	1.7	1.6	1.3	0.7
Employment effect	0.52	3.02	2.82	0.32	1.25	1.13	0.60	1.07	0.44	1.52	0.47
Covariation sign	+	+	+	+	+	+	+	+	+	+	+
Iowa											
Compensation rate	3.4	2.9	3.3	1.8	2.8	2.0	1.2	2.3	5.0	2.1	1.1
Employment effect	0.93	2.65	3.21	0.45	1.75	2.06	1.03	2.26	1.38	2.46	0.73
Covariation sign	+	+	+	+	+	+	+	+	+	+	+
Kansas											
Compensation rate	4.5	5.6	3.4	3.4	9.4	1.8	3.1		3.7	1.6	1.6
Employment effect	1.23	5.12	3.31	0.85	5.87	1.85	2.67		1.02	1.88	1.06
Covariation sign	+	+	–	+	+	+	+		+	+	+
Kentucky											
Compensation rate	4.1	4.9	5.7	1.4	4.6	3.1	1.9	2.5	6.5	2.1	2.7
Employment effect	1.12	4.48	5.55	0.35	2.87	3.19	1.63	2.45	1.79	2.46	1.79

TABLE 5.3 *continued*

State	20	2085	2511	2648	3011	3931	314	21	3711	2911	3911
Covariation sign	+	+	+	+	+	−	+	+	+	+	+
Louisiana											
Compensation rate	6.7	4.2	7.8	2.2	3.7	2.6		3.3	5.8	3.4	1.6
Employment effect	1.83	3.84	7.59	0.55	2.31	2.67		3.24	1.60	3.99	1.06
Covariation sign	+	+	+	+	+	+	+	+	+	+	+
Maine											
Compensation rate	5.5		7.1		7.2	2.8	2.0		4.9	6.4	1.8
Employment effect	1.51		6.91		4.49	2.88	1.72		1.35	7.50	1.20
Covariation sign	+		+		+	+	+		−	+	+
Maryland											
Compensation rate	5.1	10.8	4.9	4.7	5.9	2.8	2.2	4.3	5.8	5.1	3.5
Employment effect	1.40	9.88	4.77	1.17	3.68	2.88	1.89	4.22	1.60	5.98	2.33
Covariation sign	+	+	−	+	+	+	+	+	−	+	+
Michigan											
Compensation rate	7.8		8.5	6.5	18.6	7.5	3.1	2.0	7.6	6.1	4.1
Employment effect	2.14		8.27	1.62	11.61	7.71	2.67	1.96	2.09	7.15	2.73
Covariation sign	+	+	+	+	+	+	+	+	−	+	+
Minnesota											
Compensation rate	7.9	7.9	8.5	5.9	5.7	1.8	3.4	1.1	10.2	4.2	1.4
Employment effect	2.16	7.23	8.27	1.47	3.56	1.85	2.92	1.08	2.81	4.92	0.93
Covariation sign	+	+	+	−	+	+	+	+	+	+	+

Mississippi											
Compensation rate	3.2		4.0	2.8	3.5	1.4	1.10		2.7	2.5	6.1
Employment effect	0.88		3.89	0.70	2.18	1.44	0.95		0.74	2.93	4.05
Covariation sign	+		+	+	+	+	+		+	+	+
Missouri											
Compensation rate	2.9	5.2	4.3	2.4	3.0	1.9	1.1	1.6	3.6	2.8	1.0
Employment effect	0.79	4.76	4.19	0.60	1.87	1.95	0.95	1.57	0.99	3.28	0.66
Covariation sign	+	+	+	+	+	+	+	+	+	+	+
Montana											
Compensation rate	7.2	9.3	5.0		4.5	1.6			4.4	2.7	0.7
Employment effect	1.97	8.51	4.87		2.81	1.64			1.21	3.17	0.47
Covariation sign	+	+	+		−	+			+	+	+
Nebraska											
Compensation rate	3.0	3.6	4.1	1.9	2.0	2.2	2.4	29.8	3.4	1.7	1.0
Employment effect	0.82	3.29	3.99	0.47	1.25	2.26	2.06	29.24	0.94	1.99	0.66
Covariation sign	+	+	−	+	+	+	+	+	+	+	+
New Hampshire											
Compensation rate	5.8		6.7	2.7	4.4	2.9	2.9		6.4	7.9	1.8
Employment effect	1.59		6.52	0.67	2.75	2.98	2.49		1.76	9.26	1.20
Covariation sign	+		+	+	+	+	+		+	+	+
New Mexico											
Compensation rate	6.8		6.8	2.2	4.7	4.9			5.1	3.5	2.6
Employment effect	1.86		6.62	0.55	2.93	5.04			1.40	4.10	1.73
Covariation sign	+		+	+	−	+			−	+	+

TABLE 5.3 *continued*

State	20	2085	2511	2648	3011	3931	314	21	3711	2911	3911
North Carolina											
Compensation rate	2.3	6.5	2.2	1.4	2.1	2.2	1.1	0.8	1.8	1.5	1.6
Employment effect	0.63	5.95	2.14	0.35	1.31	2.26	0.95	0.78	0.50	1.76	1.06
Covariation sign	+	+	+	+	+	+	+	+	+	+	+
Oklahoma											
Compensation rate	6.9	8.3	9.8	4.8	4.6	3.5	1.3		7.4	1.7	2.5
Employment effect	1.89	7.59	9.54	1.20	2.87	3.60	1.12		2.04	1.99	1.66
Covariation sign	+	+	+	+	+	−	+		+	+	+
Oregon											
Compensation rate	11.0	10.4	12.8	6.0		5.9	3.5		11.1	6.6	2.5
Employment effect	3.01	9.52	12.46	1.50		6.06	3.01		3.05	7.74	1.66
Covariation sign	+	+	+	+		−	+		+	+	+
Rhode Island											
Compensation rate	7.0		6.2	2.7	4.1	3.4	5.5		8.1	4.5	2.8
Employment effect	1.92		6.03	0.67	2.56	3.49	4.73		2.23	5.28	1.86
Covariation sign	+		+	+	+	+	+		+	−	+
South Carolina											
Compensation rate	3.4	2.5	4.4	2.7	1.3	1.8	1.1	4.4	2.7		1.6
Employment effect	0.93	2.29	4.28	0.67	0.81	1.85	0.95	4.32	0.74		1.06
Covariation sign	+	−	+	−	+	+	+	+	−		+

South Dakota

Compensation rate	2.9	3.9	2.8		1.9	1.4		2.3		0.9
Employment effect	0.79	3.57	2.73		1.19	1.44		0.63		0.60
Covariation sign	+	+	+		+	+		+		+

Tennessee

Compensation rate	3.5	3.3	4.5	2.6	4.3	2.4	2.8	5.4	3.6	2.5	1.0
Employment effect	0.96	3.02	4.38	0.65	2.68	2.47	2.41	5.30	0.99	2.93	0.66
Covariation sign	+	+	+	+	+	−	+	+	−	+	+

Utah

Compensation rate	2.8	3.5	1.8	4.8	1.3	1.2	2.3	2.0	0.4
Employment effect	0.77	3.41	0.45	3.00	1.34	1.03	0.63	2.34	0.27
Covariation sign	+	+	+	+	+	+	−	+	+

Vermont

Compensation rate	3.3	3.5	4.5	6.5	2.4	3.3	1.2			1.0
Employment effect	0.90	3.20	4.38	1.62	1.50	3.39	1.03			0.66
Covariation sign	+	+	+	−	+	+	+			+

Virginia

Compensation rate	4.4	7.0	3.3	3.1	4.8	1.9	1.5	1.1	2.6	2.3	1.2
Employment effect	1.21	6.41	3.21	0.77	3.00	1.95	1.29	1.08	0.72	2.70	0.80
Covariation sign	+	+	+	−	+	+	+	+	+	+	+

Wisconsin

Compensation rate	3.6	5.1	5.0	4.2	4.5	1.5	1.4	2.4	2.7	1.0	1.6
Employment effect	0.99	4.67	4.87	1.05	2.81	1.54	1.20	2.35	0.74	1.17	1.06
Covariation sign	+	+	+	−	+	+	+	+	+	+	+

6 · THE ECONOMICS OF TRANSITIONAL EMPLOYMENT AND SUPPORTED EMPLOYMENT

Craig Thornton and Rebecca Maynard

Despite federal efforts to enhance the employment prospects for working-age disabled Americans who have some permanent mental or physical condition, the low level of job-holding among this population remains a serious problem. In 1982, approximately 75 percent of the working-age adult population who reported that they were limited in the amount and kind of work they could do because of their physical or mental condition did not have a job (U.S. Bureau of the Census 1983). This is a distressing situation not simply for those persons who are either unemployed or have dropped out of the labor force in discouragement, but particularly for the thousands of students with physical and mental impairments who hope to graduate from school into jobs each year. Moreover, because of the paucity of job opportunities, many individuals who are in sheltered workshops or work-activity centers are prevented from moving into regular competitive employment where wages are higher and greater opportunities are available to interact with nondisabled peers. And even among impaired workers who are employed independently, some groups, due to their own expectations or those of others, are not being employed as productively as possible in their particular positions.

This scenario of unemployment and underemployment presents a clear challenge to public policy oriented toward the disabled

We thank Thomas Good for his assistance in editing.

person's work. Two issues must be addressed in meeting such a challenge. The first is the loss in *economic efficiency*—that is, the loss of the goods and services that could be available to society as a whole if disabled persons were employed productively. The second is the loss in *equity*—the degree to which the distribution of income, wealth, and opportunities diverges from what is socially desirable. Concerns about lost efficiency reflect the growing body of evidence that many disabled persons could work productively if given appropriate training and support. Concerns about equity reflect a general sense that sufficient job opportunities are simply not available to disabled persons—an attitude reflected by President Reagan's November 28, 1983, proclamation of the "Decade of Disabled Persons," whereby the economic independence of all disabled Americans has become a "clear national goal."

Beginning with the Rehabilitation Act of 1973 (P.L. 93–112), which prohibited discrimination against handicapped persons in programs and activities receiving federal financial assistance,[1] several policies have been implemented during the past four administrations to address these efficiency and equity concerns. For example, the Vocational Education Act and provisions of the Comprehensive Employment and Training Act (1973) and the Job Training Partnership Act (1982) have actively encouraged the participation of disabled persons in vocational training and employment programs. The Revenue Act of 1978 provided tax credits for hiring disabled workers. The Education for All Handicapped Children Act of 1975 required that all such children be provided with a free and appropriate education, and that, to the extent possible, they receive that education in the same environment as nondisabled children. Amendments to the social security act in 1980 and 1984 attempted to reduce some of the work disincentives to disabled Americans that are created by the Social Security Disability Insurance (SSDI) and Supplemental Security Income (SSI) programs. In addition, a number of court cases and grow-

---

1. In addition to prohibiting discrimination, the 1973 act also mandated that architectural barriers be eliminated, and that most federal contractors take affirmative action to employ disabled individuals. (It should be noted that, although the act was passed in 1973, the implementing regulations—45 C.F.R. 84.1 et seq.—were not published until 1977.)

ing pressure from advocates (and state budgets) have led to the deinstitutionalization of many disabled adults, and have prompted a greater emphasis on community integration for disabled persons in general.

These laws and the programs they have engendered have greatly enhanced the employment prospects for persons with physical or mental impairments; despite their success, however, a high, persistent level of unemployment and underemployment remains, particularly among those persons severely affected. In response to this prevailing employment problem, further efforts have been undertaken to refine public policy, particularly the promotion of two program models that offer a more direct approach for increasing the job opportunities available to this group: transitional employment and supported employment.

Transitional employment, which provides limited-duration services that place and train persons in competitive jobs, represents a bridge to employment for persons who are in schools or sheltered workshops, or who are simply unemployed. Supported employment, which provides long-run services to enable individuals to remain in their jobs, is targeted toward more severely impaired persons who would be unable to remain employed without ongoing assistance. Both programs emphasize placement in jobs that exist in the competitive labor market, although they also recognize that subsidies and other forms of support may in some cases be necessary.

Although the basic concepts behind these programs are not new (both draw on ideas developed and used in the fields of education and training), they have only recently been used to help disabled persons. Yet the persistent unemployment rate and the slow integration of disabled Americans into the social and economic mainstream have fostered the rapid growth of transitional employment and sparked an increased interest in, if not the actual implementation of, supported employment.

The purpose of this paper is to offer an economic assessment of the two program models by exploring the rationale that underlies these direct government interventions and by examining existing evidence on their economic efficiency and equity—that is, examining whether they offer the potential for generating impacts sufficiently large to outweigh their costs. We begin our assessment by defining the transitional and supported employment models, and then by examining the specific problems addressed by transitional and supported employment and asking why they represent appropriate types of interventions. The crux of our paper analyzes the potential of transitional and supported employment to enhance the employment prospects for disabled persons. We consider the existing evidence on the feasibility of these programs, their costs, the potential magnitude of their impacts, and the types of intangible benefits they may generate. We focus on the potential of the programs, rather than on their actual performance, because currently available evaluations provide insufficient evidence to estimate accurately the impacts of the programs.

DEFINITIONS: TRANSITIONAL EMPLOYMENT AND SUPPORTED EMPLOYMENT

As suggested in figure 6.1, persons can move from school, sheltered workshops, day-activity programs, or unemployment into two types of employment: independent employment or supported employment. Both types involve jobs in which the worker produces goods and services that have economic value, in which the worker receives a wage, and in which the worker has an opportunity to interact with nondisabled peers. Independent employment is established when two distinctive features are met: the worker is paid at least the minimum wage, and the job is not subsidized.[2] Supported employment requires only that the worker be paid a wage commensurate with his or her productivity. Supported employment also provides the ongoing public support necessary to ensure the continued employment of the worker; this may include subsidies to employers (to offset training and supervisory costs), stipends to supplement the incomes of workers, ongoing training and counseling, and assistance with housing, money management, and other non-work-related activities. In general, supported work is targeted toward persons who are moderately, severely,

---

2. Independent employment programs sometimes require short-term wage subsidies, such as the targeted jobs tax credits, to enable workers to become established on the job. However, the subsidies are provided only in the expectation that the job will become unsubsidized within a well-defined time.

FIGURE 6.1
Transitional Employment and
Supported Employment Models

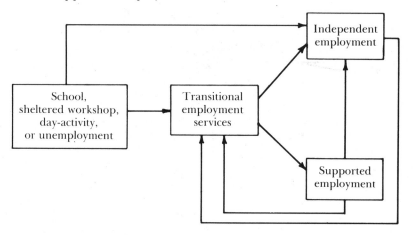

or profoundly retarded, who have multiple disabling conditions, who are autistic, or who suffer from other severe physical or mental conditions. (See Bellamy and Melia 1984 and Hill et al. 1985b for more details on the distinctive features of supported employment.)

Transitional employment provides job placement, training, and support services in order to help persons move into supported or independent employment. Services are aimed at training the program participants to perform the specific functions of the job they are expected to hold. At least part of the training is typically provided on the job, which is particularly helpful for those mentally impaired persons who experience difficulties in generalizing newly acquired skills to different settings. Such training may be combined with a variety of support services that may, for example, help clients cope with a new work supervisor, deal with disillusionment or confusion about the job in particular or working in general, handle relationships with coworkers, adapt to new job tasks, or deal with non-work-related activities. Moreover, the services may also focus on the employer, training supervisors to work with handicapped individuals or restructuring job tasks to fit the abilities of disabled workers. (See Wehman 1981, Riccio and Price 1984, and Hill et al. 1985b for more details on the distinctive features of transitional employment.)

In many cases, transitional employment will help persons who are unemployed or who are leaving school or sheltered workshops to find and hold independent employment. In other cases in which independent employment is not feasible within the time frame inherent in transitional employment, the program will help the person move into supported employment. In either case, if a person subsequently loses his or her job, transitional employment services may again become necessary to move the individual into another job. Of course, some persons may make the transition from unemployment to independent employment or from supported employment to independent employment without relying on any special transitional employment services.

Although figure 6.1 suggests a clear distinction between transitional employment and supported employment, in practice the two often overlap. The programs that have been implemented have generally offered both transitional and supported employment services, depending on the needs and abilities of their participants. At one extreme, some persons might require only a small investment in transitional training and job placement to become employed independently. Others may require more intensive transitional and support services—longer training, additional job placements, or more follow-up services. At the other extreme, some persons might never become employed independently, but might be able to work productively given the proper degree and type of support.

In addition, a growing body of literature (for example, Rusch and Mithaug 1980, Wehman 1981, and Hill et al. 1985b) indicates that more severely disabled individuals need *both* transitional and long-term support services to maintain employment. This literature argues, for example, that many disabled persons commonly lose their jobs by failing to adjust to normal changes in job tasks and the work environment—for instance, new supervisors, new job tasks, or new coworkers. Such changes can be stressful and, if the worker fails to adapt adequately to the changes, may lead to job loss. Although transitional employment services may have helped these individuals obtain and hold their jobs, ongoing support may become necessary to consolidate and maintain the employment gains generated by transitional employment. Thus, for many participants, the two programs act as complements.

Despite this functional interrelation between the two programs, specific working definitions of each are of course useful. Distinctions between them partly reflect differences in the specific clients who are served by the programs, as well as in the different methods used by each program to help those clients. They also reflect the fact that funds for short-term transitional employment would probably be obtained from different sources than would funds for ongoing supported employment. For example, a state department of vocational rehabilitation might fund short-term services consistent with their general training orientation, while state departments of developmental disabilities that have long-run responsibilities might fund ongoing support (the case in Virginia; see Hill et al. 1985b). Thus, a reasonable working definition of transitional employment would include a set of services oriented toward placing and training a person on a job, within a time frame of at most eighteen months. A reasonable working definition of supported employment would include a set of follow-up and support services of various intensities after a person is placed in independent or supported employment, or after the eighteenth month following his or her enrollment in the programs. Under these definitions, some persons in supported employment receive only minimal services;[3] persons who lose their jobs and require transitional employment services are defined as re-enrolling in transitional employment rather than as receiving those transitional services from a supported employment program.

Alternatively, supported employment could be defined to include all the services needed to place and maintain a worker with disabilities on a job. This is the case in the operational definition of supported employment currently proposed by the U.S. Department

---

3. For example, Moss (1980) reports that his program spent only ten dollars per client per month on long-run support services.

of Education (1985). This definition has four components pertaining to employment, integration, support, and target population. They require that:

1. Persons in supported employment must engage in paid work for at least 20 hours a week.

2. The work must provide for interactions with persons without disabilities who are not paid caregivers, and there must be eight or fewer persons with disabilities working together at the worksite.

3. There must be ongoing public funding for providing interventions directly related to sustaining employment.

4. Supported employment programs must serve only those persons for whom time-limited employment programs are inadequate—specifically, those not previously served by vocational rehabilitation because of a lack of ongoing support services and those currently served in day-activity programs.

PROGRAM RATIONALE

The range of laws, regulations, and programs enacted to enhance the employment prospects for disabled persons reflects the complexity of the problem and the difficulty in dealing with the numerous factors that influence job-holding by persons with physical and mental impairments. Before assessing the potential of transitional employment and supported employment to increase economic efficiency and equity, we should first examine the most important of these factors and the extent to which the programs deal with them. To do so, we will group the factors into six categories: (1) general unemployment conditions, (2) the work disincentives created by income-support programs, (3) discrimination by employers or their lack of knowledge about the skills of disabled persons, (4) market failure, (5) minimum-wage laws, and (6) the work attitudes of disabled persons.

GENERAL UNEMPLOYMENT CONDITIONS

The general level of unemployment in the economy obviously influences job-holding by handicapped persons. When an excess supply of labor exists, these persons are at a particular disadvantage in the labor market and, consequently, are likely to experience above-average unemployment.

If unemployment rose and a greater number of severely disabled persons lost jobs, transitional and supported employment services would be in greater demand. Moreover, if increases in government spending were planned in order to increase the overall aggregate demand for goods and services in the economy, investments in programs oriented toward disabled workers would represent one promising funding option. Nevertheless, transitional and supported employment programs are generally too narrowly targeted to be appropriate tools for dealing with macroeconomic problems such as general unemployment.

It should be noted, however, that the level of unemployment can be expected to influence the effects of these two programs. It will be easier for programs to place participants in jobs when overall unemployment is low. Alternatively, when unemployment is high, not only will programs have difficulty placing participants, there will also be an increased likelihood that the programs will have indirect labor-market effects—especially displacement, which occurs when an excess supply of labor exists and an employment program places participants in jobs that would otherwise have been held by someone else. (See Smith, chapter 7 of this volume, for a discussion of potential displacement effects.) Under these conditions, the employment program may find itself merely reallocating a fixed set of jobs among participants and other workers without generating any increase in overall employment. These effects would probably occur for many transitional and supported employment programs, which often place participants in entry-level jobs for which an excess supply of labor would likely exist even in relatively good economic conditions.[4] Displacement implies that the employment gains of participants are at

---

4. To the extent that participants give up jobs to enter the employment program, "replacement" is likely to occur—that is, their jobs become filled by persons who would otherwise have been unemployed (see G.E. Johnson 1979). However, given the generally low rates of job-holding among persons who enter transitional and supported employment, replacement is not likely to be substantial.

least partially offset by the employment losses to other workers. Consequently, an evaluation of these programs must weigh the interests of the two groups.[5]

WORK DISINCENTIVES

Another factor that induces a low level of job-holding among disabled workers is the work disincentive created by income-support programs such as SSDI, SSI, and Medicaid—specifically, the termination of benefits to some persons who because of their employment are no longer strictly considered to be disabled. Even if their earnings were not at a level that would cause a termination in benefits, disincentives still exist. Income-support programs generally reduce payments as earnings increase. These reductions, in conjunction with regular payroll and income taxes, create implicit marginal tax rates on earnings that often exceed 70 percent, and can exceed 100 percent when medical benefits are considered. (Leonard, chapter 3 of this volume, examines these disincentive effects in more detail.) Thus, persons may be reluctant to work either because they are afraid of losing income-support benefits or because the marginal benefits of working are less than the perceived costs of working. (See also Weaver, chapter 2 of this volume.)

Transitional and supported employment do not address this problem. Nevertheless, it is interesting to note that many employment programs have successfully enrolled and placed persons who receive benefits from income-support programs, which suggests that at least some benefit recipients are strongly motivated to work, and that these programs can increase earnings for some participants by an amount that would offset the loss of income-support benefits. In addition, recent social security legislation (particularly amendments to section 1619 of the social security act) has attempted to reduce the financial disincentives stemming from SSDI and SSI regulations.

---

5. Alternatively, an evaluation could assess the potential of the programs under conditions of full employment (that is, the potential of transitional employment given that macroeconomic policy is successful in keeping employment levels high). In this case, displacement would be ignored from the perspective of the program.

EMPLOYER DISCRIMINATION AND LACK OF KNOWLEDGE

Discriminatory practices or misperceptions about the capabilities of impaired workers cause many employers not to hire these persons. (See Johnson, chapter 9 of this volume, for a detailed discussion.) Transitional and supported employment programs can play several important roles in helping to alleviate these types of problems. First, the programs provide a source for disseminating information about the capabilities and skills of workers with specific physical and mental impairments. Second, the training and support provided by these programs to the participant and the employer may mitigate the fears of employers about their inability to provide adequate training or supervision. Finally, some programs guarantee that the job tasks required of the participant during the training period will be completed (either by the participant or by the program's own trainer). Such assurances may help overcome the initial misapprehensions of employers and give both the employer and the worker sufficient time to become comfortable with each other.

MARKET FAILURE

Many persons with physical or mental impairments lack the employment skills necessary to become employed productively. By itself, this lack of skills need not cause a problem, since the skills can generally be acquired through appropriate training. However, if these persons cannot obtain that training, either because the proper services are unavailable or because they cannot afford to pay for them, then the level of job-holding among such workers will remain quite low. It is assumed that job-skills training would generally be provided if potential trainees could pay for it, and that the trainees would be willing to pay a price that reflected their expected earnings gains.[6] However, disabled persons may not have the funds to pay for the training, nor

---

6. The price of training includes the costs of materials, supplies, and uniforms, as well as any fees paid to the training provider. The price also includes the earnings that are foregone while a person is in training. Thus, some persons might not enter training because they would be unable to support themselves and their families on what they earn during the training. This disincentive is clearly related to the manner in which income-support programs treat work and earnings that are part of training.

be able to borrow those funds. Moreover, it may be considered in-equitable to ask these persons to pay for their own training.

The inability to finance training can be viewed as a capital market imperfection. For example, loans for training would be un-secured, since no tangible assets would exist for collateral. Moreover, lenders might feel that repayments would be problematic—for ex-ample, that the training might be ineffective, or that the trainee might choose not to work after receiving the training. Thus, lenders might either refuse to give loans or set interest rates so high that potential trainees would find it uneconomical to enter the program.

Moreover, even if capital markets functioned perfectly, lenders might still refuse to grant loans to persons whose expected earnings gains would be less than the costs of training. Although investments in training under such a scenario would represent a resource cost to society, society might still want to provide the training in order to equalize opportunities for employment or to generate other social benefits.[7]

Transitional employment provides one approach for dealing with this problem, by providing training services without costs to par-ticipants and by ensuring that at least some wages are paid during the training. Thus, they eliminate funding problems for potential trainees. Further, because these programs are prepared to offer a wide range of specialized training, they allow disabled persons to seek the most appropriate training services.

It is not necessary that one program address both the funding and the training problems. Clearly, transitional employment pro-grams represent an appropriate vehicle for delivering training, but they could be funded in a variety of ways. One method would be to provide affected persons with funds in a training account, which they could use to purchase whatever services they wanted. This funding method would enable persons to choose between alternative suppliers of transitional employment services and even between transitional

---

7. As discussed in Thornton 1985, training programs can create a wide variety of social benefits (i.e., effects that create or save resources). For example, the reduced use of sheltered workshops by trainees would free up those resources to be used elsewhere in the economy. We return to this issue in the section entitled "Program Potential."

employment and other forms of training or education. Whether they would be required to reimburse their account would depend on policy judgments about the equity of transferring income from taxpayers to potential trainees.

MINIMUM WAGE LAWS

Some individuals, even if they have received training services, may be unable to work at a level that employers would find consistent with the minimum wage. This is another reason for the low level of job-holding among more severely handicapped persons. Supported employment is specifically designed to deal with this problem. In conjunction with U.S. Department of Labor programs that provide exemptions to the minimum wage, these programs provide participants, even severely disabled persons, with an opportunity to perform productive work in a socially integrated work setting. Moreover, because supported employment offers a range of support services (subsidies, stipends, counseling, help with residential matters, etc.), it helps persons who have a wide range of needs better than would more single-purpose programs or simple sub-minimum-wage programs.

WORK ATTITUDES

The attitudes of disabled persons towards working will also influence their employment. These attitudes will be formed over their lifetimes, and will reflect the attitudes of parents, relatives, teachers, counselors, friends, and other persons with whom they interact. On the basis of these attitudes, they will weigh their available options and make their decisions.

Transitional and supported employment may not be well suited to changing attitudes toward working. In fact, these programs probably do not serve many persons who have already decided that they do not want to work. However, these programs can play an important role for students who are just graduating from secondary school. The changes mandated by the Education for All Handicapped Children Act (P.L. 94–142) have created a school environment that has increasingly stressed community integration. Thus, students who are leaving this environment may express greater interest in and have higher expectations about work than did previous generations of disabled persons. Transitional employment in particular can help maintain this enthusiasm by serving as a bridge from school to work; by helping students enter the adult world of work, the program helps persons maintain their morale when faced by the difficult task of finding employment.

Transitional and supported employment address several of the factors that induce low levels of job-holding among persons with physically or mentally limiting conditions. They provide a forum for disseminating information to employers about the capabilities of such workers; they help overcome market imperfections that inhibit an adequate supply of training services; they help persons who are not employed productively in the competitive labor market at or above the minimum wage; and they help maintain positive attitudes toward work by increasing the employment opportunities available to students who are graduating from school. However, they can do little about either general unemployment levels or the disincentives created by income-support programs.

These two programs must be viewed only as components of an overall strategy for improving the employment situation of disabled persons. Clearly, they must be combined with efforts to keep overall employment levels high and to reduce the disincentives for work created by social programs. They also benefit from the training and education provided under P.L. 94–142, and from the general work environment provided by laws against discrimination. (See Johnson, chapter 9 in this volume, for a discussion of antidiscrimination legislation; see Collignon, chapter 8, for an examination of the impact of workplace accommodations.) How they fit in with other training and employment programs (for example, traditional sheltered workshops or vocational rehabilitation placement activities) will depend on their relative costs and their success in generating employment.

PROGRAM POTENTIAL

Transitional and supported employment clearly could help enhance the employment prospects for disabled persons. The experience of dozens of small programs fielded around the country and the larger statewide implementation efforts of Washington and Massachusetts indicate that these programs are feasible, and that many participants do become employed. However, whether these programs create effects that are sufficiently large to justify their costs is an issue that has yet to be resolved. That is, compared with what would have happened in their absence, do these programs create changes that are worth at least as much as the resources used to operate them? And how do these programs compare with other training and placement options?

It is difficult to determine whether the effects of the programs are large enough to justify their costs. While considerable operational experience has been gained, evidence on program performance is extremely limited. In part, this reflects the focus of most early programs on developing appropriate training protocols and demonstrating their operational feasibility. The programs generally had inadequate resources for conducting accurate evaluations of their operations; though early studies all report favorable program performance, most suffer from major technical problems that could invalidate their findings.

One exception is the U.S. Department of Labor's Structured Training and Employment Transitional Services (STETS) demonstration. This was a multimillion dollar demonstration that tested a transitional employment program for mentally retarded young adults. It was fielded in five cities and served almost three hundred participants. The demonstration included a rigorous evaluation component that randomly assigned eligible applicants to a treatment group, which was offered transitional employment services, and a control group, which was prevented from receiving the new demonstration services but could use all other services available in the community. Both groups were followed for almost two years. Riccio and Price (1984) discuss the implementation of the demonstration and Kerachsky et al. (1985) present the evaluation findings. The results of this evaluation, which are summarized later in this section, generally support the earlier findings, although the findings here are more modest than those claimed for previous transitional employment programs for mentally retarded persons.

Further evidence will be forthcoming from the Secondary Transition Intervention Effectiveness Institute, funded by the U.S. Department of Education and situated at the University of Illinois.

This institute is in the process of assessing the effects of over 110 transition-related programs. Also, the National Supported Employment Demonstration (again funded by the U.S. Department of Education) is providing seed money to ten states to enable them to expand supported employment services for persons with severe disabilities. While the current evaluation components of both these large efforts are limited, the experience provided by these demonstrations will help to resolve questions about program potential.

We begin our approach by reviewing data on the average costs of a few programs that have been evaluated. While the available data are generally limited and contain substantial inconsistencies, it is possible to judge the order of magnitude of costs for transitional and supported employment. We then examine the available evidence on the effects of the two programs (particularly with respect to increases in participant employment and earnings) to assess their potential for enhancing economic efficiency and equity. Ultimately, it will be necessary to go beyond this work to evaluate the relative performance of transitional and supported employment vis-à-vis alternative training, placement, and employment programs, so as to determine the optimal mix of government programs.

THE COSTS OF TRANSITIONAL AND SUPPORTED EMPLOYMENT

The costs of these two program models will depend on the specific populations being served, their objectives (e.g., independent or supported employment), the operational scale, the average length of participation, the range of services offered, the local service environment, local price levels, and other factors. Costs can be expected to vary across programs as different operators make different decisions about these factors. Such variation is indicated in table 6.1, which presents cost estimates for a range of programs. These include four employment and training programs funded by the U.S. Department of Labor for general populations of disadvantaged workers, the five transitional employment programs included in the STETS demonstration, the transitional and supported employment programs being operated at Virginia Commonwealth University, the transitional employment programs of seventeen operators funded by the state of Massachusetts through the Bay State Skills Corporation, and a transitional employ-

TABLE 6.1

Average Operating Expenditures
for Transitional and
Supported Employment Programs
(1984 dollars)

Program (source)	Average Expenditure per Participant-Year	Average Expenditure per Participant
U.S. Department of Labor programs (Taggart 1981)		
Job Corps	16,493	8,384
Work experience (CETA)	6,642	2,052
Public service employment (CETA)	11,292	4,630
On-the-job training (CETA)	7,613	2,049
STETS program (Riccio and Price 1984)		
Cincinnati	11,107	9,070
Los Angeles	9,418	7,848
New York	12,352	10,396
St. Paul	5,828	4,613
Tucson	7,243	7,605
Average for all participants	9,387	8,136
Virginia Commonwealth University: Rehabilitation Research and Training Center		
Transitional employment (Hill et al. 1985b)	7,668	3,539
Supported employment (Hill et al. 1985b)	2,590	n.a.
Project employability (Hill et al. 1985a)[a]	n.a.	6,264
Bay State Skills Corporation (Bailis et al. 1984)[b]	9,996	3,533
University of Washington food service program (Moss 1980)	11,602	10,319

Notes: While it was attempted to make the cost estimates as consistent as possible, differences still exist. For example, the costs for STETS and the Bay State Skills Corporation include some wage payments to participants, while the Virginia Commonwealth estimates do not include any payments to clients. Costs have been inflated to 1984 dollars by using the change in the implicit price deflator for gross national product.

N.a. means data are unavailable.

[a]Because project employability combines transitional and supported employment, the total cost per participant will depend on the length of stay. The cost estimates presented cover seventy months of operation, although most persons had not been enrolled for that long. Thus, costs per participant will continue to rise as supported employment services continue to be provided.

[b]The Bay State Skills Corporation figures reflect the experiences of seventeen vendors who enrolled 306 clients during fiscal years 1982 and 1983. Average costs per participant for these vendors ranged from about $5,500 to $1,700.

ment program with long-run follow-up operated through the University of Washington. While these programs and the persons they serve are quite different, their costs indicate the range of costs that might be expected for these general types of programs.

The first column of estimates indicates the intensity of the intervention by presenting the average expenditures for one year's worth of services to a client (participant). The second column indicates the average expenditures per participant, which reflects the average expenditures per year and the average length of participation. Because of the differences in specific program objectives, accounting procedures, and the impacts generated by the programs, these cost numbers are inappropriate for comparing the performance of the respective programs. However, they do suggest that these interventions require substantial resources, particularly when compared with traditional efforts with less disadvantaged populations sponsored by the Department of Labor.

The estimates from STETS, Bay State Skills Corporation (BSSC), and the transitional employment component at Virginia Commonwealth's Rehabilitation Research and Training Center (RRTC) provide the best indication of the expenditures necessary to operate a transitional employment program. Costs per participant-year ranged from about $6,000 to over $12,000, with a median cost of $9,400. Costs per participant varied even more because of substantial differences in the length of stay (STETS participants were enrolled for an average of 10.5 months, and BSSC participants an average of 4.2 months).[8] While it is difficult to judge from this evidence, it appears that a transitional employment program will spend at least $3,500 per person enrolled (the amount spent at RRTC and BSSC), and possibly up to 2.5 times that amount, depending on the length of stay in the program.

---

8. Differences in compensation of participants also create differences in average expenditures. Participants who were placed on jobs were generally paid at least the minimum wage in STETS. Employers paid part of this compensation, with the programs paying the rest. During the early phase of the STETS intervention, projects often paid the entire wage. In comparison, the RRTC program requires that employers pay the full wage from the beginning of employment. The RRTC model is clearly less expensive in this regard; it is unclear whether the payments enabled the STETS programs to save money in their job-development activities (e.g., by getting employers to cooperate more easily).

The best currently available estimates of expenditures for a supported employment program come from RRTC, which estimates that it would cost approximately $2,600 per year to provide ongoing support to persons who are placed and trained on a job. This expenditure encompasses an average of just over two hours of staff time per week devoted to each client. In the University of Washington food service program, long-run follow-up and support were much less extensive, and so cost only about $625 per year. The actual amount will depend on the severity of the participants' conditions and on the types of support services they need.

These expenditure levels represent only the costs of the support that would be provided by program staff. In some cases, it might also be necessary to provide subsidies to employers to compensate them for their supervisory or training costs in excess of those that they normally incur for other workers. It might also become necessary to provide stipends to the participating workers. For instance, under current social security regulations (specifically, section 1619 of the Social Security Act of 1935), cash SSI benefits and (in most states) eligibility for Medicaid continue until workers earn a substantial, state-specified amount.[9] Thus, at present, supported employment programs generally need not provide income support. However, because those social security provisions expire in 1987, it may become necessary thereafter to provide some stipends in order to counteract the disincentive effects created by losses in SSI.[10] However, because so little evidence is available on how much of a subsidy or stipend would be required, it is unclear how these costs should be estimated.

These expenditures for transitional and supported employment are not out of line with expenditures for other employment-

---

9. Workers continue to receive cash benefits, but, as earnings increase, benefits are reduced at a marginal rate of 50 percent until they reach the break-even level. The exact amount of this SSI break-even level varies across states, but, in general, it is over $10,000 per year. To earn this amount, a worker would have to work full-time at a wage of at least $4.80 per hour.

10. As defined by the permanent provisions of the Social Security Act of 1935, all except blind persons who earn more than $300 per month are engaged in substantial gainful activity and thus are no longer considered to be disabled. Consequently, participants in supported employment would run the risk of losing their cash benefits and (in most states) their eligibility for Medicaid if their program earnings were above the $300 level.

oriented interventions. If participation in transitional employment remained fairly short-term (for example, at the levels reported by RRTC and BSSC), then expenditures per participant for transitional employment would be about the same as those for the major CETA programs (other than Job Corps).[11]

Another useful comparison of the expenditures for these employment programs can be made with the expenditures for other types of programs that serve persons who have disabilities (all dollar estimates have been adjusted to 1984 dollars).[12] Nationwide studies conducted by the U.S. Department of Labor (1977) and Greenleigh Associates (1975) suggest that sheltered workshops require public subsidies of over $6,000 per year, but that work-activity centers require only approximately $2,880 per year. Hill et al. (1985a) find that day adult-service programs in Virginia cost over $5,200 per participant-year. Kakalik et al. (1981) suggest that special education services cost an average of $4,680 per student-year nationwide. On the basis of the RRTC cost estimates, it appears that supported employment is no more expensive than these long-term alternatives, and, moreover, that transitional employment may be substantially less expensive because it does not provide ongoing services.

IMPACTS OF TRANSITIONAL AND SUPPORTED EMPLOYMENT:
LIMITATIONS AND INTERPRETATIONS

The next step in our assessment is to determine whether the programs generate impacts that justify their costs. Impacts could take the form of either increased earnings or other activities that lead to increases in social resources. If these increases were sufficiently large, the programs would be justified on the grounds of improving economic efficiency. If society placed a sufficiently high value on the opportunities the programs provided to handicapped persons, they would be justified on the grounds of equity as well. A careful analysis of program-

---

11. Because Job Corps offers intensive training and, for the most part, residential services, it is more expensive than most other Department of Labor training programs; however, its expenditures per participant are roughly equivalent to those observed for the STETS transitional employment program.

12. All inflation adjustments are made by using the change in the implicit price deflator for gross national product.

induced impacts can generate an accurate assessment of economic efficiency. Assessments of changes in the distribution of resources, on the other hand, must reflect political judgments; although the magnitude of any changes can be estimated, decisions about their value must be made by policy makers.

Many of the transitional and supported employment programs that have been fielded to date have been evaluated using a variety of methods and outcome measures. Evaluations have generally examined placement rates, continued employment, and earnings over some period of time, and some have widened their focus by examining changes in the use of income-support programs and alternative or complementary service programs. The most comprehensive evaluation of a transitional employment program is the one Kerachsky et al. (1985) conducted of the STETS demonstration. There have been a few evaluations conducted of university-based transitional employment programs, notably those done by Hill et al. (1985a), Hill and Wehman (1983), Schneider et al. (1982), and Moss (1980). O'Neill and Associates (1984) have examined the statewide transitional employment effort in the state of Washington, and Bailis et al. (1984) have examined the similar efforts of Massachusetts. Very little has been written about the effects of supported employment; an exception is the report of Hill et al. (1985b) on their program at Virginia Commonwealth University.

As noted, the evidence about program impacts is extremely limited for most of these evaluations due to their lack of a valid comparison group. The principal exception is the STETS evaluation, which used an experimental design to estimate program impacts over the twenty-two months following participants' enrollment. This evaluation, which ran from 1981 to 1985, focused on transitional employment for mentally retarded young adults aged 18 to 25 in five cities. Its results are particularly relevant for the issue of the transition from school to work or for other program options aimed at young adults. Its results are more suggestive than conclusive for other populations of handicapped individuals.

The STETS evaluation concluded that transitional employment services can be instrumental in helping mentally retarded young adults achieve their employment potential. The services did not appear to increase the overall level of employment activity, but did significantly increase the fraction of participants who held regular competitive jobs rather than jobs in sheltered workshops. The net gain in unsubsidized employment twenty-two months after enrollment was an increase from 19 percent to 31 percent—an increase of more than 50 percent over what would have been expected in the absence of the transitional employment services. This represents a movement into competitive employment of 60 percent of those who otherwise would have had sheltered-workshop or activity-center jobs. The services also increased average weekly earnings of all participants by over 43 percent.

The results from this evaluation have two important implications for evaluations that lack valid comparison groups. The first is that it is easy to overestimate program impacts when considering only outcomes for participants. It is quite possible that without program intervention some participants would have obtained jobs. After twenty-two months, 19 percent of the STETS control group members had a regular job (i.e., a job that was neither a training nor a workstudy position, nor a position in a sheltered workshop or activity center), and 44 percent had some type of paid job. Thus, all postintervention employment of participants generally should not be attributed to the transitional employment services.

To illustrate this issue, consider the recent study by Hill et al. (1985a) of the RRTC program, which offers a combination of transitional and supported employment services. This study, although carefully constructed, lacks a valid comparison group. To correct this shortcoming, the study attempts to determine what would have happened to participants in the absence of the RRTC program by estimating their activities at the time of enrollment (e.g., whether they enrolled from a sheltered workshop, work-activity center, no formal program, etc.). The study assumes that participants would have continued to engage in their baseline activities in the absence of the RRTC program, and thus uses this assumption as the basis for estimating the impacts of the program. However, as indicated by the STETS results, this assumption is not necessarily accurate. Because entering a transitional employment program may indicate a participant's predisposition toward changing his or her current activities, he or she may have a greater likelihood of undergoing a change than would a person who chose not to enter the program. In STETS, for example, paid job activities among members of the STETS control group increased by 30 percent over the six months following random assignment (Kerachsky et al. 1985). Even though the RRTC sample members were generally more disabled than those in STETS, the estimates for STETS indicate the tenuousness of the RRTC assumption. Thus, the finding that the earnings of the average RRTC participant "increased" by over $5,300 during the observation period probably overstates the actual increase in earnings. Without knowing the extent of this overstatement (and encountering similar problems with other estimated impacts), it is difficult to judge whether the earnings gains and other observed benefits justify the observed cost of almost $5,500 for the same period. Such a situation illustrates even more clearly the weakness of the other studies that have failed to go so far as to develop a synthetic comparison group.

The second implication of the STETS findings pertains to program targeting. The concern here is that programs may focus on the individuals who can most easily be placed or served rather than on those for whom the programs will have the greatest impact. The STETS findings suggest that it may be the case that transitional employment services represent the only effective vehicle for helping many severely disabled persons obtain jobs, while more mildly handicapped persons may be able to obtain employment through other (less service-intensive) channels.[13] If program performance is judged only in terms of participant outcomes, and not relative to a valid comparison group, programs may tend to serve the more mildly impaired group, which can be expected to proceed more rapidly through the program and to have high rates of postprogram employment. In this case, the programs would spend fewer resources per participant, but would also generate smaller net impacts than if they had served the more severely impaired group. The most efficient targeting strategy can be determined only by examining the relative costs and the relative size of impacts as measured in a well-defined comparison study.

---

13. In STETS, the estimated program impacts on the probability of holding a regular job were essentially zero for participants with IQ scores in the "borderline" range (between normal and mildly retarded), 12 percentage points for those whose IQ scores indicated mild retardation, and 28 percentage points for those participants whose IQ scores indicated moderate retardation.

Determining whether an impact should be considered a benefit or a cost presents another difficulty in interpreting existing studies, since impacts that are perceived as benefits by some groups may be perceived as costs by others. The most notable example is a change in the receipt of income-support payments. A reduction in the average payment made to participants represents a saving to the government budget, but a cost of participation to the participants. From the social perspective, this change will be a benefit, cost, or neither according to how society regards the change in the distribution of resources.[14] If the evaluation seeks to judge the program from the perspective of the government budget, then changes in transfers (and similar outcomes, such as changes in a participant's tax payments) should be included. Alternatively, if the evaluation seeks to determine economic efficiency or equity, a more complex strategy is required.

One such strategy is reflected in table 6.2. This framework identifies three analytical perspectives. The social perspective includes only those impacts that affect (or could affect) the aggregate value of social resources. Thus, it can be used to judge economic efficiency. The participant perspective will indicate whether participants benefit on average from the program and could be expected to enroll voluntarily. The taxpayer perspective indicates whether a subsidy will be necessary to operate the program. Taken together, the participant and taxpayer perspectives can be used to assess the magnitude of the redistributional, or equity, effects. If it is assumed that a dollar of benefit or cost is equal for all persons in society, then the sum of the participant and taxpayer perspectives will equal the social perspective (i.e., all transfers between these groups will cancel out). This framework has proved useful for assessing several transitional employment programs for disadvantaged populations—specifically, Job Corps (Thornton, Long, and Mallar 1982; Long, Mallar, and Thornton 1981), the national supported work demonstration (Kemper, Long, and Thornton 1981), the RRTC program (Hill et al. 1985a), and the STETS demonstration (Kerachsky et al. 1985).

In addition to indicating the relationships among these three analytical perspectives, table 6.2 lists the major categories of benefits

---

14. Of course, resources that are used or saved because of changes in transfer payments would enter into the social perspective.

TABLE 6.2

Expected Benefits and Costs of
a Transitional or Supported Employment Program
by Analytical Perspective

Component	Analytical Perspective		
	Social	Participant	Taxpayer[a]
Program costs			
Project operations	−	0	−
Payments to participants	0	+	−
Central administration	−	0	−
Output produced by participants			
Increased in-program output	+	0	+
Increased out-of-program output	+	+	0
Reduced use of other programs			
Sheltered workshops	+	0	+
Work-activity centers	+	0	+
School	+	0	+
Job-training programs	+	0	+
Case-management services	+	0	+
Counseling services	+	0	+
Social/recreational services	+	0	+
Transportation services	+	0	+
Reduced use of residential programs			
Institutions	+	0	+
Group homes	+	0	+
Foster homes	+	0	+
Semi-independent residential programs	+	0	+
Transfer payments and taxes			
Reduced SSI/SSDI	0	−	+
Reduced other welfare	0	−	+
Reduced Medicaid/Medicare	0	−	+
Increased taxes	0	−	+
Transfer administration			
Reduced use of SSI/SSDI	+	0	+
Reduced use of other welfare	+	0	+
Reduced use of Medicaid/Medicare	+	0	+
Intangibles			
Preferences for work	+	+	+
Increased self-sufficiency	+	+	+
Increased variation in participant income	−	−	−
Foregone nonmarket activity	−	−	0
Increased independent living	+	+	+

Notes: The individual components are characterized from the three perspectives as being a net
benefit (+), a net cost (−), or neither (0).

[a]The taxpayer perspective includes all members of society who are not participants.

and costs of transitional and supported employment. Most of these categories are self-explanatory, but two deserve special mention: "other programs" and "intangibles."

Some authors argue against including reductions in the use of other, alternative, programs as a social benefit. For instance, Bailis et al. (1984) argue that, because of long waiting lists for these programs, the positions freed up by participants when they enter transitional employment will be filled by other persons, and thus no resource savings will accrue to other programs. Although this scenario is likely to hold true, the decision to serve additional persons represents only one way to use the resources freed up by reductions in the use of other programs by participants. If the resources are not reallocated to another program, taxpayers have made an implicit decision that serving additional persons in the original program is the best way to use the freed-up resources.[15]

Intangibles are difficult to evaluate. Consequently, although they are typically included in the accounting framework, they are left unmeasured. The intangibles generally include such elements as participants' preferences for work over welfare, changes in their self-sufficiency, and general improvements in the quality of their lives. They may also include such costs as increased stress or health problems associated with work. Moreover, persons who lose their eligibility for income-support benefits may face potentially more uncertainty about future income than those who remain unemployed but are still active in the income-support program. This increased risk may be an important but intangible participant cost.

These types of intangibles may be very important in evaluating transitional employment, particularly if the program is being justified on equity grounds. Thus, it is important that *indicators* of the impacts of the program on intangibles be developed. Self-sufficiency may be assessed by examining the presence of personal benefactors, the ability to handle money, the ability to travel independently, and the degree of independence in residential situations. Quality of life may be reflected in part by the estimated changes in earnings, residential situation, and program use. The difficulty with using indicators is that they may fail to reflect accurately any underlying phenomena that

---

15. Alternatively, if transitional or supported employment induces an increase in the use of complementary programs, extra costs would be generated.

change slowly. However, finding favorable impacts on intangibles would enhance arguments about the effects of the program on equity.

Given this framework and the necessity of evaluating programs relative to a defined comparison situation, what does the existing literature say about the potential of transitional and supported employment to generate benefits that would justify their costs? Although the literature indicates a great deal of potential, it provides little hard evidence on specific impacts. The studies by Schneider et al. (1982), Hill and Wehman (1983), Bailis et al. (1984), and Hill et al. (1985a) all present evidence that participants in transitional employment programs do obtain jobs, and that many participants can hold those jobs with only minimal program intervention. Because the costs of these programs are in line with the costs of common alternative programs, these types of government interventions clearly have the potential for efficiency and for increasing social equity. Moreover, all four studies present evidence that gross earnings plus the value of reduced alternative program use by participants outweighs costs over a three- or four-year time horizon. Thus it is possible that the programs are efficient as long as they have enrolled persons who would have had relatively low earnings otherwise and who would not have reduced their use of alternative programs over time. A more accurate assessment is problematic.

The STETS evaluation (Kerachsky et al. 1985), with its relatively large sample size (437 sample members) and rigorous experimental design, provides more solid evidence about the relative magnitudes of costs and benefits. These results indicate that gains in participant earnings over the twenty-two months following enrollment, coupled with reductions in participant use of other programs, offset 85 percent of the program costs. This leaves an average net social cost of approximately $1,000 per participant after the twenty-two-month period covered by evaluation data. However, trends observed during that period suggest that benefits will persist and eventually exceed costs. The data suggest that society can recoup its investment in 2.5 to 4.5 years.

SUMMARY

Transitional and supported employment programs for disabled persons have come a long way in the last fifteen years. They have developed rapidly past the prototype stage to a point where at least two states have implemented transitional employment on a statewide basis and ten states have agreed to expand supported employment services. These types of programs are clearly feasible, and many policy makers have adopted them because they address a key policy objective: they make current training technology available to disabled persons who would like to work. They also help foster the dissemination of information about the capabilities of disabled workers by helping employers and disabled persons work together.

The fact that these programs have expanded rapidly reflects this sense that they fill an important need. It also reflects the generally favorable performance measures of early programs. These measures—placement rates, starting wages, job tenure (beyond the traditional sixty days used by many rehabilitation agencies), and costs per placement—all indicate that the programs could successfully move even those persons who have severe disabilities into employment. The emphasis placed by these programs on community integration and on securing jobs in the competitive labor market also enhances their desirability.

The empirical evidence about program effectiveness is limited. Most evaluation efforts to date have lacked the valid comparison groups needed to estimate program impacts. Nevertheless, evidence from the one rigorous evaluation that has been conducted indicates that transitional employment can substantially increase participant employment rates, and that these programs can generate benefits that exceed their costs. When this finding is combined with the evidence of feasibility and potential from the other evaluation efforts, the combined weight of evidence indicates that transitional employment can be an effective means for reducing the unemployment of persons with disabilities. The feasibility and effectiveness of supported employment programs are more uncertain, since there have been many fewer programs and evaluations. The current National Supported Employment Demonstration being funded by the U.S. Department of Education should help to clarify this situation.

In the last fifteen years, the transitional and supported employment program models have grown into their adolescence. The available evidence demonstrates that they are feasible, and that they can reasonably be expected to be economically efficient and to help us achieve important equity goals. However, as these programs continue to mature, we will have to implement more sophisticated and thorough evaluations if we expect to answer the questions normally asked about mature programs:(1) are these programs cost-effective? (2) how should they be targeted? (3) with what types of administrative structures do they work best? and (4) how can training and support services be provided most economically?

These formative and summative evaluations can be expected to help operators refine the program models further and to help them enhance the employment prospects for disabled persons above the distressingly low levels noted at the outset of this paper.

7 · THE ECONOMICS OF JOB DISPLACEMENT

Robert S. Smith

It is of concern to policy makers that programs to enhance the job opportunities for certain groups of workers may increase their employment at the expense of employment among other groups. Put somewhat differently, a policy that increases employment among some "target group" by x may well increase *overall* employment by substantially less; the difference is due to the displacement of workers formerly in those jobs by members of the target group.[1] Government-subsidized programs of vocational rehabilitation of disabled persons are familiar with the charge that society may be helping one group at the expense of another. There are those who object that rehabilitating disabled persons, especially during periods of high unemployment, merely displaces others—and is therefore a waste of social resources. A somewhat more sophisticated view is put forth by some who argue that job displacement is one cost of the vocational rehabilitation program that ought to be included among other more direct costs in weighing the social gains and losses of the program.

I wish to thank Robert Aronson, Ronald Ehrenberg, Robert Hutchens, Olivia Mitchell, and Walter Oi for their helpful comments on an earlier draft. Each should be exonerated from blame for remaining deficiencies.

1. Displacement has been a central issue in the debate over public employment programs. See, for example, G. Johnson and Tomola 1977; Borus and Hamermesh 1978; Adams et al. 1983; and Fechter 1975.

The purpose of this paper is to analyze the issue of job displacement in general, with particular reference to the programs of vocational rehabilitation and targeted wage subsidies. The analysis begins with a brief consideration of the goals of, or bases for, government intervention in the labor market. These goals suggest related criteria by which to judge governmental programs, and these criteria are elaborated upon in the second section of this paper. The third section reviews concepts about how labor markets operate, and the remaining three sections discuss program-related job displacement.

GOALS OF GOVERNMENT INTERVENTION IN THE LABOR MARKET

One of the most common justifications for government programs is *income redistribution*. Government frequently acts out of compassion or a sense of equity to confer a set of benefits upon one or more disadvantaged groups in society. Often, such redistributive programs impose a direct cost on more advantaged members of society (as when the latter are taxed to finance transfers to the former). In other cases, however, the costs of subsidizing disadvantaged persons are felt only imprecisely and indirectly as relative employment opportunities are subtly altered.

Redistributive programs necessarily help one group at the expense of another. If, for example, new job opportunities are won for a particular disadvantaged group, they may tend to be accompanied by the displacement of others. The most extreme view of the job displacement allegedly accompanying vocational rehabilitation implicitly accepts the notion that this program is merely redistributive.

There is, however, another basis for governmental intervention in the labor market—one that emphasizes the net social gains that are possible to create in certain situations. Formulating programs to enhance *general* welfare (as opposed to the welfare of only a particular group) begins with the notion that social welfare is largely the sum of individual welfare. Our society relies heavily on the marketplace to accomplish transactions that are mutually beneficial to the parties involved. Exchanges that are beneficial to all parties, of course, can be voluntarily agreed upon, and the genius of the market system is that citizens are allowed to pursue the maximization of their own welfare through transactions of various kinds.

If primary reliance for the maximization of social welfare is placed on market exchanges, it is natural to wonder whether—or under what conditions—government intervention is warranted. Put briefly, markets may fail to accomplish all potential mutually beneficial transactions. With particular reference to disabled persons, for example, markets may fail for at least two reasons. First, employers may be ignorant of the productive potential of the disabled employee, in the sense that through lack of direct experience they underestimate the expected productivity of handicapped workers. Second, handicapped individuals may be prevented from securing employment opportunities that would otherwise be available to them because of an inability to obtain funds for vocational rehabilitation. That is, employers may be willing to hire suitably trained disabled persons, but the mutually beneficial transactions are blocked by capital market imperfections that prevent disabled individuals from borrowing funds to finance their rehabilitation.[2]

If either of these two barriers (or others) are present, then transactions that would enhance the social welfare (because they would benefit both employer and employee) will not be undertaken voluntarily. The role of government in these cases would be to eliminate or overcome the barriers so that social welfare could be enhanced. Programs successfully fulfilling this purpose will confer gains upon the beneficiaries that are larger than costs, a condition necessary to the enhancement of the *general* welfare.

Seen in this light, then, government programs to rehabilitate disabled persons might be considered an extension of the principle that guides market economies: the encouragement of mutually beneficial transactions. There is, however, one critical distinction between market- and government-induced transactions. Market transactions are voluntary, so that both parties must gain for them to take place.

---

2. In addition to these two reasons, government may want to intervene if it believes handicapped persons are victims of discrimination. Discriminatory preferences among employers may prevent transactions that would otherwise take place (their prejudice reduces the gains to them of transacting). In this case, the government would intervene to negate the effects of socially detrimental preferences, with the ultimate goal of changing attitudes.

Government involves compulsion, so that one party to a government-induced transaction (e.g., disabled persons) might gain while another (nondisabled persons) might lose. This asymmetry notwithstanding, a government program can be said to enhance the social welfare if the beneficiaries gain more than the losers lose; the reasoning is that the losers *could* be compensated by the gainers and the latter would still be better off than they were without the program.

The above considerations suggest that government programs must be evaluated to determine if their effects are consistent with their goals. It is to this issue that we now turn.

THE CRITERIA FOR JUDGING GOVERNMENT PROGRAMS

If redistribution of income is the goal of a government program, then the program may be judged solely by the extent to which the target group is benefited. In fact, if a particular target group can only be helped at the expense of some other group, then imposing costs on the latter is a necessary condition for the success of the program. For example, if a rehabilitated person can only acquire a job if an able-bodied worker is displaced, a program seeking only to *redistribute* advantages toward disabled persons would be considered a success only to the extent that displacement can be accomplished.

PHILOSOPHICAL FOUNDATIONS OF BENEFIT-COST ANALYSES

If redistributive programs are rejected because their benefits are too narrowly circumscribed, and it is instead insisted that government intervention must confer net benefits upon society, then a method must be found for weighing the benefits and costs of the programs. The philosophy underlying benefit-cost analysis is intimately related to the criterion of mutual benefit; such analyses simply seek to ascertain whether the gainers gain more than the losers lose. In other words, benefit-cost studies seek to determine if the beneficiaries of a program would be willing to pay its costs—for if they are, it is clear that this transaction is one that would have taken place voluntarily in a perfectly functioning market (it is therefore a mutually beneficial transaction that enhances social welfare). If the gainers are estimated *not* to be willing to pay the costs of a program, then by the same reasoning it is not a transaction that advances the general welfare.

Put differently, the goal of enhancing social welfare through government intervention requires the development and use of evaluative criteria that are analogous to those used by private actors in everyday market decisions. When a consumer is shopping in a store or a worker is considering a job offer, the question is at least implicitly asked whether the costs imposed by the decision are outweighted by the benefits. These decisions, though at times instantaneous and subjective, nevertheless characterize our everyday economic lives. Explicit formulation of these considerations by government policy makers is simply an attempt to make the decisions that private actors would have made had it not been for the existence of transactions barriers in the marketplace.

BENEFIT-COST STUDIES OF VOCATIONAL REHABILITATION

The purpose of vocational rehabilitation is to increase the productivity of disabled persons. Many are rehabilitated with paid employment as the goal, but at least some receive subsidized services whose goal it is to increase their productivity in "household production."

In terms of benefit-cost analysis, rehabilitation programs invest social resources in an attempt to increase the productivity of a certain group of citizens. That is, society commits resources (incurs costs), and in return generates the benefits of a more productive labor force. If the long-run gain in productivity exceeds the cost of achieving it, then the program is socially beneficial—in the sense that the gainers (those whose productivity is increased) could pay for the costs of the program and still be better off.

Studies that have looked at the overall costs and benefits of vocational rehabilitation have generally concluded that the benefits are very large compared to the costs. Unlike more ordinary job training programs, whose benefits are often not commensurate with the costs, vocational rehabilitation seems to generate benefits that are at least triple the size of the social costs (see Conley 1965, Bellante 1972, and Worrall 1978).

Two issues must be raised in connection with these studies, however. First, the gains to disabled persons of vocational rehabilitation are generally measured in terms of increased earnings after training. In many cases the studies implicitly assume that those who were unemployed at the start of their vocational rehabilitation program would have remained so throughout their lives had it not been for the program's "treatment"; others attempt to adjust the prerehabilitation earnings data to avoid this implausible assumption (see Worrall 1978). However, even these adjustments ignore the possibility that the disabled persons may be engaged in "household production"—doing unpaid, but valuable, work at home—that permits their spouses to seek paid employment.[3] In short, it is not necessarily true that disabled people who are not earning income in paid employment are not producing anything of social value. By assuming that disabled people who are not employed are not producing anything, the benefit-cost studies of vocational rehabilitation programs have tended to overstate the gains in productivity associated with rehabilitation.

The second issue with respect to these benefit-cost studies relates to the subject of this paper: job displacement. These studies have frequently been criticized for ignoring the costs to society when displacement of the able-bodied occurs (see, for example, Burkhauser and Haveman 1982, 68, 70). Thus, we turn now to an analysis of job displacement.

Labor Market Concepts

To analyze the issue of job displacement and determine whether such displacement represents a social cost requires a basic understanding of how labor markets accommodate changes in the demand for workers of various kinds, in the supplies of workers, or in labor costs. We also need to establish a set of simplified, or stylized, labor market contexts within which our analyses can be insightfully conducted.

---

3. One study found, for example, that slightly disabled persons tended to replace their spouses as primary household producers, so that it is quite possible for those who are not in paid employment to be producing in the home (see Conley 1965, 70). It should be noted that if rehabilitation causes the spouses to return to their original market or household roles, the social gain associated with rehabilitation is equal to the earnings of the rehabilitated worker minus the earnings of the spouse *if* both are equally productive in the household.

LABOR DEMAND AND SUPPLY

Firms employ workers in the process of manufacturing goods or services; in short, workers are hired to enhance employer profitability. The extent to which employers hire labor depends upon the demand for their product, the availability of both capital and labor, and the technology by which their product can be produced. Individuals are assumed to be attempting to maximize their welfare, or happiness, and in the course of doing so, weighing their alternatives before choosing. In choosing employment, individuals must compare alternative job offers, considering such factors as wages, fringe benefits, job location, job characteristics, and so forth. If an individual has decided to work for pay, it may be confidently assumed that an increase in the wage of one job, while holding wages in other jobs constant, would increase the attractiveness of that job (assuming that fringe benefits and job characteristics on all alternative jobs also remain unchanged). For this reason, supply curves to industries or occupations are assumed to be upward-sloping. That is, an increase in the wage of the job, holding all other factors on all other jobs constant, would result in an increased number of people seeking employment in that job.

Not all alternatives to a particular job, however, involve working for pay. Individuals also have the option of staying at home and engaging in household production. In other words, besides weighing alternative offers of paid employment, workers must also consider the value of their services on an unpaid basis at home.

In the context of deciding whether to work for pay, both income and the potential hourly wage are important considerations to the worker. Because the household is the primary locus of consumption activity, it is reasonable to assume that as family income rises, other things remaining equal, individuals will want to increase the amount of time allocated to nonmarket (or household) activities. That is, as family wealth increases, people would like to enjoy more of the good things in life, and those good things are generally consumed as part of leisure activities. Thus, as wealth increases, it is not surprising to observe workers retiring earlier or taking longer vacations.

Besides income, however, potential workers must also consider their wage rate when making decisions concerning labor supply. A high wage rate in paid employment increases the cost of spending an added hour at home. Thus, if families A and B have identical wealth, but the adult members of family A have higher hourly wages than those in family B, it is reasonable to predict that members of family A would tend to work more for pay. The reason for this, of course, is that their higher wage rates increase the opportunity costs of staying at home.

Because an increase in wage rates is generally accompanied by an increase in at least the potential wealth of workers, it is theoretically impossible to say how a general increase in the wages will affect people's decisions about seeking paid employment. The increase in potential wealth will tend to drive them toward an increase in leisure activity and reduce the time spent in paid employment. Conversely, however, the rising wage increases the cost of not working for pay, and this effect will tend to increase the propensity to seek paid employment. Thus, with respect to a general increase in the wages of paid employment, we are uncertain about the shape of labor supply curves. An increase in general remuneration for market work might generate increases, decreases, or even essentially no changes in the number of hours workers are willing to supply to the market.

CONTEXTS OF THE ANALYSES

As will be seen, the social effects of job displacement that result from programs to help disabled persons crucially depend on the cause and context of the displacement. The effects of displacement that occur because of program-related shifts in employer demand, it will be shown, are different from the effects of displacement that result from shifts in labor supply. Similarly, displacement in the context of full employment has different social effects from displacement occurring in markets that are prevented from clearing.

The general context underlying all our analyses assumes the existence of two labor markets: one in which the job requirements are such that disabled persons can hope to compete for work, and one in which disabled persons cannot compete. We might, for example, think of the former as a market for skilled workers and the latter as a market for laborers (in which physical skills and abilities are barriers to the employment of disabled workers). While in fact there are several labor markets in which disabled persons can find work, and perhaps none in which people who might be considered disabled are totally absent, our assumption allows us to derive some general principles concerning the social effects of displacement. Analyses of the market that includes disabled workers will be termed "own-market" analyses, while those of the other market will be called "other-market" analyses.

In the following sections we focus on the issue of displacement associated with two programs to help disabled persons: vocational rehabilitation and employer wage subsidies. In both cases the central issue is whether displacement of able-bodied workers *imposes a social cost* that must be accounted for in a benefit-cost study; there is *no* presumption in any of the following analyses regarding the larger issue of whether benefits exceed costs for either program. For expository purposes, displacement associated with each program will first be analyzed within the "textbook" context of a perfect labor market (full employment) and then within the context of a labor market that does not clear.

Job Displacement and Vocational Rehabilitation in a Perfectly Functioning Labor Market

Let us consider the case of government-sponsored rehabilitative training in the context of a perfect labor market. That is, assume that the government subsidizes the training of disabled workers, who then seek work in the labor market in which jobs are available to them. What types of displacement can occur, and what are their effects?

OWN-MARKET DISPLACEMENT, VERTICAL SUPPLY CURVES

The most obvious labor-market effect of a vocational rehabilitation program is to increase the number of workers seeking employment in the market in which disabled workers can compete for jobs. In graphic terms, this increase in supply is manifested by a shift to the right of the market's supply of labor curve—indicating that more workers are willing to work at each possible wage rate. Because vocational rehabilitation does not directly affect labor demand, the outward shift in labor supply will tend to reduce the equilibrium wage rate. As will be shown, however, the precise effect depends on the slope of the labor supply curve.

It is instructive to begin our analysis with a case in which the labor supply curve is vertical. A vertical supply curve depicts a situation in which the number of workers seeking jobs in the market stays the same no matter what the wage rate. Such a supply curve is illustrated by S_1 in figure 7.1.

If vocational rehabilitation is implemented, the supply of labor to this market is increased, which can be graphically depicted by shifting the supply curve in figure 7.1 to the right (from S_1 to S_2)—indicating that more workers are supplying their services than before. The result of this rehabilitation program would be to increase employment from N_1 to N_2 (which is accommodated by a fall in the wage rate from W_1 to W_2). The additional employment is equal to the number of disabled persons successfully rehabilitated ($N_2 - N_1$), so

FIGURE 7.1
Own-Market Effects of
Vocational Rehabilitation in
a Perfectly Functioning Labor Market
with Vertical Supply Curves

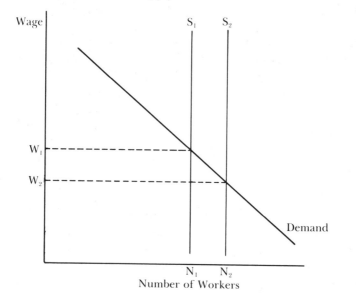

that no previously employed workers have been displaced. However, workers previously employed face lower wages than they would otherwise face, so that losses indeed have been imposed upon them.

Should these wage losses be counted as costs of the program? No, because they are directly offset by the gains *employers* reap from the lower wages. There is no overall reduction in social output because of the wage reductions—only a redistribution of income. Thus, in evaluating whether the increases in social output associated with rehabilitation are greater or less than the value of the resources used in generating that increase, one should ignore the wage changes experienced by able-bodied workers in the market.

OWN-MARKET DISPLACEMENT, HORIZONTAL SUPPLY CURVES

If own-market changes in the *wages* of other workers can safely be ignored in the context of vocational rehabilitation, what about changes in their *employment*? In a very real sense, workers are only displaced from their previous employment in the face of an increased supply of new workers if they are unwilling to accept wage reductions. Thus, the workers in figure 7.1 were not displaced because, in the face of increased competition, they accepted cuts in their wages to maintain their jobs. Had the labor supply curve in figure 7.1 been absolutely horizontal, as it is in figure 7.2, then one-for-one job displacement would occur. That is, as increased competition from previously disabled workers occurred, previously employed workers would find it better to leave their jobs than to accept even a minute wage cut. Thus, as can be seen in figure 7.2, employment remains at N_1—and presumably the newly trained workers have simply replaced some of those previously employed on a one-for-one basis. Does this job displacement impose costs on society?

Because in this case wages and paid employment levels stay the same, the question is whether a worker who quits his or her job and enters some other form of activity (such as household production), rather than accept a wage below W_1, has suffered a significant loss. The answer in this case is most likely "no." A horizontal supply curve is a graphic depiction of indifference. If the tiniest fall in wages induces someone to leave his or her employment, that person must have alternatives that are substantially equal in terms of the well-being they

FIGURE 7.2
Own-Market Effects of
Vocational Rehabilitation in
a Perfectly Functioning Labor Market
with a Horizontal Supply Curve

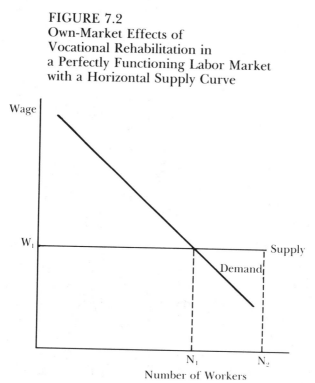

generate. Changing from one activity to another in this case involves no losses because the two are equivalent.

OWN-MARKET DISPLACEMENT, UPWARD-SLOPING SUPPLY CURVES

Having considered the losses suffered by previously employed workers in two extreme cases—one involving only wage loss and the other one-for-one job displacement—let us finally turn to an intermediate case in which a bit of both occur. Rather than assuming that labor supply curves have either infinite (vertical) or zero (horizontal) slopes, we now assume that they are positively sloped, as shown in figure 7.3.

Figure 7.3 indicates that before vocational rehabilitation, N_1 able-bodied workers were employed at a wage of W_1. While supply

FIGURE 7.3
Own-Market Effects of
Vocational Rehabilitation in
a Perfectly Functioning Labor Market
with Upward-Sloping Supply Curves

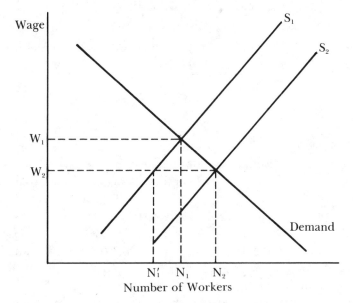

curve S_1 still represents the labor supply of able-bodied workers, the curve S_2 includes the addition of rehabilitated handicapped workers. When these latter workers join the market, wages fall to W_2 and the employment of able-bodied workers falls to N_1' (there are $N_2 - N_1'$ rehabilitated workers also employed, bringing total employment to N_2). Should this job displacement of the able-bodied be counted as a social cost of vocational rehabilitation?

The workers who leave their original employment when the wage falls are indicating that rather than accept a wage of W_2 in their old employment, they would prefer to engage in some other activity. This behavior is really telling us that the utility these displaced workers derive from some other employment is greater than the utility they would derive from continuing in their old jobs at a wage of W_2. In short, some of these workers prefer to minimize their losses by changing jobs, and they are clearly no worse off than they would be if they had stayed in the market and accepted the wage reduction. If the wage loss experienced by able-bodied workers is not a cost to society, but merely a reallocation of resources from workers to employers (or customers), then the attempt to minimize the loss of utility by workers who change jobs rather than take the wage loss is not a social cost either.

OTHER-MARKET EFFECTS

While the labor market has been assumed to consist of two submarkets, we have not made explicit assumptions about the product market. It is most plausible to assume that workers from both labor markets are employed by each firm (one may think of each firm as having two departments, one that hires "own-market" workers and one that hires "other-market" workers). As "own-market" workers become less expensive owing to vocational rehabilitation, two effects on the demand for "other-market" workers might be felt. First, by reducing the costs of production and inducing production levels to rise, this reduction in cost of "own-market" workers may cause demand for workers in the other market to increase. Second, as "own-market" workers become less expensive, firms may substitute *away* from "other-market" workers in the production process, because the wages of these latter workers have not also declined. It is impossible to say, a priori, whether the former ("scale effect") or latter ("substitution effect") will dominate.

To take a concrete example, suppose that vocational rehabilitation programs train typesetters and artists, who become employed by publishing companies. What will happen to the traveling sales people (who, we will assume, need to be able-bodied) employed to market the company's books? On the one hand, employment of sales personnel could rise (a shift in the demand curve from D_0 to D_1 in figure 7.4) if the scale effect dominated. That is, as production costs fell, more books could be produced and the employment of sales people might well rise as a consequence. However, a strong substitution effect could make the labor demand curve in figure 7.4 shift

FIGURE 7.4
Other-Market Effects
of Vocational Rehabilitation

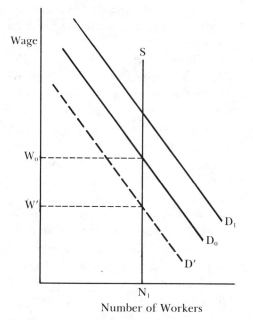

to the left from D_0 to D'. For example, the reduced costs of hiring typesetters and artists might create incentives for the firm to use printed brochures or flyers to advertise their books and rely less on the personal contact offered by sales personnel (who now are *relatively* more expensive than they once were, owing to the reduced cost of an alternative form of advertising). If the substitution effect dominates and the demand curve for sales people shifts to the left, displacement of these "other-market" workers can occur. Is this displacement a social loss?

To consider this question, let us first assume that the supply curve is vertical, as in figure 7.4. In this case the other-market wage falls from W_0 to W', and while there is no displacement, workers in this market have clearly suffered losses. Unlike the own-market case, in which the decline in wages was caused by a rightward shift in the supply curve, these other-market losses are *not* offset by gains to employers. The leftward shift in the demand curve signals a reduction in the value of other-market workers to their employers; in the context of the example above, outside sales workers become less valuable as the publishing company expands its use of mailed advertisements. Instead of enhancing profits in the "outside salesperson" department, the wage reductions there serve only to mitigate losses occurring when other forms of sales activities are increased.[4]

Suppose now that the substitution effect dominates, but the supply of labor curve in this other market is horizontal. The leftward shift in demand *would* result in displacement, but, as before, this displacement would be essentially costless to workers (a horizontal supply curve signals total indifference between working for pay in this market or engaging in some other alternative pursuit). However, the absence of wage reductions means that the fall in value of these workers to their employers can be mitigated only by cutting output and employment, so that total employer profits are reduced.[5]

If the labor supply curve to the other market is upward-sloping, the losses imposed by a leftward shift in demand will be shared by workers and owners. Displacement will occur as workers who would otherwise face wage reductions seek to minimize their losses by changing activities. However, losses occur in this other market no matter how much or how little displacement there is. As before, displacement occurring in perfect labor markets is a (voluntary) *response* to losses suffered by workers—not a *cause* of these losses.

LESSONS OF THE ANALYSES

Two major principles can be derived from our analyses of vocational rehabilitation in the context of perfect markets. First, if employees

---

4. We are assuming here that mailed advertisements and personal contact by sales personnel are not complementary. It is possible, however, to think of brochures as *enhancing* the productivity of sales people, in which case the scale effect will dominate in the other market and displacement is not a concern. It should be noted that profits for the entire firm are clearly enhanced by the availability of cheaper own-market labor. *If the substitution effect dominates,* however, the gains occur *only* in the department employing own-market workers.

5. If the capital owned by these employers is somewhat specialized, then the decline in profits will be accompanied by a fall in the market value of employer assets. Thus, even employers who adjust to their losses by leaving the industry or closing all or parts of a plant will experience declines in wealth.

are assumed to be able-bodied, there are no net social losses imposed on the able-bodied as a whole resulting from rightward shifts of the labor supply curve; losses imposed on able-bodied workers are offset by gains to employers. With respect to own-market effects of vocational rehabilitation, then, the benefits are quite legitimately measured by the gains in productivity of disabled persons.[6] However, losses imposed on the able-bodied because of a leftward shift in labor demand (as was possible, but not inevitable, in the market in which disabled workers could not compete) are not offset by gains to other able-bodied economic agents in that market. These losses therefore *should* be included among the costs in performing an evaluation of vocational rehabilitation programs.

Second, as noted above, displacement of disabled persons in a perfectly functioning market is a *response* to losses, not the cause of them. In the situations analyzed above, workers voluntarily left employment rather than accepted a cut in their wage rate. Presumably, they felt some other activity was preferable to maintaining their former job at a reduced wage.

It should be emphasized, however, that while wage loss and job displacement in the context of full employment do not always represent net social costs, their redistributive effects may themselves be of social concern. That is, to the extent that the distribution of income is altered, society may judge the effects as undesirable even in situations in which there is no net drain on overall social resources.

JOB DISPLACEMENT AND VOCATIONAL REHABILITATION IN SLACK LABOR MARKETS

Having considered the case of job displacement in a labor market characterized by full employment, let us now turn to labor markets characterized by unemployment. An example of such markets is depicted in figure 7.5, where the supply of workers (E_s) at the market wage (W_M) exceeds the demand for workers (E_1) at that wage. The reason for the unemployment of $E_s - E_1$ workers is the failure of

---

6. There are some gains in profits, or "producers' surplus," that should be counted also, but as a practical matter these are difficult to measure.

FIGURE 7.5
Effects of
Vocational Rehabilitation
in a Slack Labor Market

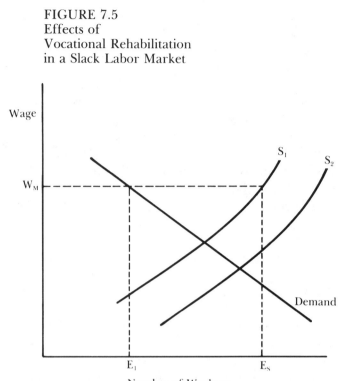

Number of Workers

wages to adjust downward—an adjustment that would encourage employers to hire more workers. In the absence of this adjustment no
more jobs will be created in this market, and any additions to the
supply of workers (as for example, from rehabilitation programs)
would not result in any more employment.

The last point above can be illustrated by referring again to
figure 7.5. To the original supply of workers in the market (along
curve S_1) are added rehabilitated workers, shifting the supply curve
to the right (curve S_2). This influx of added workers does not increase

employment above E_1 because neither wages nor the demand curve has changed. While this result looks superficially like that obtained in a perfectly functioning labor market with horizontal supply curves, there is one critical difference. In a labor market with full employment, those who are displaced by rehabilitated workers voluntarily leave their previous employment for an activity that is a perfect substitute; when unemployment prevails, displaced workers leave involuntarily and thus suffer losses.

To elaborate, let us point out again that displacement per se is not socially costly, and may even involve some net gain. After all, if the newly rehabilitated workers replace previously employed workers at the old wage, employers must believe them to be superior performers. However, the presence of unemployment clearly involves social costs, because mutually beneficial transactions are being blocked for some reason (most of those who want employment at W_M and cannot obtain it would find it preferable to work for less than W_M rather than do what they do in their unemployed state). It is straightforward to show, then, that the presence of unemployment can limit the benefits of vocational rehabilitation. While those who are rehabilitated have enhanced earning capacities—and may even be good enough to replace workers now employed—the presence of transactions barriers (which cause the unemployment) means that displaced workers cannot mitigate their losses by seeking their next best alternative. Because own-market wages and employment levels are unchanged,[7] the losses absorbed by these workers are not offset by gains to other parties (except for the productivity gains already counted above), and thus they become social losses. Therefore, if the increased productivity of rehabilitated workers is counted as a program benefit, the losses absorbed by displaced workers must be counted among the costs if unemployment is a prevailing labor market characteristic.[8]

In assessing vocational rehabilitation in the context of slack

---

7. If we assume that unemployment also prevails in the other labor market (in which disabled persons cannot compete), then wages and employment levels there are also unchanged.

8. Just as one must take into account the household productivity of unemployed disabled workers prior to rehabilitation in calculating benefits, one must also take into account the household productivity of displaced able-bodied workers in calculating costs.

labor markets, it is important to consider what the cause of the unemployment might be. Some unemployment is *frictional*—caused merely by the failure of individuals to immediately find available jobs. Frictional unemployment normally connotes at least a rough equality between job openings and job seekers, but it is recognized that search on both sides of the market cannot be instantaneous. Unemployment caused by labor market frictions may be "permanent" in the sense that there is always a pool of workers "between jobs," but the workers in the pool are constantly changing. Since frictional unemployment can occur even in labor markets that are functioning well, there is no reason to believe that it will cause vocational rehabilitation programs to be accompanied by socially costly displacement.

A second cause of unemployment is structural imbalances, such that job openings and job seekers cannot be matched without substantial investment. The jobs may be highly skilled and the job seekers unskilled, or the jobs may be in the "sunbelt" and the job seekers in the "rustbelt." With structural unemployment, vocational rehabilitation may have one of two effects. If disabled workers are rehabilitated into markets where there is an excess of labor supply already, the social benefits of rehabilitation will, of course, be minimal.[9] However, if vocational rehabilitation is designed to qualify workers for jobs for which excess supply is not a problem, then its effects will be analogous to those discussed in the above section. The simple lesson here, of course, is that if unemployment is caused by structural imbalances, vocational rehabilitation programs may still be of social value if they seek to equip rehabilitated workers for labor markets in which jobs are plentiful relative to supply.[10]

Finally, unemployment may be caused by a level of aggregate demand insufficient to fully employ all those who want work at the

---

9. That is, if structural imbalances are ignored by those running vocational rehabilitation programs, so that supply is increased to the markets in which labor is in excess supply, then the queue of unemployed workers is merely lengthened with no substantial increases in social output.

10. In this case, however, it would be wise for society to consider training or otherwise "rehabilitating" *all* structurally unemployed workers, and not only those who are physically handicapped. Relative to this latter consideration, of course, is that a society contemplating the spending of x dollars on overcoming structural imbalances must consider whether the net social gains would be larger or smaller if these resources were focused on handicapped workers as opposed to able-bodied ones.

prevailing wage. Demand-deficient unemployment, however, is relatively short-term in nature, and it tends to follow a somewhat cyclical pattern; it can be argued that evaluations of vocational rehabilitation should focus on the long-run benefits and costs to society.

The benefits of any job-training program include the discounted lifetime increases in output of trainees; a recession has only modest effects on these lifetime benefits unless its duration is long, interest rates are high, or the rehabilitated workers are old. Thus, the proposition that vocational rehabilitation should be focused away from jobs and labor markets for which the long-run prospects of employment are bleak can be extended to encompass the corollary that vocational rehabilitation should not fail to prepare workers for jobs in markets in which the demand for them is only temporarily soft. To reiterate, it is *lifetime* discounted benefits that are to be compared to costs when performing benefit-cost analyses of vocational rehabilitation programs.

In summary, it is the presence of unemployment—not job displacement per se—that limits the social benefits of vocational rehabilitation. Moreover, we have argued that the presence of unemployment need not threaten the social utility of vocational rehabilitation.

WAGE SUBSIDIES AND JOB DISPLACEMENT

The implementation of employer wage subsidies for hiring disabled persons is an alternative to vocational rehabilitation, and subsidies may be used either for redistributing a larger portion of a fixed national income to disabled persons or for enhancing national output. However, because subsidies do not directly add to the nation's stock of productive resources, their ability to enlarge national income must lie principally in whatever inducements they provide to better utilize a given set of productive factors.[11] (For example, if through ignorance or prejudice employers place a lower value on the services of disabled

---

11. It is possible that wage subsidies could *indirectly* increase the stock of national human resources by inducing some who would otherwise have been out of the labor force to acquire the necessary habits and attitudes for successful market work. However, this benefit of "industrializing" workers contributes to a net social gain only to the extent that they become more productive at work than at home.

persons than is objectively warranted, too few of them will be hired and their skills will be underutilized. An employer wage subsidy for hiring disabled persons could be used to artificially alter employer perceptions of their net productivity, and it could lead to a more socially efficient use of our labor resources.)

As pointed out earlier in this paper, job displacement is only of critical concern if the aims of a program to help disabled persons are not purely redistributive. That is, displacement or some other cost to the able-bodied is an *intended* response of a program that is purely redistributive. However, if such a program is to be evaluated on the extent to which it enlarges *net social welfare*, any adverse consequences for the able-bodied must be considered. In this section we shall consider, as before, the effects of wage subsidies in two different contexts: full employment and slack labor markets.

MARKETS WITH FULL EMPLOYMENT

Suppose that the market in which disabled persons compete is split into two sectors by employers. One sector contains the able-bodied, whose productivity is correctly assessed by employers. The other contains disabled persons, whose productivity is incorrectly (by assumption) devalued by employers. That is, all workers in this market are *actually* equally productive, but employer ignorance or prejudice reduces the perceived productivity of disabled persons by \$X per hour below their actual productivity. If the *actual* productivity of able-bodied and disabled persons alike is \$W per hour, disabled persons are perceived to be worth \$W − X and are paid accordingly (no employer is willing to pay \$W to someone perceived as worth less).

The presence of a group of workers worth \$W but paid less should clearly signal the expansion of employment for this group. If society (including employers) can get \$W in output from those who cost only \$W − X to obtain,[12] it should increase its hiring of these workers. If ignorance or prejudice is a barrier to this mutually ben-

---

12. If disabled workers can get paid only \$W − X, some may opt to perform alternative activities in which their output is close to \$W − X per hour. If they could instead be hired for the job in which they produce \$W per hour, society would gain \$W in output at a cost of \$W − X (the lost output in the alternative activity).

eficial transaction, an employer subsidy of $X per hour for every disabled worker hired would "artificially" induce the transaction to occur (by raising the perceived productivity of disabled persons to the employer by $X per hour).

While society and disabled persons could benefit in this situation,[13] we must also consider displacement-related losses imposed on the able-bodied. The subsidy of disabled workers *could* lead to a leftward shift in the demand for able-bodied workers in both the same and the "other" labor market. As we saw in the case of vocational rehabilitation, losses suffered because of a leftward shift in market demand do not entail offsetting gains to other economic agents in the market; they are therefore a cost that must be counted in evaluating the net gains of any program. Again, however, these losses are independent of the voluntary displacement that might accompany wage reductions.

MARKETS WITH UNEMPLOYMENT

In labor markets characterized by inflexible wages and by unemployment, a wage subsidy for disabled persons will cause their employment to increase if there are disabled workers among the unemployed. However, this subsidy could cause able-bodied workers in the market to be displaced—and the displacement will probably be one-for-one.[14]

---

13. Society would benefit if the subsidy overcame the barrier of ignorance or prejudice to an otherwise mutually beneficial transaction. If, however, a subsidy were implemented in a market without such barriers, disabled persons would be induced to work at jobs in which their productivity was *less* than it was before the subsidy. In this latter case, the subsidy entails a net social loss. Likewise, there are no social gains if the supply curve of disabled persons is vertical, because in this case all those potentially employed are already at work. In this case, a subsidy merely bids up wages of disabled persons, and these gains are exactly offset by taxpayers' losses. There is no increase in output.

14. Employers make hiring decisions on the basis of added revenues generated by an additional worker as compared to the added costs associated with hiring him or her. If, as seems likely, there are fewer disabled workers than the total number of workers desired by employers, the *additional* workers considered for hire (after disabled, subsidized workers are fully employed) will always be able-bodied, *unsubsidized* ones. Thus, the subsidy will not alter the marginal (added) revenues or costs of hiring, and profit-maximizing employment will remain at previous levels. In this event, previously unemployed disabled workers will simply change places with able-bodied employees.

As was emphasized in the case of vocational rehabilitation in the context of imperfect labor markets, this displacement represents a social cost and must be counted against the gains to disabled persons in evaluating the social utility of the program.

CONCLUSIONS

This paper has analyzed the general phenomenon of job displacement in the context of programs to help disabled workers. In particular, the paper's task was to ascertain the extent to which social losses result from displacement of the able-bodied when attempts are made to improve the employment prospects of disabled persons. Several general propositions distilled from the analyses bear repeating. For the sake of convenience and to facilitate applications to problems of vocational rehabilitation, the conclusions discussed below will be presented in the context of efforts to help disabled persons that result in displacement of the able-bodied. However, the observations concerning displacement are of general applicability to *any* government program affecting employment opportunities.

First, we should note that in markets that clear (i.e., where there is no unemployment), job displacement is *symptomatic* of employee losses, not the cause of them. In such markets, job loss is avoided when employees are willing to accept wage reductions. Displacement in this context is appropriately seen as a voluntary withdrawal from the market, viewed by those withdrawing as preferable to wage loss.

Second, in perfectly functioning markets, the losses imposed on able-bodied workers that result from rightward shifts in labor supply curves are offset by employer gains in profits; therefore, while there are redistribution effects, there are no net social costs associated with these employee losses. However, losses imposed on the able-bodied caused by leftward shifts in the labor demand curve *do* represent social costs, because there are no offsetting gains to employers. In the context of evaluating vocational rehabilitation programs, then, own-market displacement can be ignored in benefit-cost studies, while any displacement occurring in other markets (i.e., markets not directly affected by an influx of rehabilitated workers) should be counted among the costs.

Third, while the existence of unemployment can lead to socially costly own-market displacement of the able-bodied, it need not render vocational rehabilitation socially useless. Those responsible for administering the rehabilitation programs must take a long-term view of both benefits and costs—avoiding rehabilitation aimed at markets in which there is long-run excess supply, while at the same time not being unduly influenced by temporary (cyclical) factors causing unemployment.

8 · THE ROLE OF REASONABLE ACCOMMODATION IN EMPLOYING DISABLED PERSONS IN PRIVATE INDUSTRY

Frederick C. Collignon

The "reasonable accommodation" of disabled persons by industry has now been part of federal law and policy for a decade. While the provisions of the Rehabilitation Act of 1973 (P.L. 93–112) and the subsequent legislation enjoyed bipartisan support in Congress, the requirements of reasonable accommodation have been among the more controversial aspects of the implementation of those laws. Various horror stories have been reported in the press about how firms and public agencies have had to spend large sums of money on what popularly has been seen as unreasonable accommodations. One of the more publicized examples involved the substantial expenditure in a small Iowa town to build ramps to a library (Roberts 1980). When speakers at a large plenary session of local government officials at the 1981 national meetings of the American Planning Association in Cincinnati referred to the requirements to provide disabled persons access to public transit, loud booing came from the audience, reflecting officials' concern with the large costs being experienced across the country. *Time* magazine reported that a California firm spent $40,000 to lower all of its drinking fountains (*Time* 1977). Various business associations continue periodically to issue statements citing their concern over the large costs and government intrusion involved in the requirements for accommodating disabled employees.

The stories that capture the attention of the media may, of course, be the anomalies of overall societal experience in undertaking accommodation. Those few studies that have systematically probed the experience of firms and public institutions have, with a possible exception in the case of public transit, found that for most institutions and firms the costs and difficulty of providing accommodation have not been extensive.

In this paper, we shall examine the particular experience of private industry in adapting to the requirements of reasonable accommodation. We first briefly review the legal contexts of the provisions for reasonable accommodation. We then examine the theoretical context in which the costs and activities of accommodation should be viewed. Following that, we look at the data available concerning the actual experiences of firms in undertaking accommodation. Because of the nature of accommodation practices and the limited data available, the analysis of accommodation must necessarily be partial and limited. We rely heavily on the only large-scale national study done to date, the study of accommodations provided for handicapped workers by federal contractors under section 503 of the rehabilitation act, undertaken by the U.S. Department of Labor (DOL) and published in 1982 (U.S. Department of Labor 1982).[1] The limitations of existing studies and the areas for further research will be emphasized. Finally we draw some tentative conclusions and point out possible directions for future public policy.

LEGAL CONTEXTS

According to the most comprehensive and authoritative review of federal law and overall societal experience relating to accommodation, almost thirty different federal laws prohibit discrimination against handicapped people (U.S. Commission on Civil Rights 1983).[2] Most of the laws originated in the early 1970s when handicapped persons, along with other groups in American society as part of the larger civil rights movement, sought protections. The Rehabilitation Act of 1973,

---

1. Hereafter referred to as "BPA Accommodations Study 1982." This author served as principal investigator for the study. Other key authors were Mary Vencill, the project's manager, and Linda Toms Barker.

2. Hereafter referred to as "Civil Rights Accommodation Review 1983."

as amended in 1978, is the principal basis for the reasonable accommodation requirements for private employers. This statute combined the comprehensive federal-state program providing handicapped people with a wide variety of rehabilitation services with broadly worded civil rights protections against discrimination. The law sought to increase their employment skills and the ability to live independently in the community.[3] Title V of the act established as national policy the protection of the civil rights of handicapped people. The provisions of title V and the regulations subsequently issued that interpret the provisions have been the most controversial elements of the overall legislation. Three key sections of the title have directly affected employers: sections 504, 501, and 503, with section 503 most affecting private-sector firms.

Section 504 prohibits discrimination on the basis of handicap in any program or activity receiving federal financial assistance, as well as any discriminatory practices by the federal government itself. While the most publicized impacts of the section have been upon the access to and provision of public transportation and educational and other services to disabled persons, the section also affects employment. Employers covered by the section—those who receive financial assistance—are prohibited from discriminating in the hiring and promotion of handicapped persons. Handicapped job applicants must meet the essential qualifications for a particular job that is reasonably accommodated to their particular disabilities unless the accommodation would cause undue hardship to the employer. The interpretation of the U.S. Commission on Civil Rights is that

although the regulations do not use the phrase reasonable accommodation outside of the employment context, making modifications in program operations to permit participation by handicapped people is a consistent theme running throughout the regulations. (U.S. Commission on Civil Rights 1983, 52)

With regard to architectural barriers, the regulations require recipients to operate their programs so that they are "readily accessible to

---

3. "The purpose of this chapter is to develop and implement, through research, training, services, and the guarantee of equal opportunity, comprehensive and coordinated programs of vocational rehabilitation and independent living." 29 U.S.C. 701 (Supp. V 1981).

and useable by handicapped persons." Recipients of financial assistance were given three years from the date of agency regulations to correct existing facility barriers. New facilities and alterations to existing facilities are to be designed and constructed to be readily accessible. All recipients are required to provide assurances of compliance with the section and all its requirements, and must conduct self-evaluations of their compliance. While the U.S. Department of Justice has been assigned the responsibility for coordinating enforcement activities, the section can also be enforced through private lawsuits by aggrieved handicapped persons.

Section 501 focuses on the federal government's own responsibility to be an equal opportunity employer for handicapped persons. The section both prohibits handicap discrimination in federal employment and mandates affirmative action. Each federal department or agency, including the U.S. Postal Service, is required to establish an affirmative action plan to encourage the hiring, placement, and promotion of handicapped individuals. Each federal agency must annually provide written plans specifying goals for the employment and advancement of both handicapped applicants and current handicapped employees. Numerical goals are mandated if the agency has more than five hundred employees. Agencies must also establish special recruitment programs and goals, and timetables for providing facility accessibility. Special emphasis in employment is to be given certain targeted disabilities: deafness, blindness, missing extremities, partial or complete paralysis, convulsive disorders, mental retardation, mental illness, and distortion of the spine or limbs. The regulations for section 501 that have been issued by the U.S. Equal Employment Opportunity Commission (EEOC) lay out specific standards with regard to reasonable accommodation, employment criteria, pre-employment inquiries, and physical access to buildings. Federal employees and job applicants who believe they have been subjected to discrimination may file complaints with EEOC, and, if unsuccessful through the administrative route, may file a lawsuit in federal court.

It is section 503 that has the greatest implications, however, for the private profit employment sector. This section requires businesses with federal contracts of $2,500 or more to take affirmative action to employ and advance qualified handicapped persons. The affirmative action requirement is enforced by the Office of Federal Contract

Compliance Programs (OFCCP) of the U.S. Department of Labor; unlike the other sections, section 503 cannot be enforced by private lawsuits brought by aggrieved handicapped individuals. Under the regulations issued by the department, federal government contracts must contain clauses that prohibit employment discrimination against qualified handicapped persons and mandate affirmative action to hire and promote them. A qualified handicapped person is defined by the regulations as a handicapped person "who is capable of performing a particular job, with reasonable accommodation to his handicap." Contractors also are required to "make a reasonable accommodation to the physical and mental limitations of an employee or applicant."

What constitutes "reasonable accommodation" is not defined by the regulations, but appendix B to the regulations provides a sample notice to employees that describes such accommodations as "the accommodations which we could make which would enable you to perform the job properly and safely, including special equipment, changes in the physical layout of the job, elimination of certain duties relating to the job, or other accommodations." Contractors can plead "business necessity" and also costs as grounds for limiting their requirements for mitigating the effect on job performance of an individual's handicapping condition. Contractors must, as part of their obligations under the section, undertake a self-analysis of their personnel procedures to ensure that handicapped applicants and employees are systematically and thoroughly considered for hiring and promotions. Job qualifications must be modified to ensure they are job-related and consistent with business necessity. Depending on the outcome of the self-analysis, employers are advised to publicize their affirmative action policies for recruiting more handicapped applicants and for hiring and promoting handicapped employees.

There has, from the outset, been uncertainty among employers concerning their true obligations for "reasonable accommodation" under section 503. Case law is still evolving, and major court precedents were still lacking as of 1984.

The explanations of "reasonable accommodation" in the regulations issued for section 504, and later adopted also for section 501, were given in terms of examples:

Reasonable accommodation may include: (1) making facilities used by employees readily accessible to and useable by handicapped persons, and (2) job restructuring, part-time or modified work schedules, acquisition or modification of equipment or devices, the provision of readers or interpreters, and other similar actions. (45 C.F.R., 1982)

The civil rights commission's most recent review acknowledges the continuing uncertainty as to the boundaries of an employer's or service provider's obligations, and emphasizes the case-by-case nature of assessing what is reasonable accommodation:

Reasonable accommodation means providing or modifying devices, services, or facilities or changing practices or procedures in order to match a particular person with a particular program or activity. Its essence is making opportunities available to handicapped persons on an individualized basis. A number of legal standards have emerged, including those involving: the definition of a "qualified handicapped individual" entitled to accommodation; a requirement that equivalent opportunity be provided; limitations upon the duty to accommodate; requirements regarding the elimination of discriminatory selection criteria; and requirements regarding the removal of architectural, transportation, and communication barriers.

These general legal statements emphasize that there is a duty to accommodate unless the context and all the circumstances make accommodation unreasonable. Although accurate, general statements do not provide simple legal rules that answer in advance the questions of when, what, and how much accommodation is due in given circumstances. (U.S. Commission on Civil Rights 1983, 139)

The Department of Labor's study of section 503 accommodation practices among employers similarly concluded that the case-by-case examination of particular circumstances was needed in interpreting an employer's responsibilities. That report recommended that the department establish a series of relevant considerations or questions (see appendix) that employers could use for their self-assessment of the need for and reasonableness of specific accommodations for a particular handicapped worker (BPA Accommodations Study 1982, 104–105). In short, the obligation to make a reasonable accommodation would best be defined by a process, rather than in terms of universally specified requirements of actions for all handicapped applicants and employees. The process of the employer's consideration of a worker's need for accommodation, and subsequent follow-up action when consideration would appear to justify accommodation, could then be audited by OFCCP on the basis of specific complaints and/or randomly. The civil rights commission's review concurs that this focus on process has merit (U.S. Commission on Civil Rights 1983, 140).

The thrust of the DOL study recommendations and the position taken in the civil rights commission's review would provide a flexibility for government enforcement and for employers that would mesh more clearly with the limitations currently in the regulations whereby employers can be exempted from accommodation by business necessity or costs. Such flexibility is needed since there is little clarity in the case law concerning the latitude permitted employers to cite these exemptions. The "business necessity" defense was first developed in litigation over title VII of the Civil Rights Act of 1964. The concept has been summarized by one court as follows:

> The test is whether there exists an overriding legitimate business purpose such that the [challenged employment] practice is necessary to the safe and efficient operation of the business. Thus, the business purpose must be sufficiently compelling to override any racial impact; the challenged practice must effectively carry out the business purpose it is alleged to serve; and there must be available no acceptable alternative policies or practices which would better accomplish the business purpose advanced, or accomplish it equally well with a lesser differential racial impact. (Robinson v. Lorillard, 444 F.2d 791 (4th Cir. 1971), as cited in U.S. Commission on Civil Rights 1983, 54–55)

A satisfactory defense based on business necessity might stress the specific threat to the health and safety of a person with a particular set of disabilities if he or she were to undertake a specific set of work activities, or the threat to the safety of other workers or customers if that particular set of work activities were undertaken by an individual having certain disabilities. But the employer would have to make the assessment in the context of a particular individual's disabilities, rather than use blanket prescriptions against opening the job to all handicapped persons. Similarly, there might have to be no alternative means of restructuring the job so that it could be carried out by the disabled applicant or employee without safety risks being incurred (U.S. Commission on Civil Rights 1983, 130–33). Another successful business necessity defense might be that the accommodation would entail violation of existing collective bargaining agreements.[4] In general, the

---

4. Bey v. Bolger, 504 F Supp. 910, 926–27 (E.D. Pa. 1982). In this case, light duty assignment in violation of a collective bargaining agreement was found to constitute undue hardship to the employer.

extent to which employers could cite business necessity as grounds for avoiding accommodation requirements would appear fairly minimal if a feasible accommodation were identified.

Exemption from accommodation requirements because of costs has, to date, been given an "inconsistent" analysis by the courts, according to the civil rights commission (U.S. Commission on Civil Rights 1983, 127–28, 137–38). This is despite section 505, which was added by Congress to the rehabilitation act a year after the reasonable accommodation regulations went into effect, and which permits courts to consider "the reasonableness of the cost of any necessary work place accommodation and the availability of any alternatives therefor or other appropriate relief in order to achieve an equitable and appropriate remedy" (29 U.S.C. (Supp. V 1981)). The exemption has been more difficult to use as a defense by agencies or firms receiving federal financial assistance than by private firms receiving no federal aid.

The most extensive litigation over the cost exemption has been in the field of public transportation, not employment. Two principles have been emerging. First, as noted in regulations issued for section 504 by the U.S. Department of Health and Human Services, costs must be viewed in the light of the purpose, nature, and resources of a particular program. Second, costs of accommodations should be considered in terms of the number of people served and the benefits gained. One court has suggested that a realistic assessment of the costs of accommodation must look beyond the cost of the accommodation itself and include an assessment of the costs to handicapped persons if the accommodation is not made, and the benefits to handicapped persons if the accommodation is successful (New Mexico Association for Retarded Citizens v. State of New Mexico, 678 F.2d 847, 854 (10th Cir. 1982)). All of these considerations look more pertinent to ascertaining the reasonableness of an expensive accommodation in a public program or in a situation involving architectural barriers than they do in the context of an accommodation facilitating the specific employment of one individual. Where an accommodation would benefit not only a particular handicapped employee or applicant, but many other workers (and/or customers), it would appear that cost is less compelling a defense.

The above discussion has focused on the specific laws and regulations that have been written expressly for handicapped persons and that directly involve the mandate of reasonable accommodations. There is as well a growing tendency for advocates of disabled persons' rights to seek to make use of more general civil rights law. The legislation and regulations described above were designed to parallel earlier civil rights legislation, and indeed section 504 was added to the Rehabilitation Act of 1973 after several attempts to amend the Civil Rights Act of 1964 to include handicapped individuals had failed in Congress (New Mexico Association for Retarded Citizens v. State of New Mexico). As one legal specialist has noted:

[The] most significant difference between the handicapped and other protected classes is the fact that the condition which initially gives rise to the protected status may also affect an individual's . . . performance. (Gittler 1978, 593)

This concern for performance makes the application of civil rights protections more difficult in employment antidiscrimination suits, since employers can obviously maintain as a defense that their unwillingness to undertake an accommodation is prompted by a reasonable judgment that a handicapped applicant or worker, even with the accommodation, would be less able to provide a level of productive performance akin to that of other workers. If the use of general civil rights legislation as additional protection for handicapped persons is upheld in the courts, the kinds of precedents which have emerged may also become applicable in consideration of employment discrimination against handicapped persons.

As an example, separate legal standards have emerged for "intentional discrimination" (where a decision by an employer would include purposeful nonremedial consideration of the class characteristic of the employee or applicant, e.g., exclusion from a job category because of the general characteristic of being handicapped), and also for "effects discrimination" (where an action or criterion has a disproportionate effect on a class of people and cannot be justified by a legitimate reason, such as the safety and efficiency of an employer's operations). Statistical evidence demonstrating a numerical underrepresentation of a minority group has been given great weight by courts in demonstrating effects discrimination.[5] And if civil rights

---

5. In the conduct of the BPA Accommodations Study, the researchers found great resistance in the industry review panels that advised on the design of the study

legislation does prove applicable, aggrieved job applicants and employers would have the remedy of private lawsuits, which they lack under section 503. According to the civil rights commission's review of current legal precedent, however, court decisions to date have indicated "disagreement, inconsistency and confusion" (U.S. Commission on Civil Rights 1983, 150) concerning the applicability of the civil rights standards to the handicapped, with some court decisions being supportive of the applicability[6] and other decisions negative (Pushkin v. Regents of Univ. of Colo., 658 F.2d 1372, 1385 (10th Cir. 1981)).

The law does establish reasonable accommodation as national social policy. The questions remaining are, first, whether the law as it pertains to employment is reasonable and effective in achieving its intent of facilitating the employment and integration of disabled persons into society, and, second, who should appropriately bear the cost burden of the law.

The Economics of Accommodation

Individuals are hired and promoted on the basis of what an employer perceives to be their potential for producing goods and services. Employers want to select the most productive workers from a pool of applicants. The criteria used in hiring or promotion are, in theory, relevant to the expected job performance of the individual in the firm. The wage to be paid the worker would, in a competitive labor market, be equal to the worker's marginal contribution to the value of the firm's product.

In practice, of course, the conditions of perfect competition are rarely fully realized. The value of a worker's contribution is not easily assessed, especially in a service business or in more complex

---

to reporting full data on handicapped persons, precisely because of the fear that such data, once gathered across firms and existing in the public domain, could become the basis for statistical arguments in suits by the government or disabled advocacy groups.

6. Cf. Prewitt v. United States Postal Service, 662 F. 2d. 292, 305–307, n. 19 (5th Cir. 1981). For a review favoring the applicability of civil rights decisions, see Lang 1978.

production processes. Union rules, affirmative action policies, and larger public relations concerns may make it difficult for employers simply to hire or to promote the most productive individual or truly link wages with productivity.[7] Often well-intentioned efforts to hire on the basis of expected job performance may be misguided because of faulty information about those individual characteristics that are associated with good job performance. Wrong notions of the limitations associated with given disabling conditions, unjustified fears of customers' or fellow employees' reactions to a potentially disabled worker, incorrect assumptions about the risks that a disabled worker will suffer reinjury or illness while in a firm's employ and thus raise fringe benefit costs—all can result in hiring decisions that are not based on an individual's true job performance and that result in discrimination against the disabled worker.

The mandate of "reasonable accommodation" is a complex provision of the rehabilitation act. Unlike other provisions that focus on the fact that disabled persons may be just as productive as other potential workers, the accommodation provision recognizes that some disabled persons will *not* be as productive as other workers *unless* the accommodation occurs. If the accommodation is costly to the employer, then the accommodated worker, if employed at the same wage, will cost the employer more in a given job than another qualified applicant who does not require accommodation. Yet an employer who would then insist that the accommodated disabled worker receive a lower wage than a nondisabled worker performing the same job would be vulnerable to charges of wage discrimination under the law.

To some critics of the accommodation requirement, the fact that the accommodation represents an additional cost beyond the

---

7. It can be argued, of course, that often these practices do in fact increase the overall or long-run productivity of the firm. Firms invest in public relations because a positive image of the firm enhances sales, increases the morale and thereby presumably the productivity of most employees, may enhance the attractiveness of the firm to some investors, and may facilitate the leverage of the firm in its relationships with governments at the local, state, and federal levels. In short, good public relations may ultimately increase profits. Firms may accept union rules that appear to countermand what is the most productive arrangement of activity in one part of the firm, to avoid an overall breakdown in employee relations that could prove expensive. What may appear inefficient in a particular case may prove efficient when the larger context of consequences in an organization is understood.

wage, which may not be offset by the disabled worker's higher productivity or lower wage, makes the accommodation requirement unfair and an unreasonable economic cost for the employer to bear. Such critics would argue that because the accommodation is serving larger societal objectives, the employer should not have to bear the extra hiring cost. It may be true that taxpayers reap considerable savings in income and other transfer payments as a consequence of the disabled worker's securing employment and an income. It may be true that the disabled individual who, with accommodation, now gains the experience of working will be freed from dependency and will be a consistent contributor to social production. It may well be true that the citizenry as a whole will experience a greater sense of social justice in the increased well-being of the accommodated and now employed disabled worker. All of these social gains may justify the extra costs of making the disabled worker employable through accommodation, but, the critics would ask, why should the particular employer have to bear the costs of those social gains? The employer, under this argument, is suffering higher costs with no compensating increase in production or revenues.

The economist, on first glance at these arguments, finds them plausible. In a perfectly competitive market, the individual producer who incurs extra costs because of social regulation, but lacks any offset through a lower wage or higher productivity, indeed bears the cost, unless other competitors make similar expenditures to accommodate disabled workers. In a competitive market, the employer cannot raise the price of the firm's product to pass along these higher costs to consumers. In the longer run, those firms engaging in extensive accommodation would be relatively less profitable than other firms in their industry, and would be devalued by investors. Firms that perceive these consequences might look for loopholes in the legislation to reduce their chances of incurring these costs. They might be more aggressive at pointing disabled applicants and workers to those jobs within the firm that do not require accommodation.

The problem with this scenario is that it fails to consider actual experience and institutional practices within firms. There are a number of situations in which accommodation may not impose additional costs on the employer. First, the accommodation may provide a more efficient way of undertaking production that improves the productivity of many other workers as well. While the shift to permit more flexible work times is an accommodation for many disabled workers, this shift may also increase satisfaction and productivity for other workers as well.[8] The barrier-free design of a new building may facilitate movement and communication within the structure and increase overall productivity, while also specifically benefiting some handicapped workers (and customers). Offices may be rearranged so that not only wheelchairs but also delivery carts have easier access. At least, the cost of the accommodation per benefited worker may be lowered; in such cases, all the costs are not appropriately assigned to the particular individual whose needs prompted the change.

The extra cost of accommodation may be justified on productivity grounds if the disabled worker who is accommodated becomes more productive than the nondisabled worker who is vying for the same job. This situation can arise if the firm normally experiences high employee turnover, absenteeism, and supervisory problems with workers in the job for which the disabled worker is being considered. The government has long asserted in its "Hire the Handicapped" campaigns—and there is consistent, though unchallengeable, empirical evidence to back up the claims—that handicapped persons are more stable workers, with lower turnover, less absenteeism, lower risks of accident, and more loyalty to and satisfaction with their jobs and employers than other workers of similar characteristics in similar jobs.[9]

---

8. The survey reported in Fast et al. (1978) found that flexible work hours increased employee satisfaction and employment performance, as well as facilitated the employment of handicapped workers.

9. These claims have been fairly consistently supported to date in studies of the relative productivity of handicapped persons. Most of the more recent studies have taken place in the context of specific firms, e.g., the continuing series of studies by the Dupont Company or by Michigan Bell in the 1970s. The firm studies have not, however, made their data available for independent review and validation. The one extensive study, which is still the most widely cited and remains the major basis for many of the claims in the government's "Hire the Handicapped" publicity, is the classic 1948 study by the Department of Labor (U.S. Department of Labor 1948). That study examined employment records of 11,000 impaired and 18,000 carefully matched unimpaired workers throughout the country. Impaired workers had slightly higher productivity rates (1 percent) and fewer disabling conditions (8.9 injuries per million exposure hours on the job compared to 9.5 for unimpaired workers). The two groups had identical nondisabling injury rates. Impaired workers had slightly higher absenteeism rates (3.8 days per 100 scheduled work days compared to 3.4) and somewhat higher voluntary quit rates (3.6 per 100 employees compared to 2.6). Especially interesting was the fact

If this is true, the costs of accommodation would be a good investment because of the lower costs and higher productivity of the disabled worker.

If an employee has some special skills in scarce supply, the costs of accommodation may be justified. While the law mandates reasonable accommodation for disabled workers, it may be that for various jobs, some firms or industries routinely make "accommodations" for many nondisabled workers, but without calling them such. Firms may incur substantial recruiting costs if the supply of workers with those skills is in scarce supply. The lower the cost of the accommodation, the more likely a firm will be to undertake the accommodation even for a worker with lesser skills. With higher skills, and in positions where jobs are designed around the individual, adjustments of the specific job and even extra costs for specific equipment may be a normal firm response to bringing on a desired worker.

The most compelling incentives for the employer to pursue accommodation arise when an individual becomes disabled while an employee of the firm. In this case, if the employer does not pursue accommodation, the employer risks becoming liable for long-term maintenance of the individual's income if disability insurance is a part of the firm's fringe benefits. If an employee has a $25,000-a-year income and the firm's policies guarantee two-thirds of that income in the event of a disability that prevents the individual from working, the employer has a potential liability of over $16,500 a year. Confronted with such potential costs, the firm might see an accommodation that permits the individual to sustain work within the firm as a bargain. The employer has an incentive, of course, to look for the least costly accommodations. Shifting the individual to a comparably paying job that does not require activities for which the individual's

---

that impaired workers had considerably higher involuntary termination rates (firings). The Department of Labor attributed this to the postwar practice of firing disabled workers (just as women were also fired) to accommodate returning able-bodied veterans. In a more recent study, Zadny (1979) reports that among 448 employers surveyed in Portland and San Francisco, respondents rated the performance of disabled persons as being average or above average in comparison with other workers, and that employer attitudes were correlated with their hiring of the disabled persons. (Zadny also finds that the major reason cited by employers for not hiring more disabled persons was that disabled people were not being referred to them.

condition poses a handicap will usually be preferable to an expensive adaptation or acquisition of machinery or equipment.

Thus, the reasonableness of undertaking an accommodation involving additional costs for the employer depends on the particular circumstances of the worker and the nature of the job and the accommodation. How often accommodations are needed by disabled workers, how costly the accommodations turn out to be, whether they tend merely to bring the disabled worker up to the levels of other workers or are seen as yielding benefits to other workers and/or higher productivity—all these are empirical questions needing an answer. It does remain true that if an employer simply adapts to the requirement to accommodate a disabled worker when the employer could just as readily hire another worker with no loss in overall productivity, then the employer and society are incurring social costs due to accommodation. There may indeed be offsetting gains for society as a whole if the accommodation is made. But the issue of who should properly bear such extra social costs remains.

To the extent that the employer operates in a market that is not fully competitive, and therefore has some degree of monopolistic control over the product price, part of the cost of accommodation can be shifted to consumers. Indeed, if all firms have an equal probability of encountering disabled employees needing accommodation, and of being compelled by law to incur costs for accommodation, then even in a competitive market all firms would be able to pass on to consumers the extra costs of accommodation. The cost of accommodations are simply then a general cost of production—like a general sales tax—to be shifted forward to consumers.[10] Thus, as disabled workers are referred to *all* employers and as the law on reasonable accommodation is universally enforced, any particular employer will be less disadvantaged. Even for that employer, some of the costs may

---

10. In theory, a further consequence of such general accommodation effort could be that the costs and thus the prices of the products of American industry would be raised relative to the products of foreign competitors lacking such a social policy of accommodation, with resulting negative impacts on national employment and income. To be significant, the costs of accommodation would have to be quite large. However, our principal foreign competitors (e.g., England, Germany, and Japan) have more extensive, restrictive, and potentially more costly programs for employing disabled workers.

be substantially deflected back to the taxpayer if the accommodation consists of equipment purchase that would qualify for the favorable tax treatment (via investment tax credits and accelerated depreciation) that is afforded such capital acquisitions. Similarly, the costs are also shifted back to the taxpayer to the extent the accommodated worker is hired over other applicants who would not similarly qualify for the de facto wage subsidies now being provided (via tax credits) for hiring various classes of disadvantaged workers. These last examples again illustrate how analysis of the incidence of the costs depends on the particular situation of the firm (e.g., whether it had current profits so that tax credits and deductions were useful), the nature of the particular accommodation (e.g., involving a capital cost, or only more costs in management time), and the nature of the available labor supply for the position (e.g., whether the accommodated disabled worker is being hired instead of some other applicant in a class of worker qualifying for a wage subsidy).

Nonetheless, and despite these qualifications, some employers or even economic sectors may differentially absorb the costs of accommodation and thus be put at a competitive disadvantage. If a firm uses disproportionately less skilled labor relative to its competitors, and if disabled workers requiring accommodations turn out to be concentrated in the lower skill levels, such a firm may experience greater accommodation costs than its competitors. Industries with relatively higher proportions of less skilled labor would experience higher costs and lower profits.

We turn now to what is known about accommodations. The evidence clearly suggests that most of the fears of severe cost implication have little justification to date. After the evidence is reviewed, we shall explore the questions of whether accommodations that are less than reasonable for a particular employer might not in fact be socially desirable, and who should pay for such accommodations.

THE EVIDENCE TO DATE ON EMPLOYERS' ACCOMMODATION EXPERIENCE

The consistent finding of detailed surveys of employers has been that expensive job modification or accommodation is rarely needed by disabled workers. As early as 1970, the civil service commission had completed a survey of their placement of severely handicapped people in the federal government and found that only 15.6 percent of some 397 persons placed required any job restructuring or work-site modification. The report concluded that

contrary to the general assumption, the severely handicapped do not usually, or even often, require major alterations in a job situation. When changes are made, they were such incidental things as installing a wheelchair ramp at a building entrance, rearranging desks and file cabinets to improve mobility and accessibility, etc. (O'Neill 1976, 7)

This finding in the federal government has consistently been borne out by later studies.

The largest survey of reasonable accommodation experience with principally public agencies under section 504 similarly found few examples of expensive accommodation; most accommodations involved minimal adjustments by employers (Johnson and Associates, Inc. 1980). Handbooks issued by the federal government have made similar characterizations of what reasonable accommodation normally entails.[11] The larger survey also interestingly found that public and nonprofit agency managers were not particularly accurate in their ability to report the actual costs of accommodation; on-site validations of cost reported by managers proved discrepant with the initial survey reports, with higher costs being reported initially for those accommodations involving more than trivial expense. On the other hand, the study reported a tendency for managers to overlook the hidden costs of management time associated with the majority of accommodations that involved little or no outright expenditure of money. Management time tended not to be perceived as a "cost" to most agencies surveyed.

Only two surveys have been done on a national sampling basis of private employer experiences under section 503 with "reasonable accommodation." The most extensive of these studies is the BPA Accommodations Study (1982). The survey sought to provide a better base of information to the government for implementing section 503

---

11. Cf. U.S. Department of Health, Education and Welfare 1977, which was one of the principal handbooks for section 504. Similarly, cf. U.S. Office of Personnel Management 1980, which was one of the first major handbooks for federal agency employers implementing section 501.

of the Rehabilitation Act of 1973, which stipulates that, for any contract in excess of $2,500, "the party contracting with the United States shall take affirmative action to employ and advance in employment qualified handicapped individuals. . . ." The principal objectives of the survey were to discover the prevalence of current accommodation efforts and the types and costs of accommodations currently being provided, to explore the related practices that firms found conducive to successful accommodation, and to understand the decision-making processes involved.

The twenty-month study had four major components:

1. A survey of 2,000 federal contractors, documenting the extent, nature, and costs of the accommodations provided, together with the relationship between firms' attitudes toward accommodations and handicapped workers and the actions these firms had taken. Responses were analyzed for 367 responding firms, representing 512,000 workers, of whom 19,200 were known to be handicapped.

2. Telephone interviews with 85 firms to explore in some detail the circumstances surrounding a single accommodation: how and why it was undertaken and with what results.

3. A survey of disabled workers to learn their perceptions about any accommodations that may have been made for them.

4. Intensive case studies of 10 firms identified from their survey and/or telephone responses as having exemplary accommodation practices.

Before reviewing the findings of that study, which are totally consistent with the conclusions of the other studies reported above, we should note some of the limitations of the study. While a large number of firms and workers are covered by the survey, the overall response rate to the mail survey was low (though comparable to the response rate for other national mail surveys of industry). Industry remains one of the more difficult components of American society to survey, especially when actual data are wanted, rather than merely opinion statements from a respondent. The BPA Accommodations Study analyzed biases in nonresponse at length. There appeared to be no important bias by firm size or industry type. Follow-ups with forty nonrespondent firms, exploring reasons for nonparticipation, found no consistent pattern. Some firms reported confidentiality concerns or distrust of the use to which the data would be put. More often, firms reported their nonresponse as based on lack of staff time to complete the survey forms, or lack of records of the kind needed for the survey (e.g., centralized counts of numbers of disabled workers, their accommodations, and the costs), or the firms' not perceiving that they had any handicapped workers who had received accommodations. The very largest corporations sometimes did not respond because of the sheer difficulty of gathering data across plants at multiple sites. Some firms that did not respond nonetheless reported, in the follow-up probes by phone, accommodation experience that was consistent with the overall findings of the BPA survey. The analysis of nonrespondents thus did not yield clear indications of bias, but the possibility that firms resisting accommodation might have been disproportionately under-represented in the survey response cannot be dismissed. At the same time, the general findings are partially validated by their consistency with other studies, by the internal consistency of the various different segments of the multifaceted BPA study, and by the judgments that the study findings were consistent with previous findings. Also, there is some reason to anticipate that those firms that had experienced serious problems with accommodation and large expense might be more likely to respond and vent their frustration, rather than be less likely to respond.

A second limitation of the BPA study is the exclusion from the study of firms with fewer than fifty employees. Such firms generate a large share of the new jobs created in the economy each year. However, as we shall note subsequently, another survey of accommodation experience has focused on small businesses, and has reported findings similar to those of the BPA report.

A third limitation of the BPA findings is inherent in the ability of firms to generate data. Many firms do not centrally store data on whether employees are disabled or on the kinds of accommodation they receive. This is especially true when the accommodations are minor or of little cost. In the on-site case studies as well, central management often proved unaware of many inexpensive accommodations that were made informally at the job station by the immediate line supervisor and coworkers. Most firms also reported that many disabled workers do not choose to identify themselves as disabled or to bring themselves under the protection of the federal legislation (and thus to get themselves designated as disabled persons in the firm's records). Personnel departments were often aware of disabled workers who had not so identified themselves. (This also appears to be the general experience in federal agencies, even within the President's Committee on Employment of the Handicapped, with its high prevalence of disabled employees.) The reasons for this non-self-identification can be speculated upon. In some cases, it may be the fear of stigma or of losing a promotion if the firm's management became aware of an employee's heart condition, mental illness history, or problem with alcohol or drugs. More commonly, however, many disabled workers simply don't perceive themselves as handicapped people in need of special accommodation or protection in their employment situation. All of these factors led BPA to conclude that the data reported are probably *minimum* estimates of the extent of accommodation and hiring of handicapped workers at the responding firms.

Another limitation of the data is that in reporting costs, firms tend to look only at direct outlays of cash for accommodation—"out-of-pocket costs." Management time, the time of engineers and employees, and the cost of materials in constructing, say, a ramp are not seen as costs at many firms. The effort required in the accommodation is seen as simply part of the normal job requirements of the personnel manager, line supervisor, or maintenance engineer and crew. These are previously budgeted costs that, if not incurred for the accommodation of the disabled worker, would be incurred for some other (nondisabled) employee's needs or other plant adaptation. The BPA study was not designed to permit measurement of the opportunity costs of the resources required for the accommodation. What was striking, however, was that most firms did not perceive the resources as having a high opportunity cost. This suggests that any analysis of the behavior of firms in responding to accommodation needs and costs must be sensitive to the institutional practices and perceptions of the managers within the firm.

The strong overall conclusion of the BPA study was that, for firms that have made efforts to hire the handicapped, accommodation is "no big deal." Rarely did an accommodation involve much cost: according to the firms' reports and records (see table 8.1), 51 percent

TABLE 8.1

Total Cost of Accommodations to Company

Cost	Frequency of Response	
	Number	Percent
None	458	51.1
$1–99	169	18.5
$100–499	109	11.9
$500–999	57	6.2
$1000–1999	39	4.3
$2000–4999	35	3.8
$5000–9999	9	1.0
$10,000–14,999	8	0.9
$15,000–19,999	6	0.7
$20,000 or more	15	1.6
Total for which cost was reported	915	100.0

Source: BPA Accommodations Study, I, 29.

of the reported accommodations cost nothing; another 30 percent of the accommodations were reported as costing less than $500. Only 8 percent of the accommodations were reported as costing more than $2,000.

About 55 percent of the firms responding did have some accommodation experience. Some 17 percent of responding firms reported employing handicapped workers, but not making any accommodations. The remaining 28 percent of firms reported employing no handicapped workers. This last finding indicates a broad variance among firms in the extent of their risk of accommodation expense, since overall the sample of responding firms reported an average of 2.5 percent of their labor force as being handicapped. If accommodation did involve great expense, this wide variation in prevalence of disabled workers could indicate that some firms would be put at a competitive disadvantage relative to other firms in their markets. However, these accommodations did not appear to be expensive.

What is clear in the BPA data, however, is that larger firms are much more likely both to recruit handicapped workers and to undertake expensive accommodations. In the class of largest firms, the percentage of handicapped workers in the labor force was 3.5 percent on average, in contrast to 2.5 percent for the average firm. This finding is striking. One might expect larger firms to have larger personnel units that are perhaps better able to match disabled individuals to jobs where they can perform comparably to nondisabled workers. Larger firms also have many more jobs and a broader diversity of jobs in the internal labor market, so that a disabled employee can be more readily assigned or shifted to a job not requiring extensive or expensive accommodation. Larger firms may have internal engineering and maintenance capability at the work site for undertaking physical alterations of the work space without special expense. Larger firms often have the financial capability to justify the occasional more expensive accommodation (and derive larger public relations value from it). All of these speculative explanations were supported by the case studies and the phone interview surveys undertaken in the BPA study. In any case, it would appear that efforts to expand the employment of disabled individuals, especially those requiring accommodation, might wisely be focused on larger firms, rather than on the small business sector.

The accommodations took many forms: adapting the work environments and the location of the job within the work site; retraining or selectively placing workers in jobs needing no accommodation; providing transportation or special equipment or aides; redesigning the actual job; and reorienting or providing special training to supervisors and/or coworkers. The ranges of accommodations provided to different occupational groups and to workers of differing disabling conditions are indicated, respectively, in tables 8.2 and 8.3. No particular type of accommodation emerged as predominating. Most workers received more than one accommodation. The most expensive and extensive accommodations tended to be provided to the blind and to those in wheelchairs, as indicated in table 8.4. Consistent with earlier theoretical expectations, more skilled workers were more often provided more expensive accommodations (see table 8.5) and accommodations requiring environmental adaptation of the workplace or special equipment (see table 8.2). Less skilled workers were more likely to receive job redesign accommodations, retraining, or selective placement.

Two other patterns were notable. The basic pattern of accommodation practice was reported to be that once an individual was

TABLE 8.2
Job Category of Accommodated Employees
by Type of Accommodation

Job Category	Removed Barrier	Adjusted Work Environment	Adjusted Table, Desk	Other Rearrangement	Relocated Work Site	Modified Phone, Typewriter	Microfilm, Dictaphone	Other Special Equipment	Job Transportation or Mobility
Officials, managers	12.3%	7.7%	7.7%	4.6%	3.1%	15.4%	0.0%	6.2%	10.8%
Professionals	23.6	7.3	22.5	17.4	2.8	7.9	6.2	14.6	10.1
Technicians	11.5	3.8	10.6	8.7	4.8	3.8	2.9	11.5	4.8
Office, clerical	9.6	5.6	10.0	6.8	1.2	9.2	2.8	8.0	6.0
Sales	0.0	0.0	6.3	0.0	0.0	0.0	0.0	0.0	6.3
Crafts	4.5	0.8	4.5	4.5	0.8	0.8	0.8	3.8	2.3
Operatives	3.7	3.1	8.8	5.8	2.7	0.7	0.3	6.8	5.1
Laborers	8.4	8.4	13.7	8.4	6.3	1.1	0.0	6.3	0.0
Service workers	4.1	2.0	0.0	2.0	2.0	4.1	0.0	4.1	2.0

Job Category	Reassigned Tasks	Modified Work Hours	Other Modification of Work Procedure	Assigned Aides, Reader	Additional Training	Oriented Coworkers, Supervisors	Transferred to Another Job	Other Accommodation	Total Job Categories and Accommodation Types Reported (%)
Officials, managers	16.9%	21.5%	6.2%	0.0%	3.1%	12.3%	12.3%	9.2%	65(5.5)
Professionals	9.6	6.2	7.3	4.5	3.4	27.0	1.7	21.3	178(15.0)
Technicians	14.4	5.8	6.7	6.7	7.7	26.9	6.7	25.0	104(8.8)
Office, clerical	19.3	10.4	14.9	6.8	9.2	32.1	10.8	11.6	249(21.0)
Sales	6.3	6.3	0.0	0.0	12.5	62.5	0.0	18.8	16(1.4)
Crafts	13.5	8.3	27.1	3.8	4.5	29.3	14.3	21.8	133(11.2)
Operatives	13.6	8.1	20.0	6.8	12.5	35.3	24.7	7.1	295(24.9)
Laborers	21.1	9.5	20.0	7.4	14.7	34.7	18.9	12.6	95(8.0)
Service workers	14.3	4.1	8.2	0.0	10.2	22.4	30.6	30.6	49(4.1)
Total									1184(100.0)

Source: BPA Accommodations Study, I, 57 (company questionnaire responses).

Notes: [a]This is the number of workers in each job category for which at least one accommodation type was specified. The number of accommodations is much larger.

[b]Percentages add across rows to more than 100% because employees often received multiple accommodations.

TABLE 8.3
Handicapping Condition of
Accommodated Employee by Type of Accommodation

Handicapping[a] Condition	Removed Barrier	Adjusted Work Environment	Adjusted Table, Desk	Other Rearrangement	Relocated Work Site	Modified Phone, Typewriter	Microfilm, Dictaphone	Other Special Equipment	Job Transportation or Mobility
Wheelchair user	56.1%	7.0%	42.1%	23.7%	3.5%	6.1%	1.8%	10.5%	14.9%
Other walking limitations	15.5	7.8	18.7	12.3	4.6	0.9	0.5	6.8	12.8
Total blindness	15.4	5.8	11.5	9.6	5.8	0.0	21.2	28.8	26.9
Other impaired vision	1.4	14.1	5.6	4.2	2.8	1.4	4.2	8.5	1.4
Deaf	1.4	1.4	3.5	4.9	0.7	13.9	4.2	9.7	0.7
Other impaired hearing	1.9	1.9	1.9	1.9	1.9	48.1	0.0	14.8	0.0

Limited use of arms	7.7	2.8	20.3	11.9	3.5	4.2	2.1	16.8	6.3
Impaired speech	1.9	1.9	9.4	9.4	0.0	11.3	5.7	11.3	7.5
Cosmetic or skin	0.0	4.5	4.5	4.5	0.0	4.5	0.0	9.1	4.5
Mental retardation	0.0	4.8	0.0	2.4	9.5	0.0	0.0	0.0	0.0
Other mental or emotional	1.8	0.0	3.5	5.3	1.8	0.0	0.0	1.8	1.8
Respiratory condition	2.2	10.9	6.5	10.9	4.3	0.0	0.0	4.3	4.3
Limitation of activity	1.9	2.8	3.3	1.9	1.4	0.9	0.5	2.3	1.4
Other condition	4.1	1.4	8.2	1.4	1.4	0.0	0.0	4.1	1.4
Condition progressive	16.0	8.0	8.0	16.0	8.0	4.0	4.0	12.0	12.0

TABLE 8.3 *continued*

Handicapping[a] Condition	Reassigned Tasks	Modified Work Hours	Other Modification of Work Procedure	Assigned Aides, Reader	Additional Training	Oriented Co-workers, Supervisors	Transferred to Another Job	Other Accommodation	Total Handicaps and Accommodation Types Reported (%)
Wheelchair user	7.0%	7.0%	3.5%	2.6%	5.3%	19.3%	1.8%	13.2%	114(8.6)%
Other walking limitations	16.4	9.6	21.9	0.0	3.2	19.6	8.7	12.8	219(16.5)
Total blindness	15.4	17.3	25.0	28.8	21.2	9.6	5.8	9.6	52(3.9)
Other impaired vision	14.1	1.4	22.5	1.4	15.5	45.1	14.1	11.3	71(5.3)
Deaf	18.1	1.4	9.7	25.0	20.8	48.6	4.9	25.7	144(10.8)
Other impaired hearing	9.3	0.0	11.1	5.6	7.4	31.5	5.6	3.7	54(4.1)
Limited use of arms	16.8	8.4	14.7	0.7	8.4	25.9	28.0	6.3	143(10.8)

Impaired speech	15.1	5.7	15.1	15.1	18.9	67.9	9.4	9.4	53(4.0)
Cosmetic or skin	13.6	9.1	9.1	0.0	0.0	9.1	36.4	9.1	22(1.7)
Mental retardation	19.0	9.5	16.7	0.0	31.0	66.7	9.5	14.3	42(3.2)
Other mental or emotional	22.8	15.8	15.8	3.5	14.0	47.4	21.1	14.0	57(4.3)
Respiratory condition	21.7	8.7	21.7	0.0	0.0	28.3	39.1	2.2	46(3.5)
Limitation of activity	16.8	16.8	15.0	1.0	0.0	27.6	19.2	15.9	214(16.1)
Other condition	9.6	9.6	11.0	1.4	1.4	30.1	17.8	37.0	73(5.5)
Condition progressive	16.0	20.0	12.0	4.0	12.0	32.0	20.0	0.0	25(1.9)
Total									1329(100.0)

Source: Company questionnaire responses.

Note: Percentages are of the total number of accommodated persons with a given disability. Percentages may add across rows to more than 100%
because many individuals received multiple accommodations.

aWhere multiple handicaps exist, they are counted separately.

TABLE 8.4

Handicapping Conditions of Accommodated Employees by Total Cost of Accommodations Provided to the Employee (percent of accommodated employees)

Handicapping[a] Condition	Zero	$1–99	$100–499	$500–999	$1,000–1,999	$2,000–4,999
Wheelchair user	14.6%	14.6%	13.4%	8.5%	19.5%	12.2%
Other walking limitation	54.3	14.5	13.4	12.4	1.1	1.6
Total blindness	17.1	12.2	26.8	4.9	4.9	7.3
Other impaired vision	64.0	24.0	4.0	2.0	4.0	2.0
Deaf	44.0	17.4	14.7	12.8	3.7	7.3
Other impaired hearing	35.3	50.0	8.8	2.9	0.0	2.9
Limited use of arms	51.8	19.3	12.3	2.6	7.9	4.4
Impaired speech	54.2	2.1	20.8	12.5	6.3	4.2
Cosmetic or skin	64.7	11.8	17.6	0.0	5.9	0.0
Mental retardation	70.3	2.7	10.8	8.1	2.7	2.7
Other mental or emotional	50.0	14.3	14.3	14.3	2.4	4.8
Respiratory condition	67.7	6.5	9.7	0.0	9.7	0.0
Limitation of activity	63.5	22.6	8.2	0.0	1.3	1.3
Other condition	60.0	21.8	7.3	3.6	1.8	5.5
Condition progressive	50.0	30.0	5.0	5.0	0.0	5.0

Handicapping[a] Condition	$5,000–9,999	$10,000–14,999	$15,000–19,999	$20,000 or more	Total Handicaps and Costs Reported (%)[b]
Wheelchair user	2.4%	2.4%	6.1%	6.1%	82(8.0)
Other walking limitation	1.1	1.1	0.0	0.5	186(18.1)
Total blindness	7.3	2.4	2.4	14.6	41(4.0)
Other impaired vision	0.0	0.0	0.0	0.0	50(4.9)
Deaf	0.0	0.0	0.0	0.0	109(10.6)
Other impaired hearing	0.0	0.0	0.0	0.0	34(3.3)
Limited use of arms	0.0	0.9	0.0	0.9	114(11.1)
Impaired speech	0.0	0.0	0.0	0.0	48(4.7)
Cosmetic or skin	0.0	0.0	0.0	0.0	17(1.7)
Mental retardation	2.7	0.0	0.0	0.0	37(3.6)
Other mental or emotional	0.0	0.0	0.0	0.0	42(4.1)
Respiratory condition	0.0	0.0	0.0	6.5	31(3.0)
Limitation of activity	1.3	1.9	0.0	0.0	159(15.5)
Other condition	0.0	0.0	0.0	0.0	55(5.4)
Condition progressive	5.0	0.0	0.0	0.0	20(2.0)
Total					1025(100.0)

Source: BPA Accommodations Study, I, 66 (company questionnaire responses).

Note: Percentages add across rows to approximately 100% (rounding errors).

[a] Where multiple handicaps exist, they are counted separately.
[b] Number of accommodated workers having each handicapping condition for which costs were reported.

TABLE 8.5
Job Category of Accommodated Employees
by Total Cost of Accommodations to Employer
(percent of accommodated employees)

Job Category	Zero	$1–99	$100–499	$500–999	$1,000–1,999	$2,000–4,999
Officials, managers	49.0%	17.6%	5.9%	5.9%	11.8%	5.9%
Professionals	39.3	14.8	11.5	7.4	5.7	9.0
Technicians	36.1	19.4	11.5	8.3	12.5	4.2
Office, clerical	47.8	19.1	14.6	5.1	5.1	5.6
Sales	68.8	0.0	18.8	6.3	0.0	0.0
Crafts	67.3	19.4	5.1	3.1	4.1	0.0
Operatives	51.0	24.1	15.1	4.9	0.8	2.4
Laborers	55.1	14.6	13.5	12.4	2.2	2.2
Service workers	75.0	8.3	2.8	8.3	0.0	0.0

Job Category	$5,000–9,999	$10,000–14,999	$15,000–19,999	$20,000 or more	Total Job Categories and Costs Reported (%)[a]
Officials, managers	2.0%	0.0%	0.0%	2.0%	51(5.6)
Professionals	2.5	0.8	3.3	5.7	122(13.5)
Technicians	0.0	2.8	1.4	4.2	72(8.9)
Office, clerical	1.1	0.0	0.6	1.1	178(19.6)
Sales	0.0	6.3	0.0	0.0	16(1.8)
Crafts	0.0	1.0	0.0	0.0	98(10.8)
Operatives	0.8	0.8	0.0	0.0	245(27.0)
Laborers	0.0	0.0	0.0	0.0	89(9.8)
Service workers	0.0	2.8	0.0	2.8	37(4.0)
Total					908(100.0)

Source: BPA Accommodations Study, I, 56 (company questionnaire responses).

Notes: Percentages add across to approximately 100% (rounding errors).

[a]This is the number of workers in each category for whom accommodation costs were reported.

hired, he or she was likely to be accommodated if the need arose, regardless of occupation or seniority. Nonetheless, accommodations were more common with workers already employed by the firm, especially among less skilled workers. This is consistent with the theoretical expectation. Firms have a greater incentive to facilitate the retention of workers who become disabled after being in the firm's employ because of the greater firm-specific training and because of the firm's interest in reducing its liability for long-term disability income maintenance. Because the BPA study also focused on existing workers, it cannot be known whether there were rejected job applicants who may have needed more extensive or expensive accommodation than those workers who were hired. The study's survey of handicapped employees—the least representative sample in the study—found, however, that 21 percent of the responding disabled workers in the twenty-two participating firms reported further unmet needs for accommodation, with half of these workers reporting that management had not responded favorably when the accommodation was proposed by the worker.

A second pattern reported in the study was that accommodation efforts *did not appear* to be strongly related to upward mobility in the firm, either in terms of providing an advantage for the disabled workers or in limiting their potential (perhaps because of management's unwillingness to write off the investment in the accommodation required in the previous job slot). Only 21 percent of the surveyed workers judged that the accommodation had improved their career potential, and only 30 percent of the responding firms in the mail survey affirmed that accommodation had improved the workers' promotability and advancement potential within the firm. Instead, accommodation efforts were perceived as successful principally in allowing the worker to be effective on the job. Firms did frequently report, however, that the accommodation would still benefit the employee if he or she were promoted to a new job, and often stated that other nondisabled workers had also benefited from the accommodation.

Most interesting is the actual reported success of the firms with their accommodation efforts. The firms saw accommodation as good business practice. The majority of firms reported that accommodations had increased workers' productivity (50 percent assenting, 5 percent dissenting). More than five times as many firms reported that actual benefits had exceeded actual costs for most accommodations undertaken as reported the opposite (39 percent assenting, 7 percent dissenting). In spite of their observed tendency not to treat management time and similar previously budgeted expenditures as costs, only 9 percent of firms affirmed that their projections of either the benefits or costs of accommodation had been off target. When projections were off, reality seems to be in favor of the accommodation being more beneficial than the firm had thought; thus, while only 7 percent of firms said that actual benefits had not exceeded actual costs with their accommodations, 16 percent of firms reported that their projected costs had exceeded projected benefits.

It was earlier noted that a major limitation of the BPA study was its exclusion of the truly small business sector, the sector where new jobs in the economy are supposedly being disproportionately created. A subsequent survey of small business experience with government regulation in general, but including the reasonable accommodation requirement, was conducted by faculty of the business school at Wright State University, under funding by the U.S. Small Business Administration (Premus and Carnes 1982). That study also found very few examples of expensive accommodations undertaken by small business. The study identified management time as the big constraint on accommodation. In small firms, managers tend to perform many more functions than in larger firms; the time of the manager (who often is also the entrepreneur and owner) is one of the scarcest resources in the firm. Just as top management commitment was seen as essential to the success of changes in large firms' practices toward handicapped persons, so too was that commitment important in small firms. But whereas in larger firms the time of the immediate supervisors, line managers, and personnel staff implementing accommodation could be treated as a "free resource," such time is scarce and limited in small business and is recognized as such. As a result, extensive accommodation will be rarer in small businesses.

We have now summarized the major studies of accommodation experience, pointing out their similar findings, and some of the inherent weaknesses in their designs and in the data. The most recent literature review undertaken for OFCCP is also consistent with the depiction of the evidence above (U.S. Department of Labor 1985). Managers, firms, and public agencies do appear to consistently un-

TABLE 8.6

Firms' Reactions to Policy Options
(percent of firms)

Option	Strong Incentive	Some Incentive	No Incentive	Not Sure	Not Reported	One of Most Important Incentives
Tax credit for a portion of the cost of accommodation	19%	46%	25%	5%	5%	42%
Provision of free technical assistance for accommodation	14	42	31	8	5	25
Increased enforcement of affirmative action regulations	13	35	34	11	6	23
Placement efforts on behalf of specific applicants by vocational rehabilitation or other service-providing agencies	14	50	19	12	5	27
Direct wage subsidy for severely handicapped workers whose productivity is below standard	8	26	46	15	5	10
Funding for more technical occupational training or work experience for handicapped persons	15	39	27	14	5	25
Provision of information by the government documenting the advantages and profitability of hiring handicapped persons	4	32	42	16	6	7
Other	5	4	0	1	90	9

Source: BPA Accommodations Study, I, 71.
Note: Total adds to more than 100% because firms were asked to state the two most important incentives.

dervalue the resources consumed in accommodation, but they perceive accommodation as successful, justified in the preponderant majority (90 percent) of attempts by the benefits, and as "no big deal."

There are two large gaps in the research to date, however. First, there have been no studies of firms that are not federal contractors and thus not liable to the reasonable accommodation requirements. It would be interesting to determine whether accommodation in these firms is as prevalent as, and of similar types to, that found for OFCCP contractors. If so, it would indeed be a strong indication that the law and its enforcement are not a factor in inducing accommodations, and that accommodations truly are—as advocates but also managers attest—"good business."

Second, all of the studies have focused on accommodations actually provided and/or on the accommodation needs and experiences of workers currently employed by firms and public agencies. There have been no studies that focused on those accommodations that might have been needed by job applicants who were not hired. Such a study would require a very different design; the research would have to track individual handicapped job applicants, rather than sample firms or agencies providing accommodation. (Probing why accommodations were not given would also be threatening to the agencies and firms which had not provided accommodations.) Nonetheless, it remains a strong possibility that disabled persons, especially those with severe disabilities, who do not find it easy to enter or reenter the labor market may be precisely those individuals whose needs for accommodation are more extensive and would require greater costs to employers. If these individuals were to be pushed forward to firms for their consideration for employment, and strong emphasis was then placed by enforcement upon the reasonable accommodation requirement, the reactions of firms to making accommodations and to absorbing the costs of accommodations solely within the firm might well change.

In the next section, we shall explore the need for and the policy considerations surrounding accommodation for this group of disabled workers who are not finding entry into the labor market easy.

THE ROLE OF ACCOMMODATION IN EXPANDED EMPLOYMENT PROGRAMS FOR THE DISABLED

While the studies to date of accommodation experience in firms and agencies have not looked at the job applicants or the potential disabled job seekers not hired, there is other evidence that some have needs that accommodation would address. The Urban Institute and its consortium of research groups conducted a survey of 889 severely disabled individuals rejected for service by vocational rehabilitation agencies because of the severity of their disabilities. The Urban Institute asked the severely disabled individuals who were not currently working (94 percent of all respondents) what services they thought they would need in order to return to work (Urban Institute 1975). The most common response concerned the intensity and duration of work—the need for light work only (62 percent), for a reduced work schedule (47.5 percent), and for a flexible work schedule (40 percent). The second most frequent type of response was classified by the Urban Institute as "prework needs," though some could clearly be provided by employers: transportation (41 percent), special training or education (39 percent), ramps and elevators (27 percent), attendant help (14 percent), and regular assistance in work tasks (16 percent). These perceived service needs were particularly instructive since, on a different question, only 20 percent of respondents had reported that the employer's unwillingness to hire, union policies, or the employer's inflexible scheduling was a primary or secondary reason for their unemployment. Instead, on that question, 83 percent had cited their poor health, not any barriers erected by employers, as their main reason for being unemployed. Similarly, studies of initially successful vocational rehabilitation (VR) clients who fail to sustain employment over time have frequently reported that poor and unreliable transportation and inability to maintain regular working hours were major factors in the individual's dropping out of employment (Abt Associates, Inc. 1974).

It is important to emphasize that these studies, along with other studies of the correlates of success for individuals who go through vocational rehabilitation programs, also make it clear that for the *majority* of disabled individuals not in the labor force, accommodations at the work site are not the key in their securing employment. The principal correlates of failure in job finding for disabled individuals have fairly consistently turned out to be lack of past work experience and characteristics other than the type or severity of the disability itself—such as the individual's youth, poor education, or minority or female status.[12] For this large group, employment strategies must, at

---

12. See Berkeley Planning Associates 1975, part of the overall Urban Institute submission for the comprehensive needs study cited earlier; Berkeley Planning Asso-

least in the initial years, look at policies other than accommodation. At the same time, accommodation *is* a relevant consideration for a large segment (20–40 percent) of those outside the employed handicapped work force.

Another significant group of unemployed disabled persons, for whom accommodation is a highly important consideration, are those compelled to withdraw from the labor force because of injury and especially illness that emerges or worsens during the course of their work life.

Research has found high correlations between the physical requirements of a job and whether the worker will cease working at it when disabled (Luft 1978). More and more of the studies emphasize the need for early intervention by employers when an employee experiences major illness or injury, or confronts major surgery or a progressively worsening or severe chronic health problem, in order to prevent long-term disability and withdrawal from the labor force (Jarvikoski and Lehelma 1980; Galvin 1973; Hester and Downs 1984). Key to this early intervention is often adjustment in the design of the job and the worker's requirements (e.g., providing flexible hours)— in short, accommodation. One survey of 250 individuals in California with rheumatoid arthritis, a chronic disease normally classified as severely disabling, determined the individual's ability to control the scheduling of his or her work hours and requirements to be a key predictor of whether the individual would return to work eventually, even controlling for the severity of the medical problem (Yelin et al. 1980; Yelin, Nevitt, and Epstein 1980; Yelin 1979). Individuals who were self-employed or in managerial or white collar occupations, who worked in larger firms, who worked with relatively less supervision,

---

ciates 1978; and Worrall and Vandergoot 1982. It is also true, however, that there remains a large residual of unexplained variance in even the largest multivariate studies of nonsuccess in vocational rehabilitation. Nagi's (1975) analysis of work disability, using a large array of demographic and socioeconomic characteristics, found that all the factors combined still explained only 38 percent of variance in work disability. M. Berkowitz et al. (1972), even estimating regressions separately for different age, race, and sex cohorts, and adding more variables to the usual personal characteristics, such as area unemployment, the presence of income support, and the person's more detailed health and functional limitations, explained only half the variance in labor force participation for white and black males. Noting these findings, researchers have frequently cited the need for some measure of motivation or work socialization to improve predictability.

who could reduce or flexibly shift their hours of work, were much less likely to become disabled as a result of their health conditions, even controlling for education, income, and numerous other personal characteristics. Similar findings have emerged with other specific populations defined by medical problems, such as hip replacement (Nevitt 1984), as health researchers concerned with the low benefit-cost returns to many of the newer surgical innovations have begun to look more closely at the factors that interact with health treatment in influencing return to work.

Given these two large groups of disabled persons who may benefit from accommodation, there is a larger role for accommodation to play in federal employment programs for disabled persons. If policy and the law were to favor such accommodation, however, the costs of the accommodation should be directly borne by the public sector, not by the employer. This would be more equitable, since the employer would not reap gains offsetting the costs and would usually find it difficult to pass the costs on to consumers. Our earlier evidence showed clearly that many firms may not be hiring handicapped persons now and are not making accommodations. Those firms that are actively accommodating disabled people would thus find it difficult to pass the costs of accommodation on, since the experience of accommodation costs is not marketwide. Also, if the burden were placed uniquely on employers, the sympathetic and favorable attitudes now existing among employers toward handicapped persons might well change. In that case, it would require even greater punitive effort to secure compliance with the law. Third, in the current environment of limited enforcement and pressure for reasonable accommodation, employers have incentive to consider the maximum productive potential of disabled applicants and workers, and to try to place individuals in those jobs with as high a work skill level as their skills can justify. With knowledge that the government might require expensive accommodations not warranted by the disabled worker's short-run productive capability, employers might begin considering the disabled persons only for those jobs having the least risk of giving rise to expensive accommodation; those jobs might also be the ones that make less than optimal use of the workers' capabilities.

The creation of more incentives for employers to accommodate the disabled worker could be achieved in many ways. As the earlier analysis of incentives in the BPA Accommodation Study indicated, firms are most supportive of incentives through tax credits. The chief problem with this approach, however, is that it would end up giving tax credit subsidies to employers for every accommodation they are currently making, and yet 90 percent or more of the current accommodations appear not to be causing difficulty for employers. By subsidizing all accommodations, one would have to pay a much greater cost than is necessary simply to finance the needed accommodations at the margin. Employers would also have less incentive to look for less expensive forms of accommodation. The sounder approach would be to give the individual disabled worker who is judged to have a strong need for accommodation a "voucher" for the special costs of accommodation, or alternatively, to give that voucher to a private employment agency to spend on behalf of the worker. Payment schemes could be structured so that the intermediary agency would have incentive to provide technical assistance to the employer in placing and accommodating the worker, but also incentive to keep the cost of the accommodation down and to get the employer to pay that share of the costs that might be justified by productivity benefits the employer will receive. The size of the voucher could be increased to reflect the expected difficulty of the worker's securing and sustaining employment—as with the Diagnosis Related Group (DRG) ceilings on cost reimbursement negotiated with health providers currently in some states. Bonuses (here potentially exploiting tax credits) could be built in to reward firms that sustained the worker for more than a year, or for even longer periods. Yet a third approach would be simply to have a public agency pay the costs of accommodation that are reported as needed by an employer to accept in placement a disabled job applicant who is judged deserving by the public agency. In many ways, state vocational rehabilitation agencies have now the authority to pay for special equipment and aids and other accommodations, but few of those agencies have made use of that authority.

A good program model for the second intermediary approach above would be some of the transitional employment or work support models being set up in Massachusetts and other states for public assistance recipients and other disadvantaged groups. Under such models, a private service agency collects funds under the Job Training Partnership Act of 1982, or other state funds, if the worker is placed and trained, while the agency also sells the worker's services directly to employers, as with an employment agency. The private agency provides some training prior to placement, but focuses principally on providing on-the-job training after placement, often supplementing the firm's own supervisors of entry-level workers with a private agency supervisor on site during the early months of employment. This model, where the private intermediary firms spend a lot on placement, tends to correct for the often weak management capability of many firms in handling entry-level workers. (This is in stark contrast to the vocational rehabilitation model, where it is usually desired that workers place themselves after training, although with counseling during the worker's placement effort.) With the substantial growth of the private rehabilitation counseling industry over the last decade (albeit more linked to the handling of reentry of job-experienced disabled and workers' compensation claimants), a supply of such intermediary firms does appear available.

In the provision of such incentives, it would appear that the target group should be those disabled persons who have never yet been in the labor market or have long since withdrawn from the market, *not* the workers who, because of illness and injury, are being compelled to withdraw from the labor market. The latter group has the greater (and a unique) need for accommodation to stay employed, but they also offer a high enough payoff, both to the insurance firms that will pay the disability income maintenance benefits and to the firms buying those insurance policies, that public subsidy should not be necessary. The market on its own should be capable of substantial innovation in early intervention to prevent disability in the workplace. However, a target group of only those disabled individuals having difficulty entering the labor market is not trivial, involving at least several million disabled persons. With both groups, however, it may well prove true that the income disincentives to work must be reduced before accommodations will be successful.

In launching such accommodation efforts aimed at those having difficulty entering the labor market, there are several tentative lessons from the current accommodation studies. First, a major problem in getting more disabled persons into firms appears to be that they do not apply for the jobs and identify themselves as disabled. Even the firms most aggressive in accommodating disabled persons insisted that they nonetheless saw few disabled applicants. It is probably true that active, aggressive placement has been one of the real shortcomings in past vocational rehabilitation and training programs. Also, if the applicant does not identify himself or herself as a disabled person, the firm is not bound by the law on reasonable accommodation. Second, the key to getting active accommodation from a firm appears to be the worker's possession of skills the firm needs. Because of the widespread belief that handicapped individuals are more stable and reliable workers, firms may even be predisposed toward handicapped persons in entry-level positions, where turnover is highest; yet it is likely that many of the disabled persons wanting to get into the labor market have not had the minimum kind of work socialization and adjustment training that would allow a firm to see them as comparable to other applicants. The training in such basic skills needs to be provided either prior to placement or in conjunction with placement.

Third, because the lower turnover and greater dependability of handicapped workers is a successful selling point to firms for engaging in accommodation, the focus of manpower program placement efforts should be on what labor economists call the primary, rather than the secondary, labor market. The latter market is structured around the expectation of employee turnover, and thus there is much less interest in accommodation and the downstream profitability that a stable worker offers. Since currently the large majority of vocational rehabilitation placements are in jobs paying the minimum wage or less, it is likely that many of these jobs are in the secondary labor market. Fourth, placement efforts linked to accommodation should focus on larger firms, since they have been clearly shown by the data to be more active in hiring and accommodating handicapped individuals, to have more of the internal resources to dedicate to accommodation, and to perceive it as no major burden.

Reasonable accommodation and job modification thus remain an important part of overall government policy for bringing disabled persons into the workplace and helping them achieve greater self-sufficiency. For most disabled workers, the existing laws and levels of enforcement appear adequate. For workers who become ill or injured while in the work force, more accommodation effort is justified, but will probably be forthcoming as income disincentives are reduced and

as the private rehabilitation industry and American employers recognize their financial stake in early intervention and accommodation
to prevent disability. For some of the more severely disabled persons,
and for those who are having the hardest problems entering the labor
market, there may be a need for government efforts to facilitate more
accommodation. Such efforts should neither attempt to force onto
the employer all those extra costs of accommodation not justified by
productivity, nor simply give the private employer a blank check to
pay for the costs of accommodation, as a generalized tax credit might
provide. Such accommodation efforts might well be linked to the
growth of Projects With Industry, where employers also design the
training programs. For many other disabled persons, however, accommodation is not an immediate major element in a government
employment strategy. Many disabled persons without past work experience probably need major work socialization and adjustment skills
before ongoing employment is feasible. The transitional employment
and work support options currently being proposed will provide for
some of their needs, if only through providing work experience. For
many disabled individuals, what will remain needed is longer-term
sheltered employment within private industry (perhaps the ultimate
form of accommodation by a private employer), or even the kind of
highly subsidized employment made feasible by the nation's sheltered
workshops.

APPENDIX: RECOMMENDED QUESTIONS TO ASK WHEN ASSESSING WHETHER A JOB ACCOMMODATION FOR A HANDICAPPED INDIVIDUAL IS REASONABLE

General

1. Can it be demonstrated that the accommodation has an adverse effect on business (undue hardship due to effect on productivity)?

2. Can it be demonstrated that the business cannot afford the accommodation (undue hardship due to financial cost and expenses)?

3. Does the accommodation conflict with a valid federal or state law, regulation or standard impinging on job requirements, e.g., OSHA or architectural standards?

4. Does the accommodation conflict with a valid collective bargaining agreement?*

5. Is the accommodation a reasonable investment in the employee given:
   a. the value of the employee to the organization (monetary or otherwise)?
   b. the likely time the individual will spend in the job and future jobs requiring the same accommodation?

6. Will the accommodation enhance the ability of the organization to recruit individuals with similar handicapping conditions?

7. Is the accommodation likely to jeopardize the safety of other employees?

Building Modification (Example: Installing a ramp at the entrance of a building.)

1. Is the removal of an architectural barrier considered a capital expenditure?

2. Does the modification improve the utilization of a building by all employees?

3. Does the modification limit the utilization of the building by other individuals?

4. If the modification limits the utilization of the building by other individuals, is it readily accessible?

5. Does the modification qualify for a tax deduction under federal law (P.L. 96-167 which extended the provisions of the Tax Reform Act of 1976 until December 1982)?

---

*Regulations issued pursuant to section 503 of the Rehabilitation Act of 1973 do not exempt employers bound by a collective bargaining agreement from the requirement to provide reasonable accommodation. If covered by section 503, you *must* notify unions of the company's obligation to take affirmative action toward handicapped workers . . . including your obligation to make reasonable accommodation. If a revision of your collective bargaining agreement is necessary to comply with this requirement and you cannot facilitate such revision yourself, the union may then make their views known to the Director, Office of Federal Contract Compliance Programs, Department of Labor, who is required to use his or her "best effort" to assure that the union cooperates and assists you in meeting your affirmative action obligations.

Worksite Modification (Example: Rearranging furniture or equipment to make the work area accessible to a person in a wheelchair.)

1. Does the modification limit the utilization of the worksite by other individuals?
2. If the modification limits the utilization of the worksite by other individuals, is it readily reversible?

Machinery or Equipment Modification (Example: Lowering a machine or workbench so that it can be operated by a person from a sitting position.)

1. Once modified, is the machine or equipment usable by other employees?
2. Is the modification readily reversible?
3. Is the modification likely to affect the productivity of other employees who use the machine or equipment?
4. If modified, will the machine or equipment continue to meet safety standards?

Aids and Devices (Example: Providing a dictating machine or tape recorder to accommodate a blind worker.)

1. Is the aid or device of a purely personal nature and not directly related to performance of the job, e.g., hearing aid?
2. Can the device be taken with the individual as he or she advances in the organization?
3. Is the device likely to be usable by other disabled individuals if the original employee leaves?
4. Does the device have a resale value if the original employee leaves?
5. Will State Vocational Rehabilitation agencies or consumer organizations provide the device free or subsidize its purchase?

Personal Assistance (To enable a person to understand work directions and/or instructions [Example: Providing an interpreter for a deaf individual.])

1. Is the reader or interpreter able to perform other job duties in addition to assisting the disabled individual?
2. Will other employees be required to take time away from their jobs to assist the disabled individual?
3. Is the assistance provided by an aide of a purely personal nature or is it related to performance of the job?

Modification of Job Tasks (Example: Allowing a mobility-impaired sales worker to conduct some sales calls over the telephone rather than in person.)

1. Do other employees in the same unit do the same or similar jobs?
2. Does the job task modification require that other employees accept additional job duties?
3. Would the individual have to perform all job duties if one or more employees in the same job were absent?

Modification of Work Hours or Schedule (Example: Allowing a diabetic employee to take regular meal breaks during a shift or instituting a "flextime" schedule.)

1. Does modification of the individual's work schedule affect the productivity of self or other employees?
2. Does the schedule modification conflict with company work rules or personnel practices?

Special Privileges (Example: Allowing a mobility-impaired employee to park in a restricted parking space near the work area.)

1. Does the additional privilege conflict with company work rules or personnel practices?

Job Restructuring (Example: Creation of an "Aide" or "Assistant" position.)

Job restructuring describes the formal process of examining the relationship of a number of jobs within an organization and through the application of job analysis, rearranging the tasks performed in these jobs to achieve the organization's goals. Job restructuring is commonly used to create entry level jobs by separating out certain tasks of other jobs and combining them into new jobs. Another purpose of job restructuring is to eliminate dead-end jobs and create job ladders so that workers can advance to a position of greater responsibility, skill and pay.

Job restructuring opens up new opportunities for employment and benefits handicapped workers in the same manner as other workers. Job restructuring is generally not used to accommodate an individual handicapped worker, except where no alternatives are available.

Source: BPA Accommodations Study, I, 106.

9 · THE REHABILITATION ACT AND DISCRIMINATION AGAINST HANDICAPPED WORKERS: DOES THE CURE FIT THE DISEASE?

William G. Johnson

Persons with mental or physical impairments have become the "unexpected minority" in search of freedom of access to jobs, education, and public services (Gliedman and Roth 1980), and in search of the legal protection afforded blacks, Hispanics, and women.

Before 1973, federal government policy toward impaired persons was a combination of assistance in finding jobs, public service advertising (e.g., "hire the handicapped" campaigns), social insurance for work disability, and vocational rehabilitation.[1] Civil rights protection for impaired persons was introduced by the Rehabilitation Act of 1973 (P.L. 93–112), which applies to federal agencies and to private institutions that receive federal funds.[2] The act assumes that impairment, like sex, unambiguously defines minority group membership but (all else equal) does not affect productivity. In reality, attitudes toward impaired persons vary with the type and severity of impairments, and any one impairment affects productivity differently in different jobs. A low back impairment, for example, may prevent work as a truck driver but not limit the ability to work as a truck

---

1. For studies of federal disability programs, see: M. Berkowitz and Johnson 1970; M. Berkowitz, Johnson, and Murphy 1976; Levitan and Taggart 1977; M. Berkowitz and Rubin 1977; and Burkhauser and Haveman 1982.

2. Forty-five state laws complement the act. Because the state laws vary greatly, our discussion is restricted to federal legislation.

salesperson. To be effective, antidiscrimination laws must reflect the differences between impaired persons and other minorities. This paper explores these differences and shows how the failure to completely recognize them weakens the Rehabilitation Act of 1973.[3] We also apply economists' models of discrimination to impaired persons. Little is known concerning the nature and intensity of discrimination against the unexpected minority. Our discussion suggests a set of questions that should be tested by much-needed empirical research.

There are six sections in this paper: definition of terms; description of three types of economic discrimination and a review of empirical studies of discrimination against impaired workers; discussion of gains in efficiency that might be obtained by reducing discrimination; discussion of the effectiveness of markets in reducing discrimination; discussion of government intervention, using the example of the Rehabilitation Act of 1973; and conclusions and suggestions for further research.

CONCEPTS AND DEFINITIONS

The terms *disability, impairment,* and *handicap* are often used synonymously, but there are important differences in their meaning. The World Health Organization (1980) definitions, used here, are as follows:

Impairment is a psychological, anatomical, or mental loss, or some other abnormality. *Disability* is any restriction on or lack of ability (resulting from an impairment) to perform an activity (work, schooling) in the manner or within the range considered normal. *Handicap* is a disadvantage resulting from an impairment or a disability. Hence, an impairment subject to prejudice is a handicap, whether or not it is disabling.

Prejudice has been defined as "an aversive or hostile attitude toward a person who belongs to a group, simply because he belongs to that group and is, therefore, presumed to have objectionable qualities ascribed to that group" (Allport 1954, 8).

---

3. We discuss efficiency rather than social justice as an objective. Our emphasis is appropriate since economics is not a guide to the importance of equity or social justice to a society.

THE SOURCES OF LABOR MARKET DISCRIMINATION

Economic discrimination exists if offers of employment or wages differ among individuals of equal productivity. Economic discrimination can be caused by prejudice (Becker 1957); imperfect information (Arrow 1973; Phelps 1972); or by monopsonistic exploitation (Thurow 1969).[4] No one has studied the relative importance of the three sources of discrimination, and there are but two studies of wage discrimination against handicapped workers (Fechter and Thorpe n.d.; W.G. Johnson and Lambrinos 1985). Fechter and Thorpe, using 1967 data, find differentials in the employment and wages of handicapped workers but are reluctant to conclude that the differentials are measures of discrimination. The Johnson-Lambrinos results decompose wage differentials between majority and minority workers into endowments, selectivity bias, and a residual, attributed to discrimination. The minority group is composed of employed men and women who have impairments of the type believed to be subject to prejudice. The majority group consists of persons with less visible impairments and persons who are not impaired. The results show that one-third of the difference in offered wages for men and close to one-half of the difference for women can be attributed to discrimination. Handicapped women are also subjected to sex discrimination.

PREJUDICE AGAINST IMPAIRED WORKERS

According to the model of Gary Becker, who developed a theory of economic discrimination caused by prejudice (1957), prejudiced employers prefer to avoid minority workers. They hire majority persons until the difference between majority and minority wage rates is greater than the amount the employer is willing to pay to satisfy his or her prejudice. The employer foregoes profits by using an inefficiently large number of majority workers. The firm's profits are less and majority workers' wages more than they would be in the absence of

---

4. None of the models consider discrimination against impaired workers. For simplicity, we substitute the terms "handicapped" for "minority" and "not handicapped" for "majority" in our discussion.

prejudice. Since nonprejudiced employers require no differential to hire minority workers, the marginal cost of minority labor to them is less than to the prejudiced employer. Becker predicts that discrimination disappears in competitive markets if one or more employers is not prejudiced.

There is evidence of substantial employment prejudice related to mental or physical impairments. A summary of the pre-1966 literature shows that the intensity of prejudice varies with the nature and severity of impairments (Yuker, Block, and Young 1966). Nondeforming physical impairments are subject to less prejudice than are disfiguring or sensory impairments. Prejudice is most extreme against mentally retarded persons (Yuker, Block, and Young 1966).

More recent studies suggest that prejudice against impaired persons is more intense than that against other minorities. Bowe (1978) concludes that employer attitudes toward impaired workers are "less favorable than those . . . toward elderly individuals, minority group members, ex-convicts, and student radicals," and Hahn (1983) finds that handicapped persons are victims of "greater animosity and rejection than many other groups in society." Bowe and Hahn agree with Yuker that prejudice increases with the visibility of an impairment.

In an unpublished study, Johnson and Lambrinos use data from their previous (1985) study of discrimination to test for a relationship between wage differentials and the visibility of impairments. Wage equations estimated for workers with back problems, cancer, or heart diseases are compared with the same equations for handicapped workers. The results show that the handicapped workers receive lower rates of return to education, experience, and health. The only exception is a higher rate of return to health for handicapped women than for women with back, cancer, or heart problems. (Results available from the authors.)

Prejudice is not the only source of discrimination against impaired workers. The inherent uncertainty in predicting the effect of an impairment on productivity may contribute to "statistical discrimination." In the next section, we explore the possibility that statistical discrimination is more important for impaired workers than for other minorities.

STATISTICAL DISCRIMINATION AND OTHER PROBLEMS OF INFORMATION

The theory of statistical discrimination predicts that employers offer minority workers lower wages because they believe that minority workers are, on average, less productive than majority workers (Arrow 1973; Phelps 1972).[5]

Employers use education, job histories, and pre-employment test scores as proxy measures of productivity. Although these proxies are not very accurate, they are often the most efficient way to screen job applicants. What the employer needs most to know about an impaired worker is the effect of impairment on his or her productivity in a particular job. An impairment that is disabling on one job may not affect the worker's productivity in a different job. Methods for matching physical capacities to job requirements are available (Koyl 1970), but are used in few, usually large, firms.

Standardized pre-employment tests are a source of information, but one seldom used by firms with less than 500 employees, although the prevalence of testing increases sharply among firms who employ 1,000 workers and reaches a maximum among firms with 25,000 or more employees (Sherman and Robinson 1982). A large investment has been made to eliminate bias due to gender or race from standardized tests, but bias against impaired persons is more difficult to correct.

Test scores are biased when an impairment limits test-taking skills but does not limit performance on the job for which the test is required. Modifications in standardized tests (audio vs. written, for example) are, however, difficult to validate because validation requires very large samples. Some firms flag test results for impaired persons or waive the test requirement for their employment. Unfortunately, both solutions increase the subjectivity of the hiring decision.

The infrequent use of pre-employment tests by small firms and the problems of validating tests suggest that employers rely more on judgment than on test scores in hiring impaired workers. Studies of hiring decisions show that employers believe that all impairments limit productivity and that they evaluate impaired workers by reference to

---

5. See Aigner and Cain 1977 for an extension of the model and a critique of Phelps's work.

stereotypes. Employers believe, for example, that it is difficult to shift impaired workers among jobs; that the costs of supervision and train- ing are higher for impaired workers, and that impairments increase the costs of insurance and other fringe benefits (Schroedel and Ja- cobsen 1978).[6] Employers also tend to overstate the limiting effects of impairment (Schroedel and Jacobsen 1978). Employers' rankings of impairments by expected productivity tend to agree with the rank- ings of the same impairments by intensity of prejudice, suggesting that employers are prejudiced or are misinformed by the conventional (prejudiced) wisdom.

The models of "statistical discrimination" predict that discrim- ination is reduced by increasing information on worker productivity. Although information reduces statistical discrimination, it is not nec- essarily true that it eliminates wage differentials created by problems of information.

A firm that employs handicapped workers can be expected to acquire good information on the workers' productivity by observing their work. Estimates of productivity based on stereotypes should be corrected as true productivity is observed over time. An empirical test of the effect of length of employment on wage differentials with one firm, however, finds that differentials *increase* with the duration of employment (Johnson and Lambrinos 1985). Because there are few empirical studies of employers' responses to information after a worker is hired, we do not know whether this result is general or peculiar to impaired workers. The results are consistent with Medoff and Abra- ham's (1981) finding that changes in wages with greater job experience only weakly reflect changes in productivity.[7]

Even if firm-specific experience reduces discrimination, its total effect on handicapped workers is limited because no firm is likely to employ enough impaired workers to observe a representative distri- bution of impairments. Moreover, informed nonprejudiced employ-

---

6. Many of the same beliefs are expressed by employers as reasons for their reluctance to hire older workers (see Brennan, Taft, and Schupack 1967).
7. The results are approximate because duration of employment is not an exact measure of employer information, and the results could reflect employers' cor- rections of their previous underestimates of the productivity of their impaired em- ployees.

ers will not voluntarily pay handicapped workers more than they can earn in their next best job. In monopsonistic markets, employers are insulated from competition for workers. Wage differentials, even though created by statistical discrimination, will not change unless employers are both informed and subject to competition.[8] In the next section, we describe how employers can acquire monopsony power over handicapped workers, and discuss monopsony as a limit on the use of information to reduce discrimination.

MONOPSONISTIC DISCRIMINATION

A discriminating monopsonist is a firm that can pay each worker his or her reservation wage rather than the wage paid to the last worker hired. In this discussion, we assume that the firm has monopsony power only over workers who are impaired and that employers can easily distinguish between impaired and nonimpaired workers. We discuss only those aspects of monopsony power that are unique to handicapped workers. The influence of licensing and geographic barriers to mobility is not discussed, even though they contribute to monopsonistic labor markets.

Monopsonistic power is perpetuated by barriers to the labor force mobility of workers. The barriers that affect handicapped workers are prejudice, the interaction of job requirements with impairments as a determinant of worker productivity, barriers to physical mobility that are external to the firm (e.g., accessibility of public transportation), imperfections in information, and job-related health insurance.

If other employers are prejudiced, the nonprejudiced firm can pay handicapped workers more than the discriminatory market wage but less than the workers' productivity.

We mentioned previously that a given impairment affects productivity differently in different jobs. The loss of a foot, for example, would not affect the productivity of a concert violinist, but would totally disable a ballerina. More subtle variations in the effects of an

---

8. If workers are unionized, the market might be one of bilateral monopoly and the differentials might be bargained away.

impairment on job performance occur with variations in the extent to which the individual controls the work flow (Yelin et al. 1980).

A firm could gain monopsony power over impaired workers if, among the jobs in the labor market, its jobs alone did not require the functions affected by the workers' impairments. Assume that only one firm in a labor market has jobs that require working in the dark (e.g., processing film). Persons with severe visual impairments will be as productive or more productive in these jobs than nonimpaired workers. This example shows how the interface between job requirements and impairments can create monopsony power. In this situation, an impaired worker receives a better wage than in other jobs, but the employer pays the worker less than his or her productivity. Obviously, this type of discrimination is difficult to identify or to prove in court.[9]

A firm can also gain monopsony power by modifying its workplace to compensate for workers' limitations. Workers with mental or physical impairments are more productive in the modified environment, and wage and employment effects are the same as in the previous example except that the firm must obtain a rent sufficient to recover the costs of modification.[10]

Health insurance may be as important a constraint on job mobility as are pensions and seniority rules, for impaired persons who may not be able to obtain insurance if they leave their current jobs. A worker who becomes chronically ill after being employed does not lose his job-related health insurance, but will be rejected for health insurance in a new job. Since the incidence of chronic illness increases with age, job-related health insurance reinforces the limits that pensions and seniority rules place on mobility. An older worker who becomes chronically ill, therefore, may face a very restricted set of

---

9. This example ignores compensatory technologies and skills that permit visually impaired persons to be as productive as nonimpaired persons in many occupations.

10. An unusual example of how an impairment can affect firm-specific productivity is the recent decision of a firm to hire a number of Social Security Disability Insurance beneficiaries who require a product produced by the firm. These workers are especially beneficial to the firm because, in addition to the work that they perform, they are proof of the firm's contention that its new product is effective.

job opportunities even though the illness does not affect his or her productivity.

The death of the "company town" has made monopsony a textbook curiosity, but monopsony may be an important characteristic of labor markets for impaired workers. Because legal proof is so difficult, the costs of eliminating monopsonistic discrimination through legislation appear to be high relative to the benefits gained. The question can only be answered by empirical studies. We hope that our discussion convinces others of the need to initiate research on the subject.[11]

SUMMARY

Although the absolute effects can only be determined by empirical studies, the information we have presented suggests that impaired workers, relative to other minority groups, are: more likely to encounter statistical discrimination because of uncertainty concerning the effect of an impairment on the worker's productivity in a particular job; more likely to be subject to monopsonistic discrimination; and subject to prejudice, although the intensity of prejudice varies with the nature and visibility of impairments.

Efficiency losses due to discrimination differ with the source of discrimination. The next section discusses how efficiency can be increased by eliminating labor market discrimination.

---

11. Monopsony can also be created by employer investment in information or training specific to impaired workers. Rents obtained to recover investments in firm-specific training or workplace modification are *not* a form of discrimination. Oi's (1962) model of firm-specific training is an example of such a situation. In that model, a worker's productivity in one firm is enhanced by investments that do not affect his or her productivity in other firms. The employer, as in our previous example, can pay a wage that is higher than the worker's next best offer but less than the worker's contribution to output. Determining the productivity of an impaired worker is costly and the results uncertain, making proof of discrimination very difficult. When the differences in the worker's productivity between firms results from the employer's investment (e.g., job modification), one faces the additional dilemma of identifying the portion of the wage differential that is a return to that investment.

THE EFFECT OF DISCRIMINATION ON EFFICIENCY

Inefficiencies due to discrimination result from the misallocation of labor, distortion of criteria for private and public investment in human capital, and disincentives to labor force participation.

ALLOCATION OF LABOR

In competitive labor markets, discrimination due to prejudice reduces efficiency by inducing firms to overutilize nonhandicapped workers. If handicapped and nonhandicapped workers are perfect substitutes in the production process, the prejudiced employer hires only nonhandicapped workers at the market wage. Given diminishing returns to the use of labor, discrimination in hiring increases the cost of producing a given level of output relative to an efficient allocation of labor.

One benefit of reducing discrimination, therefore, is the reduction in costs. These gains must, however, be reduced by the amount spent to bring about the change (e.g., the costs of providing information and administering antidiscrimination laws).

If monopsony rather than prejudice is the source of wage discrimination, labor may be used efficiently. In Thurow's (1969) model, a discriminating monopsonist attempts to maximize the following function:

$$(MRP_h - W_h)E_h - [K(dMP_k) + E_n (dMRP_n)]$$

where the variables are vectors "h" subscripts handicapped and "n" subscripts not handicapped; E represents employment; $MRP_h - W_h$ is the difference between handicapped (h) worker productivity and the wage rate; $K(dMP_k)$ is the change in the marginal product of capital caused by changes in the number of h workers employed; and $E_n(dMRP_n)$ is the corresponding change for variations in the number of not handicapped (n) workers. If the quantity of capital and the number of n workers employed are independent of the number of impaired workers, the employer simply maximizes monopsony rents, employing an efficient number of h workers. There are no efficiency losses in the short run but incentives for workers' investment in education and health are distorted. The net benefit of reducing monopsonistic discrimination may be entirely determined by the value placed on eliminating exploitation of handicapped workers.

Discrimination makes workers' rates of return to investment in human capital lower than the true increase in their productivity (that is, less than the marginal product of an investment in human capital).

Discrimination also lowers the measured benefits of rehabilitation programs and other efforts to return impaired adults to the labor force. Benefits are usually measured as the difference between the wages that an individual earns once rehabilitated and those that would have been earned otherwise. Worrall (1978) estimates the benefits of rehabilitation of different categories of impairments as:

$p(B_s)/[p(C_s) + (1 - p) C_n]$, where:
p = probability of a successful rehabilitation;
B_s = benefits of successful rehabilitation, defined as the difference between wages at opening and closure, adjusted for labor market influences such as unemployment; and
C_s and C_n = the costs of rehabilitation for successful (C_s) and unsuccessful (C_n) attempts at rehabilitation.

As an example of how discrimination can bias benefit-cost calculations, we use Worrall's data on white, visually impaired men, aged 35 to 44, with nine to eleven years of education. We assume that wages at opening equal zero. In this situation, the benefit equals the probability of rehabilitation multiplied by the wages earned if rehabilitated. Johnson and Lambrinos (1985) calculate the benefit-cost ratio and then adjust it for a wage differential due to discrimination among handicapped men of a similar age and educational background. If observed wages differ from productivity by the discriminatory differential, the calculated benefit-cost ratio is 12.0, but the true value is 14.2.

Persons with zero wages at opening are only one example of the distortions caused by discrimination. If the percentage differential is (as it is usually assumed to be) constant over wages, the benefit-cost ratios are also distorted for persons with positive wages at opening. If, for example, the opening wage is $4, the wage at closing is $6, and the discriminatory differential is 15 percent, the benefit-cost ratio, unadjusted for discrimination, is \$2/cost. Controlling for discrimination, the true benefit-cost ratio is (\$7.06 − \$4.71)/cost, or \$2.35/cost.

Discrimination can also distort the allocation of rehabilitation services among persons with different impairments. The benefit-cost ratios for persons whose impairments are subject to the most intense prejudice, for example, will be lower (all else equal) than the ratios for persons with impairments against which there is little prejudice. The studies of attitudes that we discussed earlier suggest that the greatest distortions in benefit-cost ratios are for persons who are mentally retarded.

In the preceding examples, we have assumed that the probability of success in rehabilitation is not affected by discrimination. If discrimination reduces the probability of employment for the men in the Worrall study by, for example, 5 percentage points, the true benefit-cost ratio is 15.0 instead of 14.2. The combined effect of discrimination on wages and employment would reduce the benefit-cost ratio in our example from 15.0 to 12.0. If a benefit-cost ratio of 12.0 is deemed an efficient level of public investment in rehabilitation, discrimination disguises the fact that a greater investment is justified, that is, an amount sufficient to reduce the benefit-cost ratio from 15.0 to 12.0. The hypothetical benefit-cost ratios demonstrate that discrimination can be an important influence on investments in rehabilitation. They show the need for a better understanding of the effects of all types of discrimination on benefit-cost analyses of public programs.

WORK INCENTIVES

Many impaired persons are eligible for cash benefits and payments for medical care from programs such as Social Security Disability Insurance (SSDI), Supplemental Security Income (SSI), veterans' compensation, and private pensions. Eligibility for the benefits is usually based on the severity and permanence of the impairment subject to limits on the person's earnings. Minimum and maximum limits on benefits create relatively high and low replacement ratios for low- and high-wage workers, respectively.

Impaired persons who are eligible for SSDI benefits but capable of working must choose between wage income (the amount that exceeds the "substantial gainful activity" limit [SGA]) and SSDI benefits.

(See Leonard, chapter 3 of this volume, for discussion of the disincentive effects of SSDI benefits.) All else equal, an individual will work if $(Yw - SGA) > (SSDI - C)$, where Yw is wage income and C is the cost of obtaining SSDI benefits.[12] Discrimination lowers wages (Yw), thereby also decreasing the cost (C) of the waiting period. The cost of application is further reduced if discrimination reduces the worker's chances of being offered a job.[13] The effect of discrimination on SSDI beneficiaries may be small if the wage and benefit elasticities reported by Leonard (1979) or Haveman and Wolfe (1984a) are correct. Parsons's (1980a) estimates are much higher, leaving us with no reasonable idea of the true influence of discrimination on SSDI applications. Even a small effect on application rates, however, can create substantial expenditures, since SSDI recipients very rarely return to the labor force. Concern with the work disincentives of SSDI and SSI is frequently expressed in Congress, but the effect of wage discrimination on the disincentives is not considered.

The benefits of eliminating discrimination in the labor market can be summarized as more efficient use of labor, improved efficiency in the human capital market, and increased incentives for labor force participation by impaired workers. In the next section we consider whether these efficiency gains can be achieved by unregulated markets.

MARKET SOLUTIONS VS. GOVERNMENT INTERVENTION

The "unregulated" market is one in which the government provides social insurance against disability, mandates a minimum wage, and prohibits discrimination based on gender or race.

---

12. The primary cost (C) is the wage income foregone during the six-month "waiting" periods during which the worker must be out of the labor force. For simplicity, situations in which $(Yw - SGA) < (SSDI - C)$, but individuals don't work because of the utility obtained from leisure time, are ignored (Toikka 1976).

13. A test of the extent to which discrimination contributes to SSDI applications would be a useful addition to the research on SSDI. The research should also investigate ethnic and gender-based discrimination, since many impaired persons are subjected to several types of discrimination.

DISCRIMINATION DUE TO PREJUDICE

If discrimination occurs solely because of prejudice, market forces should eliminate much of the problem.[14] Because the wages of minority workers are depressed by discrimination, nonprejudiced employers will substitute miniority for majority workers. The final market share of the nonprejudiced employer is determined by the elasticity of demand for his final product, by the elasticity of the minority labor supply, and by the extent to which prejudiced employers accept a reduced rate of return to capital as the price of their prejudice (Freeman 1974).

The more elastic the supply schedule, the greater is the employer's incentive to hire handicapped workers and increase output, and, *ceteris paribus*, the larger the final market share of nonprejudiced firms. No one has estimated the elasticity of the supply of labor of impaired workers, but some inferences can be derived from certain of the workers' characteristics. The most obvious limit is that the number of impaired workers is small and the nature and severity of impairments are not uniform among them.

The elasticity of labor supply of impaired workers to a firm is also limited by the variety of impairments and skills found among the impaired persons who are in the firm's labor market. The proportion of impaired workers whose impairments do not interfere with the requirements of a firm's vacancies is likely to be small.[15] The experience of Rehab Group, Inc., is an interesting example of this problem. The firm, founded by a young man who was paralyzed in an automobile accident, hires severely impaired workers whenever it is possible to do so. The founder's "greatest frustration is that he cannot locate enough severely disabled individuals whose abilities he needs" (Bowe 1978, 172–73). Rehab Group's difficulty is made more impressive by the fact that it employs only 250 workers and can fill only one-fourth of its jobs with severely impaired workers.

Disability insurance cash benefits reduce the elasticity of labor

---

14. The history of gender-based and racial discrimination limits optimism about the influence of unregulated markets on discrimination in the labor market (Cain 1984).

15. The impaired workers must, of course, also match the skill requirements of the jobs, reside within the relevant labor market, and be aware of the vacancies.

supply of impaired workers with respect to the wage, when labor earnings fall between the minimum and maximum benefit. Labor supply will be perfectly inelastic when expected earnings are less than the minimum benefit. The disincentives of disability benefits are reinforced by the provision of medical care coverage (e.g., Medicare). The costs of medical care for chronically ill persons may be so high that medical benefits alone are sufficient to keep the person out of the labor force.

The utility that some impaired persons obtain from work could increase the elasticity of their labor supply. Advocates of "mainstreaming" argue that impaired persons derive utility as well as income from working. By reducing reservation wages, one increases the elasticity of labor supply by an amount that depends upon the magnitude of the mainstreaming premium.

The information we have presented implies that the supply of labor of impaired workers is less elastic than that of nonimpaired workers. If this conclusion is correct, hiring by nonprejudiced employers will not eliminate discrimination in competitive labor markets.

Reliance on competition to eliminate the inefficiencies caused by discrimination can also be limited by concepts of social justice.[16] Becker (1957) demonstrates, for example, that segregated firms provide efficient utilization of majority and minority workers, but such a solution is not acceptable in the United States. Sheltered workshops are a rare example of segregated firms in the United States. One could speculate that some of the frequent criticisms of the wage and employment policies of sheltered workshops are an expression of discomfort with the use of segregated facilities for handicapped workers.

MONOPSONISTIC AND STATISTICAL DISCRIMINATION

We do not know the true extent of monopsonistic and statistical discrimination, but to the extent that they are important, prospects for reducing discrimination against impaired workers are reduced. Both types of discrimination are less obvious than prejudice, and both are

---

16. Cain (1984), for example, points to segregated firms (as in South Africa) as such a solution.

less susceptible to market competition. One of the most curious aspects of monopsonistic discrimination is that the monopsonist may appear to be influenced by social conscience rather than profit. An employer could both gain praise for hiring handicapped workers and earn a rent on each worker. The demonstration effect of the employers' actions could eliminate discrimination only if handicapped workers are numerous and possess the skills needed to fill most jobs in the labor market.

Since monopsony and statistical discrimination are symptoms of market imperfections, they are unlikely to disappear in unregulated markets.

Although market failure is a rationale for government intervention, it does not guarantee that intervention will be effective. The effectiveness of federal legislation against discrimination is discussed in the next section.

FEDERAL LEGISLATION

Title V of the Rehabilitation Act of 1973 (P.L. 93–112) has been characterized as the "disabled civil rights act."[17] Section 501 requires affirmative action in federal employment, section 502 requires federal buildings to be accessible, and section 503 imposes affirmative action obligations on federal contractors receiving more than $2,500.

The act also restricts job screening and testing. Where mental or physical job qualifications screen out otherwise qualified handicapped workers, the contractor must show that the requirements relate to the jobs for which handicapped workers are being considered, and are consistent with business necessity and the safe performance of the job.

The rehabilitation act is written as if "handicap" is a characteristic like race or sex that defines a group of persons who are subjected to a common set of barriers to employment. Our discussion of the sources of discrimination has made it clear that this assumption

---

17. In discussing the act, we use the term "handicapped" rather than "impaired" since the act addresses only the rights of those impaired people who are subjected to discrimination.

is only weakly true for handicapped persons. We have shown that not all impairments are subject to prejudice; that not all impairments reduce productivity; that the limiting effects of a given impairment vary among jobs; and that the cost and validity of information on worker productivity vary with the nature of the worker's impairment. (See Collignon, chapter 8 in this volume.)

The variety of problems faced by different impaired persons substantially increases the costs of enforcing the laws against discrimination. The high cost of enforcement is exemplified by the administrative and judicial struggle over the meaning of "qualified handicapped person" and "reasonable accommodation."

"QUALIFIED HANDICAPPED PERSON"

In E. E. Black v. Marshall, a federal court directed that the definition of "qualified handicapped person" be determined on a case-by-case basis, stating that

> The definitions contained in the [Rehabilitation] Act are personal and must be evaluated by looking at the particular individual. A handicapped individual is one who has a physical or mental disability which for such an individual constitutes or results in a substantial handicap to employment. . . . It is the impaired individual that must be examined and not just the impairment in the abstract. . . . A person who has obtained a graduate degree in chemistry and is then turned down for a chemist's job because of an impairment is not likely to be heartened by the news that he can still be a streetcar conductor, an attorney or a forest ranger. (quoted in Emer and Frink 1983)[18]

The Black decision demonstrates the gap between the legal model of discrimination and the situation of handicapped workers. Before a court can analyze whether an employer's behavior is discriminatory, it must first engage in a complex and lengthy evaluation of whether the plaintiff is a member of the minority that the law intends to protect. Recent court decisions on what constitutes a handicap include: AIDS (contagious diseases are a handicap, but whether

---

18. It is worth noting that the court's language appears to conflict with the Social Security Administration's criteria that the inability to perform one's usual job does not constitute work disability. Social security disability benefits are based on the inability to perform any job in the economy.

persons with such diseases can be reasonably accommodated must be decided on a case-by-case basis); marijuana use (not a handicap); varicose veins (not a handicap, but condition was mild to moderate); diabetes (a handicap); crossed eyes (not a handicap). (See *In the Mainstream* 1986.)

The courts are given the task, for which they have little expertise, of deciding whether an impairment affects the plaintiff's ability to perform a job for which the plaintiff's education and experience make her or him eligible. Only if the court finds the plaintiff capable of performing the job, can it proceed to the issue of whether the plaintiff was rejected *because of his or her impairment,* and then, whether the rejection is appropriate under the rule of "reasonable accommodation."

"REASONABLE ACCOMMODATION"

Case-by-case determinations of the effect of an impairment on the capacity to perform a job are difficult to generalize. Decisions must be influenced by the combined, idiosyncratic effects of an individual's qualifications and impairment compared to the workplace and job of one employer. This type of decision does not establish strong precedents that would inform employers and impaired workers of their respective rights and responsibilities. Establishing rules which can be generalized to many transactions at little cost is one of the important benefits of administrative rule making and decisions by the courts. Although the question of the costs of case-by-case determinations relative to the benefits of reducing discrimination is an empirical one, it seems likely that the costs of enforcing the laws relating to handicap discrimination are high relative to enforcement costs for other forms of discrimination.

Rulings without precedential value are an ineffective and costly method of reducing discrimination. The problem is made worse by Congress's failure to adequately define the meaning of "reasonable accommodation."

The administrative regulations for the implementation of section 504 of the rehabilitation act provide that employers should make "reasonable accommodations" to permit a handicapped worker to perform a job unless accommodations result in "undue hardship" to the employer.

The regulations direct that the cost of accommodations and the size, purpose, and structure of the employer's budget be considered in defining "reasonable accommodation" (*Harvard Law Review* 1984). The regulations do not, however, indicate the relative importance to be given to each factor, nor do they provide a decision-making rule that is consistent across cases.

A concept of "reasonable accommodation" that would be consistent with efficiency objectives would direct employers to invest up to an amount where the marginal cost of accommodations is equal to the marginal benefit (that is, the increase in the productivity of the impaired worker for whom an accommodation is made). Although precise measures of marginal costs and benefits are difficult to obtain, the comparison of costs and benefits could be accomplished with some consistency among cases, thus creating an understandable, if general, code of conduct for employers.

It would also be useful to eliminate contradictory incentives in the current law. Consider the employer who invests in job modifications that increase the productivity of impaired workers. Because the employer is prohibited from paying the worker less than his productivity, the employer loses the returns from investing in the impaired worker. If employer and worker were permitted to share the increase in productivity from such investments, incentives for workplace modification and training would be increased. The definition of reasonable accommodation should, therefore, address the question of how the benefits of investment in accommodations are to be shared. If sharing between workers and employer is permitted, incentives for hiring impaired workers are substantially increased.[19]

This discussion indicates the need for an extensive revision of the concept and definition of "reasonable accommodation." The revision should state the concept in terms of a level of expenditure, relative to the benefits to be obtained, rather than as the ambiguous list of unweighted characteristics provided by the administrative regulations which accompany the rehabilitation act.

---

19. Several points in this discussion were suggested by James Lambrinos.

CONCLUSIONS

Prejudice is an important cause of discrimination against impaired workers. Because of this fact, the Rehabilitation Act of 1973 (P.L. 93–112) and many state laws are direct extensions of the civil rights statutes developed to deal with the problems of racial and sexual minorities. We suggest that the effectiveness of these laws is severely limited by their failure to consider some important differences between impaired workers and other minority groups.

The most fundamental difference is that impairments limit productivity in many but not all cases. Much of the variation in the effect of an impairment on work depends on the nature of a job or the work environment.

The struggles of the courts to define "handicap" reflect the failure of the law to recognize the complexity of the process that links impairment and work disability. The inherent uncertainty concerning the influence of an impairment on the ability to work is an important source of statistical discrimination. The influence of the workplace environment on the productivity of impaired workers may contribute to monopsonistic discrimination. Until more adequate definitions of "handicap" are enacted into law, the statutes are unlikely to reduce discrimination in any important way. This conclusion does not imply that government intervention is a mistake. Indeed, if monopsony and statistical discrimination are as important as we suspect, the market will not reduce discrimination.

It is obvious, however, that the Rehabilitation Act of 1973 (P.L. 93–112) is limited first by a failure to adequately distinguish between the concepts of impairment and handicap and second by the absence of cost criteria that could provide a functional interpretation to the term "reasonable accommodation." These failures have created a statute whose rules are idiosyncratic rather than general, requiring the courts to decide cases on narrow rather than precedential issues. Decisions or rules that cannot be generalized are not the objective of an efficient legal approach to social problems. Insofar as the goal of the antidiscrimination laws is to increase the efficiency with which we use labor, the current process raises serious doubts about whether the benefits of litigation outweigh its costs.

10 · DISABILITY POLICY IN THE UNITED STATES, SWEDEN, AND THE NETHERLANDS

Richard V. Burkhauser

Over the past decade and a half, a remarkable shift has occurred in the overall size and configuration of government programs targeted to disabled workers. There can be little doubt that the differences in the amounts of social resources committed to disabled persons and the manner in which that commitment has changed in Western industrialized countries are more a reflection of government policies than of underlying demographic differences in their disabled populations.

In this chapter, the two most comprehensive disability systems in Western Europe, those of Sweden and the Netherlands, are described and compared to that of the United States. As in this country, during the 1970s both European countries dramatically increased expenditures on disability programs and experienced rapid increases in the populations of disability income transfer recipients and in government-supported work for disabled persons. Yet the reliance on these two program responses—income support and employment—differed significantly among the three countries, as did the response of government policy makers to the added budgetary costs generated by these programs.

The first section of this paper discusses the goals of disability policy and the approaches used by Sweden and the Netherlands to achieve them over the past decade and a half. Because of the complexity of programs that touch disabled persons, only the principal disability transfer and work programs are considered. The second section reviews, within the context of the European experience, the magnitude and direction of change in U.S. programs in the early 1970s, and the subsequent responses of policy makers to this change. The final section evaluates the success of policy in achieving its stated goals in the three countries and speculates on prospects for further change in the second half of this decade.

PROGRAM GOALS AND STRUCTURE

Disability policy is shaped as much by a government's overall strategy for income maintenance and employment policy as by the health status of its working population. To deny this linkage to more general economic and social policy, one must believe that the per capita disabled population in need of income transfers in Sweden was 180 percent of that of the United States in 1970. One would also have to believe that over the subsequent decade, the population in need of income transfers in each country would have expanded so rapidly that despite an increase of over 50 percent in the disabled population in the United States, the per capita disabled populations of Sweden and the Netherlands were respectively 166 and 300 percent of that of the United States in 1980. Finally, one would have to believe that this same needy population that grew so rapidly over the decade in the United States fell by over 5 percent in absolute numbers between 1980 and 1982.

Even more difficult to explain solely with a health-based model of need is the remarkable change in the number of disabled workers who required government-supported employment. It is in this aspect of disability policy that Sweden, the Netherlands, and the United States dramatically differ.

From 1970 to 1982, U.S. policy concerning the numbers of disabled persons needing government-supported employment veered in direction. The ratio of the number of persons provided government-supported work because of a disability to the number receiving disability-related income transfers amounted to less than one quarter that in either Sweden or the Netherlands in 1970. That ratio in the United States reached near parity with Sweden and the Netherlands by the end of the decade, then returned to approximately its 1970 level by the close of 1982.

Such dramatic shifts in supposed need can only be explained by looking beyond demographic considerations of health to the subtle but more important considerations of social policy.

The overriding goal of Swedish disability policy is the provision of medical rehabilitation to ensure the return to work of disabled persons.[1] Neither knowledge of the location where the illness or accident occurred nor proof of its cause is required for treatment, nor is ability of the individual to pay.[2] Income maintenance programs provide substantial benefits, but are regarded as a temporary remedy until a return to work has been achieved.

In Sweden, work is considered necessary to the self-worth of an individual and hence essential to "making whole" an impaired person. It is seen as such an important aspect of well-being that only those considered unable to work are permitted to refuse supported employment.

The first level of protection against income loss is the sickness benefit. All workers over age 16 are assured 90 percent of the earned income lost because of sickness. The benefit is temporary: after ninety days the local social insurance office investigates to see if rehabilitation is needed. Medical care is provided at no direct cost to all Swedish citizens.

Since 1963 Sweden has had a two-tier disability pension system, the benefits of which are indexed to inflation. A flat pension amount, based on degree of diminished working capacity, is paid to all disabled workers. A supplement is then added, based on years worked and earnings. In 1970 a special bonus supplement was established for those with little or no regular supplement.

Eligibility for pension benefits is determined on medical grounds,

1. The sketch of Swedish social policy in this section is based on Wadensjo 1984. His is one of a set of papers on industrialized countries that form the basis for a cross-national evaluation of disability policy in Haveman, Halberstadt, and Burkhauser 1984.

2. The removal of cause was a nontrivial change in the law during the 1970s that made it much easier for those suffering from alcoholism, drug addiction, and sociopathology to enter the system.

but labor market conditions are also taken into consideration. In an important change in emphasis during the 1970s, workers over the age of 60 could become eligible owing solely to labor market conditions (i.e., those jobless whose unemployment benefits had run out could receive disability benefits).

Most pension recipients are initially granted temporary benefits for one year. This provides time for an evaluation of their long-term job prospects before a decision is made to award them permanent benefits. The decision is made by the Labor Market Administration (LMA).

In 1950, 3 percent of the LMA budget went to the provision of jobs for disabled persons; by 1970, the amount had grown to 20 percent. This occurred during a period when overall labor market programs administered by the LMA grew from 0.5 to 3.0 percent of GNP. Hence, supported work for disabled persons is an integral and growing part of overall employment policy in Sweden.

The assignment of individuals to various work programs is made by local public employment offices. To be included in a disability work program, an applicant must have an impairment sufficient to make it difficult to perform work on the open labor market. Government policy stresses that eventual return to the open market is the goal of all job programs.

Table 10.1 shows the numbers of participants in, and expenditures on, the disability pension program and the three major work programs for disabled persons. Sheltered employment includes jobs in sheltered workshops operated by local municipalities and counties as well as employment subsidized by the central government in the private sector and at the local government level.

Special relief work is part of two more general public relief work programs, one aimed at stabilizing the business cycle, the other an industrial relief work program employing older industrial workers affected by structural changes in industry. "Disability" eligibility in this program thus extends considerably beyond a narrow health-based definition.

Vocational rehabilitation centers provide evaluations of work capacity and some general work training. Specific job-related training for disabled persons is provided by centers open to all workers.

Participation and expenditures grew dramatically in both work

TABLE 10.1

Participants and Expenditures in
Programs for Disabled Persons in Sweden, 1970–79

	1970	1975	1979	Increase 1970–79
Disability Pensions				
Participants	187,885	288,884	284,132	51%
Expenditures[a]	1,244	4,492	8,350	571
Sheltered Work[b]				
Participants	20,301	38,961	46,705	128
Expenditures[a]	164	586	1,254	664
Special Relief				
Participants	11,400	15,600	14,900	31
Expenditures[a]	303	670	1,068[c]	252
Vocational Rehabilitation				
Participants	1,881	2,559	2,733	45
Expenditures[a]	—	33	57	—
Total Work Programs				
Participants	33,582	57,120	64,338	92
Expenditures[a]	467	1,289	2,379	409

Source: Derived from Wadensjo 1984, 464, 482, 494.
Notes: [a]Millions of kroner. The exchange rates fluctuated between 4.1 and 5.2 kroner per dollar during this period (5.16 in 1970 and 4.15 in 1979).

[b]Includes archive work, sheltered work, and semisheltered work.
[c]Amount for 1978.

and transfer programs over this period. The sheltered work programs showed the most substantial gains.

In addition to these specific job-creation programs, Sweden in 1974 passed legislation aimed at further ensuring job protection for disabled persons. A firm now can dismiss an employee only if he or she is incapable of performing any work at all; age, illness, or reduced working capacity are not sufficient individual reasons for dismissal. In addition, the local labor board may force a firm to negotiate agreements to retain or hire disabled workers. In the absence of such an agreement, the board can require a firm to increase the number of disabled workers it hires. Enforcement of these two legal changes has been sporadic, however, and their effectiveness is open to question.

SOCIAL GOALS AND PROGRAMS IN THE NETHERLANDS

Like Sweden, the Netherlands is strongly committed to providing employment for disabled workers.[3] But in most cases disabled workers are not required to accept a job, and there is considerably more reliance on income support programs to ensure the well-being of disabled persons.

The whole adult working population is covered by one or more disability transfer programs. The Sickness Benefit Act of 1934 provides a minimum of 80 percent of earnings for those in the private sector during the first year an employee is unable to work because of illness, accident, or pregnancy. All medical expenses are provided without direct cost to citizens of the Netherlands.

The Disability Security Act of 1967, which took effect in 1967, mandates the principal income maintenance program for disabled persons in the private sector. Benefits begin after one year of sickness and are based on previous earnings and degree of disability. They range from a maximum of 80 percent of previous net-of-tax wages to a minimum of the net-of-tax legal minimum wage, and are indexed to reflect changes in general wage levels. The Dutch minimum wage is based on a notion of a socially acceptable minimum consumption level, which can provide replacement rates in excess of 100 percent for low-income workers.

Eligibility for a disability pension is based on health and employment criteria. Any person who, as a consequence of illness, is unable to earn what a healthy person of the same training and at the same location can earn, is eligible for benefits. This definition, which has been in existence for several decades, allows wide latitude of interpretation.

Similar programs exist for public sector workers. Those with little work history are covered by the General Disability Act of 1976, which provides a flat-rate benefit equal to the after-tax minimum wage. In addition, the Temporary Social Assistance Program for the Less Able (1965) protects those with no work record—children, nonworking spouses, etc.

---

3. The sketch of Dutch social policy in this section is based on Emanuel, Halberstadt, and Petersen 1984.

Social employment programs began as early as 1950 in the Netherlands. The government recognizes the "right to work" of handicapped people and an obligation to ensure that work is available. The Social Employment Act of 1969 set the standards and guidelines for sheltered workshops. Under this program, employees are covered by the social insurance laws and are paid a wage that approximates that of regular private or public sector workers performing similar functions. The workshops are run at the municipal level but financed by the central government.

Table 10.2 shows the numbers of participants in the major disability programs in the Netherlands. As in Sweden, growth over the period in terms of both transfer programs and supported work was substantial, although the larger increase was in income maintenance programs.

An explicit quota system, requiring every employer with a work force of twenty or more to hire at least one disabled person for every fifty employees, has been in existence since the end of World War II. Disabled workers have the right to be paid the usual wage for that type of work unless it can be shown that their productivity does not warrant it. However, because no organization is charged with inspection, compliance has not been enforced.

TABLE 10.2

Participants in Disability Programs
in the Netherlands, 1971–80

Year	Pension Programs[a]	Work Programs[b]
1971	260,000	44,000
1974	420,000	52,000
1980	483,000	74,000
Increase, 1971–80	86%	68%

Source: Derived from Emanuel, Halberstadt, and Petersen 1984, 419.

Notes: [a]Includes those covered by the Disability Security Act, General Disability Act, Public Employees Disability, and Temporary Social Assistance Program for the Less Able.

[b]Includes those in the social employment program.

A CROSS-NATIONAL COMPARISON
OF POLICY GROWTH AND DIRECTION

U.S. disability policy can also be characterized as a mixture of income transfer and employment programs. This section discusses the level and directions of growth in the U.S. system in the context of the European experience over the same period.

INCOME MAINTENANCE PROGRAMS

The Carter administration recommended a series of actions to reduce what was perceived as excessively rapid growth in disability transfers. That same perception led the Reagan administration to continue this policy by tightening eligibility rules and reevaluating qualifications of the existing population of beneficiaries. Weaver, in chapter 2 in this volume, provides a detailed discussion of these policy changes.

In table 10.3 it can be seen that a rapid expansion in disability transfer expenditures took place in the United States between 1968 and 1978, when overall program expenses rose at an annual rate of 6.3 percent in real terms. But what was perceived as an insupportable increase in the United States pales before a rate of change over the same period that was nearly twice as great in Sweden and nearly three times as great in the Netherlands.

TABLE 10.3

Disability Income Support
Expenditures, 1968 and 1978

| Country | Portion of National Government Expenditures | | Annual Rate of Growth in Real Terms |
	1968	1978	
United States	5.8%	8.0%	6.3%
Sweden	2.6	4.3	11.7
Netherlands	5.8	13.6	18.6

Source: Haveman, Halberstadt, and Burkhauser 1984, 84.

TABLE 10.4

Net Replacement Rate
in Income Support Programs
for Disabled Workers, 1968 and 1978

	1968			1978		
Country	One-half Median Income	Median Income	Twice Median Income	One-half Median Income	Median Income	Twice Median Income
United States						
Disability Insurance	45	35	21	59	49	35
Supplemental Security Income:						
High state	77	41	21	78	42	23
Low state	48	25	13	46	25	13
Sweden Disability Pension and Supplement	105	73	55	117	88	66
Social Assistance	114	64	38	109	69	50
Netherlands Disability Security Act	92	80	55	92	80	76
General Disability Act	n.a.	n.a.	n.a.	100	77	41

Source: Haveman, Halberstadt, and Burkhauser 1984, 128.

These increases in expenditures were due in part to substantial increases in the generosity of program benefits. This can be seen in table 10.4, which compares the net replacement rates of disability pension and disability welfare programs for low-, middle-, and high-wage workers in the three countries. Program benefits considerably increased from the initial level in each country.

In the United States, benefits for low-income and even for middle-income workers in 1978 were considered to have reached the level at which substantial labor supply disincentives might occur.[4] Yet

4. See Burkhauser and Haveman 1982 for a detailed discussion of policy issues during this period.

even these historically high replacement rates were far below the 1968 rates in either Sweden or the Netherlands.

The increased generosity of benefits was accompanied by a broadening of the eligibility definition in each country. In Sweden this was particularly the case with regard to older workers. In the Netherlands, there was a general broadening of definitions to include unemployed workers and those with what were previously considered partial disabilities.

In the United States, liberalization involved the increasing use of "vocational" characteristics in the determination of eligibility for Social Security Disability Insurance and the creation of a federally run welfare program—Supplemental Security Income—that did not require disabled people to have work experience for eligibility. The benefit levels of that new welfare program were higher than that of general assistance in many states, and the program was financed primarily at the federal level; both characteristics made substitution of funds in this program desirable to local welfare clients and to local welfare providers.[5]

Growth in benefit generosity and in the size of the targeted populations led to increases in the size of the beneficiary population in each country. Table 10.5 highlights not only that population growth, but also the shifts in the age distributions of those populations. In addition, for the United States, the analysis is taken past the peak year of 1978, allowing us to see the consequences of the responses of the Carter and Reagan administrations to expenditure growth.

As can be seen, population growth in income transfer programs was substantial in the 1970s. Of equal interest, however, is the shift in the makeup of that population. A major change occurred in Sweden, where the growth in beneficiary numbers shifted toward middle-aged and especially older workers. The number of younger workers grew in absolute terms, but fell as a share of the total recipient population. The conclusion is that, at least for older workers, income maintenance now appears to be a permanent rather than a temporary ameliorative response. If true, this is a major break with Sweden's traditional work-oriented policy goal.

---

5. See Sunshine 1979 for a discussion of attempts by New York State to shift its welfare clients to SSI.

TABLE 10.5

Numbers and Age Distribution of
Recipients in Major Disability Transfer Programs,
Selected Years (in thousands)

Age	United States[a]				Sweden[b]			Netherlands[c]		
	1970	1975	1980	1982	1970	1975	1980	1970	1974	1980
15–44 years										
Number	573	1,080	1,308	1,353	37	45	52	n.a.	113	171
Percent of total	24.0	25.6	28.3	31.1	22.6	18.8	17.7		26.9	35.4
45–59 years										
Number	1,103	1,915	2,018	1,753	72	103	130	n.a.	228	236
Percent of total	46.2	45.5	43.6	40.3	43.9	42.9	44.2		54.3	48.9
60–64 years										
Number	713	1,217	1,299	1,244	55	92	112	n.a.	79	76
Percent of total	29.8	28.9	28.1	28.6	33.5	38.3	38.1		18.8	15.7
Total	2,389	4,212	4,625	4,350	164	240	294	260	420	483

Sources: For the United States: U.S. Dept. of Health and Human Services 1970, 1975, 1980, 1983. For Sweden: Wadensjo 1984. For the Netherlands: Emanuel, Halberstadt, and Petersen 1984. All population data are from International Labour Organization (1970–83).

Notes: N.a. means that data are not available.

[a] Includes SSDI and SSI (blind or disabled) recipient.

[b] Includes temporary and regular disability recipients.

[c] Includes Disability Security Act and estimates of Temporary Social Assistance Program, and General Disability Act.

The age distribution of recipients in the Netherlands and in the United States was far more stable. However, both countries had increasingly higher shares of younger beneficiaries in their programs, and both experienced more growth of that population than did Sweden.

In the United States, public policy changes substantially altered the growth pattern of the early 1970s. By 1982 the absolute size of the beneficiary population in the United States was 4.3 million, a 6 percent decline from its 1980 level. Although still substantially above the 1970 level, this change in direction nearly returned population levels to those of the mid-decade.

Table 10.6 provides additional evidence of changes in the age distribution and in the willingness of policy makers over the last years of the decade to accept the consequences of the increases in benefit levels of, and accessibility to, disability-related programs. Not surprisingly, in all three countries, in any given year, the ratio of disability transfer recipients per 1,000 active working-age people increases as you move from younger to older age groups. Clearly, deterioration in health is positively related to age and thus to the size of the disabled population relative to the working population.

More interesting from a policy perspective, the United States has substantially lower ratios than either Sweden or the Netherlands, in all age categories for all years. It is hard to believe that underlying differences in health are responsible for such differences across countries.

The rapid increase in the middle- and older-age populations in Sweden from 1970 to 1975 confirms the increased use of transfers as a permanent solution for workers this age. As will be shown in the next section, the great majority of temporary pensioners eventually move into the permanent benefit program, while movement into the work force from either of these programs is rare.

The surge of growth that is reflected in the ratios for the first part of the period appears to have continued in the later part of the decade only in the Netherlands. The overall increase in the ratio in Sweden between 1975 and 1980 was slight, and actually decreased for younger workers.

The U.S. ratio of disabled to working people had dropped by 1980 and continued to fall in 1982. It is significant to note that while

TABLE 10.6
Disability Transfer Recipients
per Thousand Active Labor Force Participants
by Age, Selected Years

Age	United States[a]				Sweden[b]			Netherlands[c]		
	1970	1975	1980	1982	1970	1975	1980	1970	1974	1980
15–44 years	11	17	16	16	18	20	19	n.a.	21	36
45–59 years	33	68	83	71	66	95	99	n.a.	186	265
60–64 years	154	265	285	273	229	382	382	n.a.	417	585
Total	27	42	41	39	49	67	68	n.a.	87	130

Sources: See table 10.5.

Notes: N.a. means that data are not available.

[a]Includes SSDI and SSI (blind or disabled) recipients.
[b]Includes temporary and regular disability recipients.
[c]Disability Security Act per insured population. Ages are 25–29, 50–54, 60–64.

the overall drop between 1975 and 1980 was primarily caused by an increase in the share of younger workers in the active population, the major cause of the drop between 1980 and 1982 was in the population of older and especially middle-aged workers. This is very likely the result of a more restrictive use of "vocational" characteristics put in motion by the Carter administration and the reevaluation of beneficiaries pushed by the Reagan administration.

In contrast to the slowdown in Sweden and the reverse in direction in the United States, the ratio in the Netherlands continued to grow steadily throughout the decade. Perhaps most disturbing in terms of future costs was the dramatic 71 percent rise in the proportion of those of younger age who received pension benefits.[6]

GOVERNMENT-SUPPORTED EMPLOYMENT

Policy makers in the United States have been less willing than those in Europe to bring the power of government to bear on the workings of the marketplace. This is particularly true with respect to employment policy, and it is therefore not surprising that this characteristic is reflected in U.S. disability policy. Prior to the 1970s, policy aimed at bringing disabled workers back to work was confined to training programs operated under the vocational rehabilitation program. Most jobs earmarked for disabled persons were in sheltered workshops, which were usually run by nonprofit organizations with substantial federal subsidies.

The advent of the Comprehensive Employment and Training Act of 1973 (CETA) and the subsequent provision of public service employment for disadvantaged and handicapped workers dramatically shifted U.S. employment policy toward that of Sweden and the Netherlands.

Table 10.7 documents the changes that occurred in the provision of jobs and rehabilitation for disabled persons in the three countries over the 1970s by providing a measure of the importance of job provision relative to income maintenance (last row). A distinc-

---

6. The ratios for the Netherlands are not strictly comparable to those in the other countries since they are of beneficiaries per one thousand insured in the General Disability Act (GDA) program.

TABLE 10.7
Supported Work and
Vocational Rehabilitation Populations,
Selected Years

Supported Work	United States				Sweden			Netherlands		
	1970	1975	1980	1982	1970	1975	1979	1971	1974	1980
Narrowly defined job population[a] (in thousands)	100	168	262	200	20.3	39.0	46.7	n.a.	n.a.	n.a.
Broadly defined job population[b] (in thousands)	100	506	1,096	200	32	52.0	61.6	44	52	74
Jobs (narrow) per 100 transfer recipients	4	4	6	5	12	16	16	n.a.	n.a.	n.a.
Jobs (total) per 100 transfer recipients	4	12	24	5	19	22	21	17	12	15

Vocational rehabilitation population (in thousands)	876	1,244	1,095	n.a.	1.9	2.6	2.7	—	—	—
Vocational rehabilitation per 100 transfer population	37	30	24	n.a.	1	1	1	—	—	—

Sources: See table 10.7.

Notes: N.a. means that data are not available.

[a]The narrowly defined population consists of those in jobs provided primarily to physically or medically handicapped workers. For the United States this includes those in sheltered workshops and in CETA-Public Service Employment (PSE) who are defined as handicapped or disabled veterans. For Sweden this includes those in semisheltered and sheltered work and in archive work.

[b]The broadly defined population includes those with economic or social handicaps. For the United States this includes the entire population of CETA-PSE as well as those in sheltered workshops. For Sweden it adds those in special relief work.

tion is made between jobs targeted to a narrow health-related disability population and a broader population including those "socially or economically" disabled persons. In the United States, the broad definition includes all categories of disadvantaged workers, not just disabled veterans and those physically or mentally handicapped persons, who held public service jobs under CETA. In Sweden, it includes older, structurally unemployed workers doing special relief work. In the Netherlands, jobs provided under the Netherlands Social Employment Act would best fit under the broader definition, but further differentiation in specific job populations over the period is not possible.

The birth and death of public service employment (titles I, II, and VI of CETA) in the United States was the single most remarkable policy change of the period covered in table 10.7. At its peak in 1980, this program, combined with sheltered workshop programs, provided over one million jobs to a broadly defined disabled population. This resulted in a ratio of work recipients of twenty-four per one hundred income transfer recipients, which was greater than that of Sweden or the Netherlands in 1980. The collapse of the job provision sections of CETA at the end of fiscal year 1982 returned this ratio to five, about the level of the pre-CETA days.

In comparison, the number of Swedish government-supported jobs grew at a rate faster than that of its transfer population over the period 1970 to 1975, and continued to grow, but at a slower pace, from 1975 to 1979. This is evidence that, despite a shift in focus away from older workers, the Swedish commitment to jobs for the disabled remained strong over the period.

The Netherlands experienced rapid growth in supported work, but neither at the pace of Sweden nor at the pace set by its own burgeoning transfer population. By the end of the decade, the ratio of supported employment to transfer recipients had fallen below the level at the start.

Nevertheless, both European countries maintained a commitment to direct job provision for disabled persons that far exceeded that in the United States, where public service employment was terminated. The United States returned to a policy dominated by income maintenance, leaving it up to vocational rehabilitation and other training programs to prepare the disabled population for the marketplace.

EVALUATION OF POLICY AND A LOOK TO THE FUTURE

The preceding section has shown that U.S. policy, after moving closer to that of Sweden and the Netherlands in terms of generosity and accessibility of income transfers and in the use of direct public service employment, dramatically changed course near the end of the 1970s. As in Sweden, the growth of income maintenance programs slowed perceptibly in the second part of the decade, but in contrast with Sweden or the Netherlands, this slowdown was followed by a dramatic cut in public-supported work. Although by the end of the decade both European countries relied relatively less heavily on job support, there is no evidence that they ever seriously considered a similar change in policy.

What has sustained the use of public service employment in these European countries? Two possible explanations can be considered. One is that European employment programs more effectively achieve their stated goals than do those in the United States. The other is that their policy goals and the weights used in evaluating them are quite different from those of the United States.

A common policy assumption in all three countries during the 1970s was that the provision of *temporary* jobs by government would lead to permanent jobs in the open market. The failure of public service employment under CETA to achieve this goal was one reason for its demise. Yet the evidence suggests that employment programs in Europe have not fared much better, and that placements have tended to become permanent.

In a study of Swedish participants who entered subsidized work in 1978, the National Labor Market Board (1980) found that only 11 percent were not participating in the same program at the end of the year; and only a little over 10 percent of those who left went on to obtain a job in the open labor market. Thus barely more than 1 percent of all new sheltered workers actually made the transition to a regular job by the end of the year.[7]

---

7. The number of temporary pension beneficiaries who leave the pension rolls is also quite small. A National Social Insurance Board study found that only 4.9 percent of men aged 20, 1.4 percent of men aged 40, and 0.2 percent of men aged 60 were rehabilitated. See Wadensjo 1984 for details.

An evaluation of the Dutch social employment program (Haveman 1978) reports similar findings. The number of participants who made the transition from the program to normal public- or private-sector employment was so low that Haveman assigned a lower-bound estimate of zero to the benefits derived from this aspect of the program.

But even if a return to regular work is not achieved, it is still possible that the actual productivity generated by targeted jobs might make them a less costly means than income maintenance of providing support to disabled persons. This goal, expressed either in the narrow sense of reduced budgetary costs or more broadly in terms of social costs and benefits, has often been the subject of policy analysis in the United States.[8]

The narrow productivity perspective was the motivation for using Social Security Disability Insurance trust funds for vocational rehabilitation in the 1970s.[9] A variation of this narrow view is often expressed by people of different political persuasions in more general debate when they assert that providing government-supported jobs to welfare recipients is less costly than giving them welfare.

Project evaluations employing this criterion, as well as a broader social cost-benefit criterion, have been performed on various forms of supported work in the United States. The results have been mixed, but provide little encouragement to the position that increasing such programs to the level of those in either the Netherlands or Sweden would be warranted.

Fewer studies of this type have been performed in Europe. One is by Haveman (1978), who in a detailed analysis that applies a range of assumptions about cost and benefits finds that none of the 155 supported work centers he investigated in the Netherlands display positive values when his least favorable assumptions are used, and that only 27 centers yield positive net social benefits under his most favorable assumptions. At a minimum, average net social costs are

8. For a discussion of the methodologies of such analyses as applied to U.S. disability policy, see Burkhauser and Haveman 1982.

9. For a discussion of the change in policy goals in vocational rehabilitation over this period, see Burkhauser and Haveman 1984.

over 2,000 guilders per worker or 65 million total, and under worst-case assumptions, net costs range to 274 million guilders.[10]

Such evidence suggests that if the United States initiated job creation programs like those currently in effect in Europe, the programs would not be likely to pass either type of policy evaluation. Another explanation must be sought for the sustained commitment of European countries to supported work despite the enormous burden of program costs experienced in the 1970s.

Both Swedish and Dutch social policy must weigh the employment of a disabled worker far in excess of the productivity generated by that job as measured in the marketplace. In these countries, efficiency arguments must implicitly value the social and psychological well-being associated with work at a much higher level than is likely to be the case in the United States.

That value, however, is not infinite, and the shift in Swedish policy toward the permanent use of income maintenance for older workers, as well as the extensive use of income maintenance in the Netherlands, is evidence that increases in prices are taken into account even by European policy makers.[11]

Table 10.8 shows the labor force participation rates of men over our period of analysis. Simple comparisons of labor supply in these countries do not provide conclusive evidence of the consequences of employment policy in general or of disability policy in particular, nor is a higher or lower level of work effort in any sense evidence of efficient policy. Nevertheless, labor supply is one indicator of the effectiveness of government policy in achieving broadly defined goals.

One issue that looms large in the debate on U.S. disability policy concerns program effects on work effort. It is argued that generous benefits may achieve equity goals but must be weighed against efficiency losses, and that the sharp increase in disability expenses in the

---

10. Exchange rates have fluctuated between 3.6 and 1.9 guilders per dollar in the 1970s.

11. See Halberstadt 1978 for an example of an early warning, by a Dutch economist and policy maker, of the enormous budgetary costs and productivity losses associated with Dutch disability policy.

TABLE 10.8

Male Labor Force Participation Rate
for Older and Prime-Aged Groups,
1970–82

Country	1970	1977	1982
United States			
25–54	93.7%	93.8%	93.6%
55–59	86.8	82.9	81.3
60–64	73.0	62.0	56.4
Sweden			
25–54	90.5	94.4	95.8
55–59	88.4	88.8	87.2
60–64	75.7	72.3	68.3
Netherlands			
25–54	96.4	96.7	96.0
55–59	86.9	79.9	73.0
60–64	73.9	58.0	43.0

Source: International Labour Organization (1970–83).

1970s resulted in a major reduction in work effort.[12] Table 10.8 also provides some evidence that the sharp rise in disability pension benefits did affect work effort. In all three countries, labor market activity fell dramatically for men aged 60 to 64. This decline is no doubt in part a direct result of increases in the size and accessibility of disability income transfers and of the relative shift away from job-supported work programs for men in this age group.[13]

For men aged 55 to 59 the decline was not as steep, but was still substantial in the Netherlands. In the United States, work reduction in this age group was smaller but still important between 1970 and 1977, then slowed considerably between 1977 and 1982, after the tightening of benefit accessibility. In Sweden, where job support still

---

12. A sense of this concern can be seen in the recent exchange between Haveman and Wolfe (1984a) and Parsons (1984a; see also 1980a). Leonard, in chapter 3 of this volume, discusses these issues in detail.

13. In the case of the United States and the Netherlands, it is also a result of increases in the generosity of retirement pensions. In Sweden, it is partly the result of both generosity of benefits and a lowering of the retirement age.

dominates income transfer policy for this age group, there was little change over the entire period. For middle-aged workers, labor market activity held virtually constant over the entire period in both the United States and the Netherlands, and actually increased in Sweden.

In sum, the table offers some evidence that disability policy in the 1970s accelerated the trend toward reduced work effort, and that cutbacks in transfer program accessibility in the United States at the close of the decade may be responsible for slowing this trend.

What does the experience of the last decade and a half portend for U.S. policy in the second half of this decade?

A dramatic change in U.S. disability policy has already occurred. Although it is unlikely that the numbers of disability transfer recipients will ever return to the levels of the early 1970s, a rollback to mid-decade levels has been accomplished. Recent court restrictions imposed on the Social Security Administration in reevaluating recipients will make it more difficult to reduce the beneficiary rolls in this manner, but budget deficits make increases in program benefits or accessibility unlikely.

It is impossible to say with confidence whether the decrease in social commitment to the disabled population in the form of government transfer and job support that began in the late 1970s is merely a downward blip in substantial program growth, or whether it is a permanent return to a narrower definition of disability and of the role government should play in meeting that population's needs. Perhaps the scales will be tipped one way or the other by the answer to an unanswered policy question: Where have all the potential disabled beneficiaries gone as a result of the Carter-Reagan disability policy?

One answer could be that these people were fringe workers who would have left the labor force under the inducement of high and easily obtainable disability benefits. Because they were denied access to these benefits, they may have suffered during the economic downturn at the start of the decade, but at least they stayed in the active work force. The general economic recovery which began in 1983, then, provided a private market demand for their services that would not have been heeded if they had become disability income recipients. If this answer is correct, the result, while painful in the short run, would constitute a policy success and portend its continued implementation in the United States.

A less happy answer is that these people fell through the holes of a noticeably weaker social safely net and have not been touched by economic recovery. They remain for the most part unemployed and exist with the support of a private network of charities and extended families. If this characterization is accurate, policy would be judged much less favorably.

The same types of answers can be suggested for questions regarding the termination of public service employment. Has the subsequent economic recovery returned these workers to permanent private sector jobs—a feat that public sector employment seems incapable of achieving?

The stubborn refusal of U.S. unemployment rates to fall below the level at which the decade began casts doubt on the probability that events indicated by the first answer have occurred as yet. Still, even if the less optimistic answer turns out to be a better description of reality, a move toward European disability programs or goals is not likely to occur. On efficiency grounds, neither the Swedish nor the Dutch job support programs seem likely to generate much support here.

It will more likely be a belated concern for disabled people who fall through the holes of the present safety net of disability policy, rather than appeals to the efficiency of new disability programs, that will cause policy in the United States to change.

REFERENCES

Abt Associates, Inc.
    1974   *The Program Services and Support System of the Rehabilitation Services Administration: Final Report.* Prepared for the Rehabilitation Services Administration, U.S. Dept. of Health, Education and Welfare. Cambridge, Mass.

Adams, Charles F., Jr., Robert F. Cook, and Arthur J. Maurice
    1983   "A Pooled Time-Series Analysis of the Job Creation Impact of Public Service Employment Grants to Large Cities." *Journal of Human Resources* 18 (Spring): 283–94.

Aigner, Dennis J., and Glen G. Cain
    1977   "Statistical Theories of Discrimination in Labor Markets." *Industrial and Labor Relations Review* 30, 2 (January): 175–87.

Allport, Gordon
    1954   *The Nature of Prejudice.* Garden City, N.Y.: Doubleday.

Anderson, Kathryn H., and Richard V. Burkhauser
    1983   *The Effect of Actual Mortality Experience with a Retirement Decision Model.* Working Paper no. 83-WO8. Vanderbilt University.

Angell, Frank J.
    1963   *Health Insurance.* New York: Ronald Press.

Arnould, Richard J., and Lem M. Nichols
    1983   "Wage-Risk Premiums and Workers' Compensation: A Refinement of Estimates of Compensating Wage Differentials." *Journal of Political Economy* 91, 2: 332–40.

Arrow, Kenneth J.
    1963   "Uncertainty and the Welfare Economics of Medical Care." *American Economic Review* 53 (December): 941–73.

1973   "The Theory of Discrimination." In *Discrimination in Labor Markets*, ed. Orley Ashenfelter and Albert Rees. Princeton, N.J.: Princeton University Press.

Bailis, L. N., R. T. Jones, J. Schreiber, and P. L. Burstein
1984   *Evaluation of the BSSC Supported Work Program for Mentally Retarded Persons*. Boston, Mass.: Bay State Skills Corporation.

Bartel, Ann P., and Lacy Glenn Thomas
1982   *OSHA Enforcement, Industrial Compliance, and Workplace Injuries*. Working Paper no. 953. Cambridge, Mass.: National Bureau of Economic Research.

Bayo, Francisco, Stephen Goss, and Samuel Weissman
1978   *Experience of Disabled-Worker Benefits under OASDI, 1972–1976*. Actuarial Study no. 75. Washington, D.C.: Social Security Administration.

Becker, Gary
1957   *The Economics of Discrimination*. Chicago: University of Chicago Press.

Bellamy, G. Thomas, and Richard Melia
1984   *Summary of OSERS Conference on Supported Employment*. Washington, D.C.: National Institute on Handicapped Research.

Bellante, Donald M.
1972   "A Multivariate Analysis of a Vocational Rehabilitation Program." *Journal of Human Resources* 7 (Spring): 226–41.

Berkeley Planning Associates
1975   *An Evaluation of the Costs and Effectiveness of Vocational Rehabilitation Service Strategies for Individuals Most Severely Handicapped*. Report to the U.S. Dept. of Health, Education and Welfare.

1978   *Implementing the Rehabilitation Act of 1973: The VR Program Response*. 2 vols. Report to the U.S. Dept. of Health, Education and Welfare, Office of Assistant Secretary for Planning and Evaluation, contract DHEW-100-76-0005.

1981   *Analysis of Policies of Private Employers toward the Disabled*. Report to the U.S. Dept. of Health and Human Services, contract HEW-100-79-0180.

Berkowitz, Edward D., ed.
1979   *Disability Policies and Government Programs*. New York: Praeger.

Berkowitz, Edward D., and Monroe Berkowitz
1984   "The Survival of Workers' Compensation." *Social Science Review* 58, 2 (June): 259–80.

1985   "Challenges to Workers' Compensation: An Historical Perspective." In *Workers' Compensation Benefits: Adequacy, Equity, and Efficiency*, ed. John D. Worrall and David Appel, 158–79. Ithaca, N.Y.: ILR Press.

Berkowitz, Edward D., and Kim McQuaid
    1978   "Businessman and Bureaucrat: The Evolution of the American Social Welfare System." *Journal of Economic History* 38 (March): 120–41.

Berkowitz, Monroe
    1973   "Workmen's Compensation Income Benefits: Their Adequacy and Equity." In *Principles of Workmen's Compensation,* ed. Monroe Berkowitz, vol. 1 of *Supplemental Studies of the National Commission on State Workmen's Compensation Laws,* 189–268. Washington, D.C.: U.S. Government Printing Office.

    1985a   *Disability Expenditures 1970–82.* Report to the National Institute of Handicapped Research (Project no. 133AH3005). Bureau of Economic Research, Rutgers University.

    1985b   "Forestalling Disincentives to Return to Work." *Business and Health* 2, 4 (March): 30–32.

Berkowitz, Monroe, and John F. Burton, Jr.
    1986   *Permanent Disability Benefits in the Workers' Compensation Program: A Multistate Study of Criteria and Procedures.* Kalamazoo, Mich.: Upjohn Institute, forthcoming.

Berkowitz, Monroe, John F. Burton, Jr., and Wayne Vroman
    1979   *An Evaluation of State Level Human Resource Delivery Programs: Disability Compensation.* Washington, D.C.: National Science Foundation.

Berkowitz, Monroe, and David Dean
    1975   "An Evaluation of the Structure and Functions of Disability Programs." Bureau of Economic Research, Rutgers University. Mimeo.

    1980   "Medical Care Costs of Disabled Persons." Department of Economics, Rutgers University. Mimeo.

Berkowitz, Monroe, Martin Horning, Stephen McConnell, Jeffrey Rubin, and John D. Worrall
    1982   "An Economic Evaluation of the Beneficiary Rehabilitation Program." In *Alternatives in Rehabilitating the Handicapped: A Policy Analysis,* ed. Jeffrey Rubin, 1–87. New York: Human Sciences Press.

Berkowitz, Monroe, and William G. Johnson
    1970   "Towards an Economics of Disability: The Magnitude and Structure of Transfers and Medical Costs." *Journal of Human Resources* 3 (Summer): 271–97.

Berkowitz, Monroe, William G. Johnson, and Edward H. Murphy
    1971   *Measuring the Effects of Disability on Work and Transfer Payments: A Multivariate Analysis.* Report for the Social Security Administration. Bureau of Economic Research, Rutgers University.

1976 *Public Policy toward Disability.* New York: Praeger.
Berkowitz, Monroe, and Jeffrey Rubin
    1977 "The Costs of Disability: Estimates of Program Expenditures for Disability, 1969–1975." Bureau of Economic Research, Rutgers University. Mimeo.
Borus, Michael, and Daniel Hamermesh
    1978 "Estimating Fiscal Substitution by Public Service Employment Programs." *Journal of Human Resources* 13 (Fall): 651–65.
Bound, John
    1977 "Variation in Social Security Disability Beneficiary Rates and Labor Force Participation across States." Harvard University. Mimeo.
    1985 "The Health and Earnings of Rejected Disability Insurance Applicants." Harvard University. Mimeo.
Bowe, Frank
    1978 *Handicapping America.* New York: Harper and Row.
Braithwait, Steven D.
    1977 *An Empirical Comparison of Alternative Multi-Level Demand Systems for the U.S.* Working Paper no. 75. Bureau of Labor Statistics, Office of Research Methods and Standards.
    1980 "The Substitution Bias of the Laspeyeres Price Index: An Analysis of Using Estimated Cost-of-Living Indexes." *American Economic Review* 70, 1 (March): 64–77.
Brennan, Michael, Phillip Taft, and Mark Schupack
    1967 *The Economics of Age.* New York: W. W. Norton.
Buchanan, James M., and Gordon Tullock
    1962 *The Calculus of Consent.* Ann Arbor: University of Michigan Press.
Burkhauser, Richard V., and Robert H. Haveman
    1982 *Disability and Work: The Economics of American Policy.* Baltimore: Johns Hopkins University Press.
    1984 "United States Policy toward the Disabled and Employment Handicapped." Discussion paper, Labor Market Policy Group of the International Institute of Management, Wissenschaftszentrum, Berlin.
Burton, John F., Jr.
    1983 "Compensating for Permanent Partial Disabilities." In *Safety and the Work Force: Incentives and Disincentives in Workers' Compensation,* ed. John D. Worrall, 61–86. Ithaca, N.Y.: ILR Press.
Burton, John., Jr., and Wayne Vroman
    1979 "A Report on Permanent Partial Disabilities under Workers' Compensation." In *Research Report of the Interdepartmental Workers' Compensation Taskforce,* vol. 6, 11–77. Washington, D.C.: U.S. Government Printing Office.

Butler, Richard J.
      1983   "Wage and Injury Rate Response to Shifting Levels of Work-
                ers' Compensation." In *Safety and the Work Force: Incentives
                and Disincentives in Workers' Compensation*, ed. John D. Worrall,
                61–86. Ithaca, N.Y.: ILR Press.
Butler, Richard J., and John D. Worrall
      1983   "Workers' Compensation: Benefit and Injury Claim Rates in
                the Seventies." *Review of Economics and Statistics* 65, 4: 580–
                89.
      1985   "Work Injury Compensation and the Duration of Nonwork
                Spells." *Economic Journal* 95: 714–24.
Cain, Glen G.
      1984   "Economic Discrimination against Women and Racial and
                Ethnic Minorities." Discussion paper DP 745–84. Institute
                for Research on Poverty, University of Wisconsin (Madison).
Calabresi, Guido, and Philip Bobbit
      1978   *Tragic Choices*. New York: W. W. Norton.
Chelius, James R.
      1973   "An Empirical Analysis of Safety Regulation." In *Supplemental
                Studies for the National Commission on State Workmen's Compen-
                sation Laws*, vol. 3, 53–66. Washington, D.C.: U.S. Govern-
                ment Printing Office.
      1974   "The Control of Industrial Accidents: Economic Theory and
                Empirical Evidence." *Law and Contemporary Problems* 38 (Sum-
                mer/Autumn): 700–29.
      1977   *Workplace Safety and Health*. Washington, D.C.: American En-
                terprise Institute.
      1982   "The Influence of Workers' Compensation on Safety Incen-
                tive. *Industrial and Labor Relations Review* 35:235–42.
      1983   "Workers' Compensation and the Incentive to Prevent In-
                juries." In *Safety and the Work Force: Incentives and Disincentives
                in Workers' Compensation*, ed. John D. Worrall, 154–60. Ithaca,
                N.Y.: ILR Press.
Chelius, James R., and Robert S. Smith
      1983   "Experience Rating and Injury Prevention." *Safety and the
                Work Force: Incentives and Disincentives in Workers' Compensation*,
                ed. John D. Worrall, 128–37. Ithaca, N.Y.: ILR Press.
Chirikos, Thomas N., and Gilbert Nestel
      1981   "Impairment and Labor Market Outcomes: A Cross-sectional
                and Longitudinal Analysis." In *Work and Retirement: A Lon-
                gitudinal Study of Men*, ed. Herbert S. Parnes, 93–101. Cam-
                bridge, Mass.: MIT Press.
Coase, Ronald
      1960   "The Problem of Social Cost." *Journal of Law and Economics*
                3 (October): 1–44.

Conley, Ronald
    1965   *The Economics of Vocational Rehabilitation.* Baltimore: Johns
            Hopkins University Press.
Craft, James A., Thomas J. Benecki, and Yitzchak M. Shkop
    1980   "Who Hires the Seriously Handicapped?" *Industrial Relations*
            19, 1 (Winter): 94–99.
Crawford, David, and Mark R. Killingsworth
    1984   "Toward a Strategy for the Measurement of VR Program
            Impact." Bureau of Economic Research, Rutgers University.
            Mimeo.
Danzinger, Sheldon, Robert H. Haveman, and Robert Plotnick
    1981   "How Income Transfers Affect Work, Savings and the In-
            come Distribution." *Journal of Economic Literature* 19 (Septem-
            ber): 975–1028.
Darling-Hammond, Linda, and Thomas J. Kniesner
    1980   *The Law and Economics of Workers' Compensation.* Santa Monica,
            Cal.: Rand Corporation.
Deutermann, William
    1977   "Another Look at Working Men Who Are Not in the Labor
            Force." *Monthly Labor Review* 100 (June): 9–14.
Diamond, Peter A., and J. A. Mirlees
    1978   "A Model of Social Insurance with Variable Retirement."
            Journal of Public Economics 10 (December): 295–336.
Dixon, R. G., Jr.
    1973   *Social Security Disability and Mass Justice: A Problem in Welfare
            Adjudication.* New York: Praeger.
Dorsey, Stuart
    1983   "Employment Hazards and Fringe Benefits: Further Tests
            for Compensating Differentials." In *Safety and the Work Force:
            Incentives and Disincentives in Workers' Compensation,* ed. John
            D. Worrall, 87–102. Ithaca, N.Y.: ILR Press.
Dorsey, Stuart, and Norman Walzer
    1983   "Compensating Differentials and Liability Rules." *Industrial
            and Labor Relations Review* 36 (July): 642–54.
Ehrenberg, Ronald G.
    1984   "Workers' Compensation, Wages and the Risk of Injury."
            Paper presented at the Conference on New Perspectives on
            Workers' Compensation, 16 October, New York State School
            of Industrial and Labor Relations, Cornell University, Ithaca,
            N.Y.
Emanuel, Han
    1979   "Factors behind the Growth in the Number of Disability Ben-
            efits in the Netherlands." Mimeo.
Emanuel, Han, Victor Halberstadt, and Carl Petersen
    1984   "Disability Policy in the Netherlands." In *Public Policy toward
            Disabled Workers: Cross-National Analyses of Economic Impacts,*

ed. Robert H. Haveman, Victor Halberstadt, and Richard V. Burkhauser. Ithaca, N.Y.: Cornell University Press.

Emer, William H., and Catherine B. Frink
1983   "*E.E. Black* and Beyond: Update on Hiring the Handicapped." *Labor Law Journal* 34 (October): 643–53.

Fast, James
1978   *Rearranged Work Schedules for Handicapped Employees in the Private Employment Sector.* Report to the U.S. Dept. of Labor, Employment and Training Administration. NTIS DLETA 20-51-77-37-1.

Faulkner, Edwin J.
1960   *Health Insurance.* New York: McGraw-Hill.

Fechter, Alan E.
1975   *Public Employment Programs.* Washington, D.C.: American Enterprise Institute.

Fechter, Alan E., and Charles O. Thorpe, Jr.
N.d.   *Labor Market Discrimination against the Handicapped: An Initial Inquiry.* Working Paper. Washington, D.C.: Urban Institute.

Fenn, Paul
1981   "Sickness Duration, Residual Disability and Income Replacement: An Empirical Analysis." *Economic Journal* 91 (March): 158–73.

Ferguson, Charles E.
1965   "Time Series Production Function and Technological Progress in American Manufacturing Industries." *Journal of Political Economy* 73 (April): 135–47.

Flinn, C., and J. Heckman
1982   "Models for the Analysis of Labor Dynamics." In *Advances in Econometrics*, ed. R. Basmann and G. Rhodes, vol. 1, 35–95. Greenwich, Conn.: JAI Press.

Franklin, Paula A.
1976   "Impact of Substantial Gainful Activity Level on Disabled Beneficiary Work Patterns." *Social Security Bulletin* 39 (August): 20–29.
1977   "Impact of Disability on the Family Structure." *Social Security Bulletin* 40 (May): 3–18.

Freeman, Richard B.
1974   "Alternative Theories of Labor-Market Discrimination: Individual and Collective Behavior." In *Patterns of Racial Discrimination*, ed. George M. von Furstenberg, Ann R. Horowitz, and Bennett Harrison, vol. 2, 33–50. New York: Lexington Books.

Frohlich, Philip
1975   "Income of the Newly Disabled: Survey of Recently Disabled Adults." *Social Security Bulletin* 38 (September): 3–18.

Gallichio, Sal, and Barry Bye.
    1980   *Consistency of Initial Disability Decisions among and within States.* Staff Paper no. 39, Publication no. 13-11869. U.S. Dept. of Health and Human Services, Social Security Administration, Office of Policy, Office of Research and Statistics.

Galvin, Donald E.
    1973   "Health Promotion, Disability Management and Rehabilitation at the Workplace." *The Interconnector* 6, 2: 1–6.

Garrad, J.
    1974   "Impairment and Disability: Their Measurement, Prevalence and Psychological Cost." In *Impairment, Disability, and Handicap*, ed. Dennis Lees and Stella Shaw. London: Heineman.

Gastwirth, Joseph L.
    1972   "On the Decline of Male Labor Force Participation." *Monthly Labor Review* 95 (October): 44–46.

General Accounting Office
    1981   *More Diligent Followup Needed to Weed out Ineligible SSA Disability Beneficiaries.* Report to the Congress by the Comptroller General, Report no. HRD81-48.

Gittler, Amy Jo
    1978   "Fair Employment and the Handicapped: A Legal Perspective." *DePaul Law Review* 27: 593, 967.

Gliedman, John, and William Roth
    1980   *The Unexpected Minority.* New York: Harcourt Brace Jovanovich.

Goldstein, Morris, and Robert S. Smith
    1976   "The Predicted Impact of the Black Lung Benefits Program on the Coal Industry." In *Evaluating the Labor-Market Effects of Social Programs*, ed. Orley Ashenfelter and James Blum, 133–82. Princeton, N.J.: Industrial Relations Section, Princeton University.

Greenleigh Associates, Inc.
    1975   *The Role of Sheltered Workshops in the Rehabilitation of the Severely Handicapped.* New York: Greenleigh Associates, Inc.

Griliches, Zvi, B. Hall, and J. Hausman
    1978   "Missing Data and Self-Selection in Large Panels." *Annales de l'Insee* 30 (April): 137–76.

Haber, Lawrence
    1985   "Trends and Demographic Studies on Programs for Disabled Persons." In *Social Influences in Rehabilitation Planning: Blueprint for the 21st Century*, ed. Leonard G. Perlman and Gary F. Austin, 27–37. Alexandria, Va.: National Rehabilitation Association.

Hahn, Harlan
    1983   "Paternalism and Public Policy." *Society* 20, 3 (March/April):
            36–47.
    1984   *The Issue of Equality: European Perceptions of Employment for
            Disabled Persons*. New York: World Rehabilitation Fund.
Halberstadt, Victor
    1978   "Comments on the Dutch Social Employment Program." In
            Public Employment Programs and Wage Subsidies, ed. John
            Palmer, 270–75. Washington, D.C.: Brookings Institution.
Hall, R. E.
    1979   "Comments on the Labor Market Displacement Effect in the
            Analysis of the Net Impact of Manpower Training Programs,
            by George Johnson." In *Evaluating Manpower Training Pro-
            grams*, ed. Farrell E. Bloch, 255–57. Greenwich, Conn.: JAI
            Press.
Halpern, Janice, and Jerry Hausman
    1984   "Choice under Uncertainty: A Model of Applications for the
            Social Security Disability Insurance Program." Mimeo.
Hambor, John C.
    1975   *Unemployment and Disability: An Econometric Analysis with Time
            Series Data*. Staff Paper no. 20. U.S. Dept. of Health, Edu-
            cation and Welfare, Social Security Administration, Office of
            Research and Statistics.
Hamermesh, Daniel
    1979   "New Estimates of the Incidence of the Payroll Tax." *Southern
            Economic Journal* 45 (April): 1208–19.
Harris, Milton, and Arthur Raviv
    1978   "Some Results on Incentive Contracts with Applications to
            Education and Employment, Health Insurance, and Law En-
            forcement." *American Economic Review* 68, 1 (March): 20–30.
Harvard Law Review
    1984   "Employment Discrimination against the Handicapped and
            Section 504 of the Rehabilitation Act: An Essay on Legal
            Evasiveness." Vol. 97 (February): 997–1015.
Haveman, Robert H.
    1978   "The Dutch Social Employment Program." In *Public Employ-
            ment Programs and Wage Subsidies*, ed. John Palmer. Washing-
            ton, D.C.: Brookings Institution.
Haveman, Robert H., Victor Halberstadt, and Richard V. Burkhauser
    1984   *Public Policy toward Disabled Workers: Cross-National Analyses of
            Economic Impacts*. Ithaca, N.Y.: Cornell University Press.
Haveman, Robert H., and Barbara L. Wolfe
    1984a   "The Decline in Male Labor Force Participation: Comment."
            Journal of Political Economy 92, 3 (June): 532–41.

1984b   "Disability Transfers and Early Retirement: A Causal Relationship?" *Journal of Public Economics* 24: 47–66.

Haveman, Robert H., Barbara Wolfe, and Jennifer Warlick
1984   "Disability Transfers, Early Retirement, and Retrenchment." In *Retirement and Economic Behavior*, ed. Henry Aaron and G. Burtless, 65–93. Washington, D.C.: Brookings Institution.

Hayek, Friedrich A.
1945   "The Use of Knowledge in Society." *American Economic Review* 35 (September): 519–30.

Health Insurance Association of America
1982   *New Group Disability Insurance, 1981.* Washington, D.C.: HIAA.

Heckman, James J.
1976   "The Common Structure of Statistical Models of Truncation, Sample Selection and Limited Dependent Variables and a Simple Estimator for Such Models." *Annals of Economic and Social Measurement* 5 (Fall): 475–92.

Heckman, James J., and Burton Singer
1982   "The Identification Problem in Econometric Models for Duration Data." In *Advances in Econometrics*, ed. W. Hildebrand, 39–77. Cambridge: Cambridge University Press.
1984   "A Method for Minimizing the Impact of Distributional Assumptions in Econometric Models for Duration Data." *Econometrica* 55 (March): 271–320.

Hester, Edward J., and Paul G. Decelles
1985   *The Disability System: A Dynamic Analysis.* Topeka, Kans.: Menninger Foundation.

Hester, Edward J., and John D. Downs
1984   *Preventing Disability Dependence.* Topeka, Kans.: Menninger Rehabilitation Research and Training Center.

Hill, Mark, and Paul Wehman
1983   "Cost Benefit Analysis of Placing Moderately and Severely Handicapped Individuals into Competitive Employment." *The Journal of the Association for the Severely Handicapped* 8: 30–38.

Hill, M., J. W. Hill, P. Wehman, and P. D. Banks
1985   "An Analysis of Monetary and Nonmonetary Outcomes Associated with Competitive Employment of Mentally Retarded Persons." In *Competitive Employment for Persons with Mental Retardation: From Research to Practice*, ed. Paul Wehman and Janet Hill, vol. 1, 110–33. Richmond, Va.: Virginia Commonwealth University, Rehabilitation Research and Training Center.

Hill, M., J. W. Hill, P. Wehman, G. Revell, A. Dickenson, and J. Noble, Jr.
1985   "Time Limited Training and Supported Employment: A Model for Redistributing Existing Resources for Persons with Severe Disabilities." In *Competitive Employment for Persons with Mental*

Retardation: From Research to Practice, ed. Paul Wehman and Janet Hill, vol. 1, 134–68. Richmond, Va.: Virginia Commonwealth University, Rehabilitation Research and Training Center.

Hirshleifer, Jack, and John G. Riley
>1979 "The Analytics of Uncertainty and Information: An Exploratory Survey." *Journal of Economic Literature* 17 (December): 1375–1421.

Houthakker, H. S., and Lester D. Taylor
>1966 *Consumer Demand in the United States, 1929–1970*. Cambridge, Mass.: Harvard University Press.

Huebner, S. S., and Kenneth Black, Jr.
>1982 *Life Insurance*. 10th ed. Englewood Cliffs, N.J.: Prentice-Hall.

Hunter, Arthur, and James T. Phillips
>1932 *Disability Benefits in Life Insurance Policies*. New York: Actuarial Society of America.

Inman, Robert
>1983 "Disability Indices, the Economic Costs of Illness and Social Insurance: The Case of Multiple Sclerosis." Paper presented at the Vancouver Symposium of the International Federation of Multiple Sclerosis Societies, August. Vancouver, Canada.

International Labour Organization
>Various
>Years *Yearbook of Labour Statistics*. Geneva: ILO.

Jarvikoski, A., and E. Lehelma
>1980 *Early Rehabilitation at a Workplace*. New York: World Rehabilitation Fund.

Jensen, Michael C., and William H. Meckling
>1976 "The Theory of the Firm: Managerial Behavior, Agency Costs and Ownership Structure." *Journal of Financial Economics* 3 (October): 305–60.

Johnson, George E.
>1979 "The Labor Market Displacement Effect in the Analysis of the Net Impact of Manpower Training Programs." In *Evaluating Manpower Training Programs*, ed. Farrell E. Bloch, 227–54. Greenwich, Conn.: JAI Press.

Johnson, George E., and James Tomola
>1977 "The Fiscal Substitution Effects of Alternative Approaches to Public Service Employment." *Journal of Human Resources* 12 (Winter): 3–26.

Johnson, Lawrence, and Associates, Inc.
>1980 *Reasonable Accommodations: Research and Remedies*. Report for the U.S. Dept. of Education, Office of Civil Rights.

Johnson, William G.
>1979 "Disability, Income Support, and S. I." In *Disability Policies*

and Government Programs, ed. Edward D. Berkowitz, 87–130. New York: Praeger.

1983 "Work Disincentives of Benefit Payments." In *Safety and the Work Force: Incentives and Disincentives in Workers' Compensation*, ed. John D. Worrall, 138–53. Ithaca, N.Y.: ILR Press.

Johnson, William G., Paul Cullinan, and William Curington
1978 "The Adequacy of Workers' Compensation Benefits." Health Studies Program no. 33. The Maxwell School, Syracuse University.

Johnson, William G., and James Lambrinos
1985 "Wage Discrimination against Handicapped Men and Women." *Journal of Human Resources* 20, 2 (Spring): 264–77.

Joskow, Paul L.
1984 *Controlling Hospital Costs: The Role of Government Regulation.* Cambridge, Mass.: MIT Press.

Kakalik, J. S., W. S. Furry, M. A. Thomas, and M. F. Carney
1981 *The Costs of Special Education, Summary of Study Findings.* Santa Monica, Cal.: Rand Corporation.

Kaplan, Robert S.
1982 *Advanced Managerial Accounting.* Englewood Cliffs, N.J.: Prentice-Hall.

Katz, Lawrence
1985 "A Competing Risks Model of Unemployment Duration." University of California, Berkeley. Mimeo.

Keifer, Nicholas M., and George R. Neuman
1979 "An Empirical Job Search Model with a Test of the Constant Reservation Wage Hypothesis." *Journal of Political Economy* 87: 89–108.

Kemper, P., D. A. Long, and C. Thornton
1981 *The Supported Work Evaluation: Final Benefit-Cost Analysis.* Princeton, N.J.: Mathematica Policy Research.

Kerachsky, S., C. Thornton, A. Bloomenthal, R. Maynard, and S. Stephens
1985 *Transitional Employment Impacts on Mentally Retarded Young Adults: Results of the STETS Demonstration.* Princeton, N.J.: Mathematica Policy Research.

Killingsworth, Mark R.
1985 "Substitution and Output Effects on Labor Demand: Theory and Policy Applications." *Journal of Human Resources* 20, 1 (Winter): 143–51.

Koitz, David
1980 "Social Security's Disability Programs: Amendments of 1980." Issue Brief no. IB79084 (July 22), Library of Congress, Congressional Research Service.

1985 "Social Security: Reexamining Eligibility for Disability Benefits." Issue Brief no. IB82078 (August 12), Library of Congress, Congressional Research Service.

Koyl, Leon F.
1970   "A Technique for Measuring Functional Criteria in Placement and Retirement Practices." In *Towards an Industrial Gerontology*, ed. Harold L. Sheppard, 140–46. Cambridge, Mass.: Schenkman Publishing Co.

Kurtzke, J. F.
1975   "Epidemiology of Spinal Cord Injury." *Experimental Neurology* 48: 163–236.

Lancaster, T.
1979   "Econometric Methods for the Duration of Unemployment." *Econometrica* 47: 939–56.

Lancaster, T., and Stephen Nickell
1980   "The Analysis of Re-Employment Probabilities for the Unemployed." *Journal of the Royal Statistical Society* A143, pt. 2: 141–65.

Lando, Mordechai E.
1979   "Prevalence of Work Disability by State, 1976." *Social Security Bulletin* 42 (May): 41–44.

Lando, Mordechai E., Malcolm B. Coate, and Ruth Kraus
1979   "Disability Benefit Applications and the Economy." *Social Security Bulletin* 42 (October): 3–10.

Lando, Mordechai E., Aline Farley, and Mary Brown
1982   "Recent Trends in the Social Security Disability Insurance Program." *Social Security Bulletin* 45, 8 (August): 3–14.

Lando, Mordechai E., and Timothy R. Hopkins
1977   "Modeling Applications for Disability Insurance." Paper presented at the American Economic Association Meetings, 28–30 December, New York City.

Lando, Mordechai E., and Aaron Krute
1978   "Disability Insurance: Program Issues and Research." *Social Security Bulletin* 39 (October): 3–17.
        "The Growth in Observed Disability Incidence Rates 1967 to 1974." Unpublished paper.

Lang, Jonathan
1978   "Protecting the Handicapped from Employment Discrimination: The Job-Relatedness and Bona Fide Occupational Qualification Doctrines." *DePaul Law Review* 27: 989–90, 1011.

Larson, Lloyd, and John F. Burton, Jr.
1985   "Special Funds in Workers' Compensation." In *Workers' Compensation Benefits: Adequacy, Equity, and Efficiency*, ed. John D. Worrall and David Appel, 117–56. Ithaca, N.Y.: ILR Press.

Lee, Lung Fei
    1979   "Identification and Estimation in Binary Choice Models with Limited (Censored) Dependent Variables." *Econometrica* 47: 977–96.

Leonard, Herman B., and Richard J. Zeckhauser
    1983   "Public Insurance Provision and Non-Market Failures." *The Geneva Papers on Risk and Insurance* 8 (April): 147–57.

Leonard, Jonathan S.
    1976   "On the Decline in the Labor Force Participation Rates of Older Black Males." Master's thesis, Harvard College.

    1979   *The Social Security Disability Program and Labor Force Participation.* Working Paper no. 392. National Bureau of Economic Research.

    1985   "Incentives and Disincentives for Disabled Employees." Paper presented at the Meeting on Economics of Disability, 10 April, Washington, D.C.

Levitan, Sar A., and Robert Taggart
    1977   *Jobs for the Disabled.* Baltimore: Johns Hopkins University Press.

Long, D. A., C. D. Mallar, and C. Thornton
    1981   "Evaluating the Benefits and Costs of the Job Corps." *Journal of Policy Analysis and Management* 1, 1: 55–76.

Luft, Harold
    1975   "The Impact of Poor Health on Earnings." *Review of Economics and Statistics* 57 (February): 43–57.

    1978   *Poverty and Health: Economic Causes and Consequences of Health Problems.* Cambridge, Mass.: Ballinger.

Mainstream, Inc.
    1981   *In the Mainstream*, vol. 11 (January-February).

Marvel, Howard P.
    1982   "An Economic Analysis of the Operation of Social Security Disability Insurance." *Journal of Human Resources* 17 (Summer): 393–412.

Mashaw, Jerry L.
    1979   "The Definition of Disability from the Perspective of Administration." In *Disability Policies and Government Programs*, ed. Edward D. Berkowitz. New York: Praeger.

    1983   *Bureaucratic Justice: Managing Social Security Disability Claims.* New Haven, Conn.: Yale University Press.

Mashaw, Jerry L., Charles J. Goetz, F. I. Goodman, W. F. Schwartz, P. R. Verkuil, and M. M. Carrow
    1978   *Social Security Hearings and Appeals.* Lexington, Mass.: Lexington Books.

Mayers, David, and Clifford W. Smith, Jr.
    1982   *Toward a Positive Theory of Insurance.* Monograph Series in

Finance and Economics. New York: New York University Press.

McGill, Dan M.
    1967   *Life Insurance.* Homewood, Ill.: Richard D. Irwin.

Mechanic, David
    1977   "Illness Behavior, Social Adaptation, and the Management of Illness." *Journal of Nervous and Mental Disease* 165: 79–87.

Medoff, James L., and Katherine G. Abraham
    1981   "Are Those Paid More Really More Productive? The Case of Experience." *Journal of Human Resources* 16 (Spring): 186–216.

Meer, C. W.
    1979   *Social Security Disability Insurance: The Problems of Unexpected Growth.* Washington, D.C.: American Enterprise Institute.

Moss, James
    1980   *Postsecondary Vocational Education for Mentally Retarded Adults.* Reston, Va.: ERIC Clearinghouse on Handicapped and Gifted Children.

Muller, L. Scott
    1980   *Receipt of Multiple Benefits by Disabled Worker Beneficiaries.* Working Paper Series no. 15. U.S. Dept. of Health, Education and Welfare, Social Security Administration, Office of Research and Statistics, Office of Policy.

Nagi, Saad Z.
    1965   "Some Conceptual Issues in Disability and Rehabilitation." In *Sociology and Rehabilitation*, ed. Marvin B. Sussman. Washington, D.C.: American Sociological Association.
    1969   *Disability and Rehabilitation: Legal, Clinical and Self-Concepts and Measurements.* Columbus, Ohio: Ohio State University Press.
    1975   *An Epidemiology of Disability among Adults in the United States.* Columbus, Ohio: Mershon Center, Ohio State University.
    1979   "The Concept and Measurement of Disability." In *Disability Policies and Government Programs*, ed. Edward D. Berkowitz, 1–15. New York: Praeger.

Nagi, Saad Z., and L. Hadley
    1972   "Disability Behavior, Income Change and Motivation to Work." *Industrial and Labor Relations Review* 25 (January): 223–33.

National Commission on State Workmen's Compensation Laws
    1972   *The Report of the National Commission on State Workmen's Compensation Laws.* Washington, D.C.: U.S. Government Printing Office.
    1973   *Compendium of Workmen's Compensation.* Washington, D.C.: U.S. Government Printing Office.

National Council on Compensation Insurance
    1981a   *ABC's of Experience Rating.* New York: NCCI.
    1981b   *The Pricing of Workers' Compensation Insurance.* New York: NCCI.
    1984   "A Report Concerning the Incidence of Vocational Rehabilitation." Mimeo.

National Labor Market Board (Sweden)
    1980   "Job Placement for Older and Disabled Persons." Report 1980-06-09.

Nevitt, Michael W.
    1984   "Social Policy, Medical Care, and Disability: Rehabilitation Outcomes of Medical Technology for Chronic Disease with a Case Study of Artificial Joint Implant Surgery." Ph.D. diss., Department of City and Regional Planning, University of California, Berkeley.

Nickell, Stephen
    1979   "The Effect of Unemployment and Related Benefits on the Duration of Unemployment." *Economic Journal* 89: 34–49.

Oi, Walter
    1972   "Labor as a Quasi-Fixed Factor." *Journal of Political Economy* 70 (December): 538–55.
    1973   "An Essay on Workmen's Compensation and Industrial Safety." In *Supplemental Studies for the National Commission on State Workmen's Compensation Laws*, ed. Monroe Berkowitz, vol. 1, 44–106. Washington, D.C.: U.S. Government Printing Office.
    1974   "Economics of Industrial Safety." *Law and Contemporary Problems* 38 (Summer/Autumn): 669–99.
    1978   "The Impact of Disability on Full Income." Paper presented at the American Economic Association Meetings, 29–30 August, Chicago.

O'Neill and Associates
    1984   "Status of DDD County Services Programs." Seattle, Washington. Mimeo.

O'Neill, David
    1976   *Discrimination against Handicapped Persons: The Costs, Benefits, and Inflationary Impact of Implementing Section 504 of the Rehabilitation Act of 1973 Covering Recipients of HEW Financial Assistance.* Report to the Office for Civil Rights. Arlington, Va.: Public Research Institute.

Parsons, Donald O.
    1980a   "The Decline in Male Labor Force Participation." *Journal of Political Economy* 88, 1 (February): 117–34.
    1980b   "Racial Trends in Male Labor Force Participation." *American Economic Review* 70 (December): 911–20.

1982a   "The Male Labour Force Participation Decision: Health, Reported Health, and Economic Incentives." *Economica* 49 (February): 81–91.

1982b   "A Time Series Analysis of Male Labor Force Participation and Social Security Disability Recipiency." Ohio State University. Mimeo.

1982c   "Male Labor Force Participation and Disability: A Cross-State Analysis." Ohio State University. Mimeo.

1984a   "Disability Insurance and Male Labor Force Participation: A Response to Haveman and Wolfe." *Journal of Political Economy* 92, 3: 542–49.

1984b   "Social Insurance with Imperfect State Verification: Income Insurance for the Disabled." Ohio State University. Mimeo.

Pati, Gopal C., and Glenn Morrison
1982   "Enabling the Disabled." *Harvard Business Review* 60, 4(July/August): 162–68.

Pauly, Mark V.
1974   "Overinsurance and Public Provision of Insurance: The Role of Moral Hazard and Adverse Selection." *Quarterly Journal of Economics* 88: 44–54.

Pear, Robert
1983   "New York and Other States Flout U.S. Rules for Disability Benefits." *New York Times*, September 12.

1984   "Disability Reviews Spur Legal Crisis." *New York Times*, September 9.

Peck, Cornelius
1983   "Employment Problems of the Handicapped: Would Title VII Remedies Be Appropriate and Effective?" *Journal of Law Reform* 16, 2 (Winter): 343–85.

Phelps, Edmund S.
1972   "The Statistical Theory of Racism and Sexism." *American Economic Review* 62 (September): 659–61.

Premus, Robert, and David A. Carnes
1982   *Regulation and Small Business Participation in the Federal Contract Market: The Effect of Section 503*. Report for the U.S. Small Business Administration, SBA-1A-00022-01. Wright State University School of Business Administration.

Reno, Virginia, and Daniel N. Price
1985   "Relationship between the Retirement, Disability, and Unemployment Insurance Programs: The U.S. Experience." *Social Security Bulletin* 48, 5 (May): 24–37.

Riccio, James A., and Marilyn L. Price
1984   *A Transitional Employment Strategy for the Mentally Retarded: The Final STETS Implementation Report*. New York: Manpower Demonstration Research Corporation.

Roberts, Steven
  1980   "Harder Times Make Social Spenders Hard Minded." *New York Times*, August 3, E-3.
Rosenblum, Marcus, ed.
  1973   *Compendium on Workmen's Compensation.* Washington, D.C.: U.S. Government Printing Office.
Rothschild, Michael, and Joseph E. Stiglitz
  1976   "Equilibrium in Competitive Insurance Markets: An Essay on the Economics of Imperfect Information." *Quarterly Journal of Economics* 90, 4 (November): 629–49.
Rusch, Frank, and Dennis Mithaug
  1980   *Vocational Training for Mentally Retarded Adults: A Behavior Analytic Approach.* Champaign, Ill.: Research Press.
Ruser, John W.
  1984   "Workers' Compensation Insurance, Experience Rating and Occupational Injuries." U.S. Bureau of Labor Statistics, Office of Research and Evaluation. Washington, D.C. Mimeo.
Scheffler, Richard M., and George Iden
  1974   "The Effect of Disability on Labor Supply." *Industrial and Labor Relations Review* 28 (October): 122–32.
K. Schneider, F. Rusch, R. Henderson, and T. Geske
  1982   "Competitive Employment for Mentally Retarded Persons: Costs versus Benefits." University of Illinois at Champaign-Urbana. Mimeo.
Schobel, Bruce D.
  1980   *Experience of Disabled-Worker Benefits under OASDI, 1974–1978.* Actuarial Study no. 81. Social Security Administration.
Schroedel, John G., and Richard Jacobsen
  1978   *Employer Attitudes towards Hiring Persons with Disabilities.* Albertson, N.Y.: Human Resources Center.
Sherman, Susan W., and Nancy M. Robinson, eds.
  1982   *Ability Testing of Handicapped People.* Washington, D.C.: National Academy Press.
Siskind, Frederic B.
  1975   "Labor Force Participation of Men, 25–54, by Race." *Monthly Labor Review* 98 (July): 40–42.
Slade, Frederick P.
  1984   "Older Men, Disability Insurance and the Incentive to Work." *Industrial Relations* 23, 2 (Spring): 260–77.
Smith, Robert S.
  1979   "Compensating Differentials and Public Policy: A Review." *Industrial and Labor Relations Review* 32, 3 (April): 339–52.
Social Security Administration
  1981a   "Social Security Disability Amendments of 1980: Legislative

History and Summary of Provisions." *Social Security Bulletin* 44, 4(April): 1–18.

1981b   *Social Security Bulletin: Annual Statistical Supplement, 1980.* Washington, D.C.: U.S. Government Printing Office.

Social Security Administration, Office of Legislative and Regulatory Policy

1984   "Social Security Disability Benefits Reform Act of 1984." *Legislative Report*, no. 2, September 21.

Soule, Charles E.

1984   *Disability Income Insurance: The Unique Risk.* Homewood, Ill.: Dow Jones-Irwin.

Spence, A. Michael

1974   *Market Signaling: Information Transfer in Hiring and Related Screening Processes.* Cambridge, Mass.: Harvard University Press.

Spence, A. Michael, and Richard Zeckhauser

1971   "Insurance, Information, and Individual Action." *American Economic Review* 61, 2 (May): 380–87.

Staten, Michael, and John Umbeck

1982   "Information Costs and the Incentive to Shirk: Disability Compensation of Air Traffic Controllers." *American Economic Review* 72: 1023–37.

1983   "Compensating Stress-Induced Disability: Disincentive Problems." In *Safety and the Work Force: Incentives and Disincentives in Workers' Compensation*, ed. John D. Worrall, 103–27. Ithaca, N.Y.: ILR Press.

Statistics Canada, Labour Force Surveys Section

1972–

1979   *Labour Force.* Ottawa, Canada.

Sunshine, Jonathan

1979   "Disability." Office of Management and Budget Staff Technical Paper. Mimeo.

Swisher, Idella G.

1973   "The Disabled and the Decline in Men's Labor Force Participation." *Monthly Labor Review* 96 (November): 53.

Taggart, R.

1981   *A Fisherman's Guide: An Assessment of Training and Remediation Strategies.* Kalamazoo, Mich.: Upjohn Institute.

Thompson, Lawrence H.

1983   "The Social Security Reform Debate." *Journal of Economic Literature* 21, 4 (December): 1425–67.

Thornton, Craig

1985   "Benefit-Cost Analysis of Social Programs: Deinstitutionalization and Education Programs." In *Living and Learning in the Least Restrictive Environment*, ed. Robert H. Bruininks and K. Charlie Lakin, 225–44. Baltimore, Md.: Paul H. Brookes Publishing Co.

Thornton, C., D. Long, and C. Mallar
    1982   *A Comparative Evaluation of Job Corps after Forty-Eight Months of Postprogram Observation.* Princeton, N.J.: Mathematica Policy Research.

Thurow, Lester
    1969   *Poverty and Discrimination.* Washington, D.C.: Brookings Institution.

Time
    1977   "Helping the Handicapped: Without Crippling Institutions." December 5: 34.

Toikka, Richard S.
    1976   *Household Participation in Non-Linear Subsidy Programs.* Washington, D.C.: Urban Institute.

Treitel, Ralph
    1975   "Effects of Financing Disabled-Beneficiary Rehabilitation." *Social Security Bulletin* 38 (November): 16–18.
    1976   *Appeal by Denied Disability Claimants.* Staff paper no. 23. U.S. Dept. of Health, Education and Welfare, Social Security Administration, Office of Research and Statistics.
    1979a   "Recovery of Disabled Beneficiaries: A 1975 Followup Study of 1972 Allowances." *Social Security Bulletin* 42 (April): 3–23.
    1979b   "Disability Claimants Who Contest Denials and Win Reversals through Hearings." Working Paper Series no. 3. U.S. Dept. of Health, Education and Welfare, Social Security Administration, Office of Research and Statistics, Office of Policy.
    1979c   "Disability Beneficiary Recovery." Working Paper no. 2. U.S. Dept. of Health, Education and Welfare, Social Security Administration, Office of Research and Statistics.

Urban Institute
    1975   *Report of the Comprehensive Needs Study.* Report to the U.S. Dept. of Health, Education and Welfare, Rehabilitation Services Administration. Washington, D.C.

U.S. Bureau of the Census
    1983   *Labor Force Status and Other Characteristics of Persons with a Work Disability: 1982.* Current Population Reports, Special Studies Series, no. 127, 23. Washington, D.C.: U.S. Government Printing Office.

U.S. Chamber of Commerce
    1983   *Analysis of Workers' Compensation Laws, 1983.* Washington, D.C.: U.S. Chamber of Commerce.

U.S. Commission on Civil Rights
    1983   *Accommodating the Spectrum of Individual Abilities.* Clearinghouse Publication 81.

U.S. Congress, Senate Committee on Finance
    1979   *Issues Related to Social Security Act Disability Programs.* Staff Report, 96th Cong., 1st sess. Committee Print no. 96-23.
    1982   *Staff Data and Materials Related to the Social Security Disability Insurance Program.* 97th Cong., 2d sess. Committee Print no. 97-16.
    1983   *Staff Data and Materials Related to the Social Security Act Disability Program.* 98th Cong., 1st sess. Senate Print no. 98-93.
    1984   *Report on the Social Security Disability Amendments of 1984.* 98th Cong., 2d sess. Report no. 98-466.
U.S. Dept. of Commerce
    1983   *1981 Annual Survey of Manufacturers.* Washington, D.C.: U.S. Government Printing Office.
U.S. Dept. of Education
    1984   *Digest of Data on Persons with Disabilities.* Washington, D. C.: National Institute of Handicapped Research.
U.S. Dept. of Education, Office of Special Education and Rehabilitative Services
    1985   *Special Projects and Demonstrations for Providing Vocational Rehabilitation Services to Severely Disabled Individuals: Supported Employment.* Washington, D.C.: U.S. Government Printing Office.
U.S. Dept. of Health and Human Services
    1982   *Report to the Congress on Implementation of Section 304(g) of Public Law 96-265.* Washington, D.C.: U.S. Government Printing Office.
U.S. Dept. of Health and Human Services, Social Security Administration
    Various *Annual Statistical Supplement of the Social Security Bulletin.* Washington, D.C.: U.S. Government Printing Office.
    years
U.S. Dept. of Health, Education and Welfare, Office of Civil Rights. Contract Research Corporation, Education and Human Development, Inc.
    1977   *Handbook for the Implementation of Section 504 of the Rehabilitation Act of 1973.* Washington, D.C.: U.S. Government Printing Office.
U.S. Dept. of Labor
    1948   "Hire the Handicapped." In *The Performance of Physically Impaired Workers in Manufacturing Industries.* Washington, D.C.: U.S. Government Printing Office.
    1977   *A Nationwide Report on Sheltered Workshops and Their Employment of Handicapped Individuals. A Statistical Appendix to Volume I.* Washington, D.C.: U.S. Government Printing Office.
U.S. Dept. of Labor, Division of State Workers' Compensation Programs
    1983   *State Workers' Compensation Laws.* Washington, D.C.: U.S. Government Printing Office.

U.S. Dept. of Labor, Employment Standards Administration

1982   *A Study of Accommodations Provided to Handicapped Employees by Federal Contractors: Final Report.* 2 vols. Prepared by Berkeley Planning Associates, under Contract no. J-9-E-1-0009.

1985   *Draft Report: A Study of Direct and Indirect Costs for Hiring the Handicapped in Three Industries: Annotated Bibliography.* Report prepared by Applied Management Sciences.

U.S. Dept. of Labor, ESA-OWCP

1981   *State Compliance with the 19 Essential Recommendations of the National Commission on State Workmen's Compensation Laws, 1972–1980.* Washington, D.C.: U.S. Government Printing Office.

U.S. House of Representatives

1975   *Staff Survey of State Disability Agencies under Social Security and SSI Programs.* 94th Cong., 1st sess.

1980   *Conference Report on the Social Security Disability Amendments of 1980.* 96th Cong., 2d sess. Report no. 96-944.

1984a   *Conference Report on the Social Security Disability Benefits Reform Act of 1984.* 98th Cong., 2d sess. Report no. 98-1039.

1984b   *Staff Report on the Disability Insurance Program.* Washington, D.C.: U.S. Government Printing Office.

U.S. House of Representatives, Committee on Ways and Means

1984   *Committee Report on the Social Security Disability Benefits Reform Act of 1984.* 98th Cong., 2d sess. Report no. 98-618.

U.S. House of Representatives, Subcommittee on Social Security

1982   *Social Security Continuing Disability Investigation Program: Background and Legislative Issue Paper.* 97th Cong., 2d sess. Committee Print no. 97-37.

U.S. Office of Personnel Management

1980   *Handbook of Reasonable Accommodation.* PMS Series 72-A. Washington, D.C.: U.S. Government Printing Office.

Victor, Richard B.

1983   *Workers' Compensation and Workplace Safety: The Nature of Employer Financial Incentives.* Santa Monica, Cal.: Rand Corporation.

1985   "Experience Rating and Workplace Safety." In *Workers' Compensation Benefits: Adequacy, Equity, and Efficiency,* ed. John D. Worrall and David Appel, 71–88. Ithaca, N.Y.: ILR Press.

Victor, Richard B., Linda Cohen, and Charles Phelps

1982   *Workers' Compensation and Workplace Safety: Employer Response to Financial Incentives.* Santa Monica, Cal.: Rand Corporation.

Vroman, Wayne

1978   "Serious Work Injuries: Examining Some Consequences." In *Policy Analysis with Social Security Research Files,* 117–42. U.S.

Dept. of Health, Education and Welfare, Social Security Administration. Washington, D.C.: U.S. Government Printing Office.

Wadensjo, Eskil
1984   "Disability Policy in Sweden." In *Public Policy toward Disabled Workers: Cross-National Analyses of Economic Impact*, ed. Robert H. Haveman, Victor Halberstadt, and Richard V. Burkhauser, 444–516. Ithaca, N.Y.: Cornell University Press.

Wehman, Paul
1981   *Competitive Employment: New Horizons for Severely Disabled Individuals*. Baltimore, Md.: Paul H. Brookes Publishing Co.

Wehman, Paul, and Mark Hill, eds.
1982   *Vocational Training and Placement of Severely Disabled Persons*. Richmond, Va.: Virginia Commonwealth University, Rehabilitation Research and Training Center.

World Health Organization
1980   *International Classification of Impairments, Disabilities and Handicaps*. Geneva: WHO.

Worrall, John D.
1978   "A Benefit-Cost Analysis of the Vocational Rehabilitation Program." *Journal of Human Resources* 13, 2 (Spring): 285–98.
1980   "An Analysis of Some Aspects of the U.S. Dept. of Labor's Draft Interim Report to the Congress on Occupational Disease." Paper for National Council on Compensation Insurance. Mimeo.
1982   "Overlapping Benefits: Workers' Compensation and Other Income Sources." Paper for National Council on Compensation Insurance. Mimeo.
1983   "Compensation Costs, Injury Rates and the Labor Market." In *Safety and the Work Force: Incentives and Disincentives in Workers' Compensation*, ed. John D. Worrall, 1–17. Ithaca, N.Y.: ILR Press.

Worrall, John D., and David Appel
1982   "The Wage Replacement Rate and Benefit Utilization in Workers' Compensation Insurance." *Journal of Risk and Insurance* 49, 3 (September): 361–71.
1985   "Some Benefit Issues in Workers' Compensation." In *Workers' Compensation Benefits: Adequacy, Equity, and Efficiency*, ed. John D. Worrall and David Appel, 1–18. Ithaca, N.Y.: ILR Press.

Worrall, John D., and Philip S. Borba
1985   "Compensating Wage Differentials, Wage-Risk Premiums and Workers' Compensation Insurance." Mimeo.

Worrall, John D., and Richard J. Butler
   1984   "Heterogeneity Bias in the Estimation of the Determinants of Comp Loss Distributions." Paper presented at the 1984 American Risk and Insurance Association Meetings, August, Minneapolis, Minnesota.
   1985   "Workers' Compensation: Benefits and Duration of Claims." In *Workers' Compensation Benefits: Adequacy, Equity, and Efficiency*, ed. John D. Worrall and David Appel, 57–70. Ithaca, N.Y.: ILR Press.
Worrall, John D., Richard J. Butler, Philip Borba, and David Durbin
   1985   "Age and Incentive Response: Illinois Low Back Workers' Compensation Claims." Paper presented at the Annual National Council on Compensation Insurance Seminar on Insurance Research, November 19, New York City.
Worrall, John D., and Jennifer Field
   1981   "Report on the Use of the 1978 Survey of Disability and Work to Estimate the Number of People with Self-Reported Work Disability Attributed to Bad Working Conditions." Paper for National Council on Compensation Insurance. Mimeo.
Worrall, John D., and David Vandergoot
   1982   "Additional Indicators of Nonsuccess: A Follow-Up Report." *Rehabilitation Counseling Bulletin* 26, 2 (November): 88–93.
Yelin, Edward
   1979   "From Social Theory to Social Policy: Social Class and the Epidemiology of Disability among Persons with Rheumatoid Arthritis," Ph.D. diss., Department of City and Regional Planning, University of California, Berkeley.
Yelin, Edward, R. Meenan, M. Nevitt, and W. Epstein
   1980   "Work Disability in Rheumatoid Arthritis: Effects of Disease, Social and Work Factors." *Annals of Internal Medicine* 93: 551–56.
Yelin, Edward, Michael Nevitt, and Wallace Epstein
   1980   "Toward an Epidemiology of Work Disability." *Milbank Memorial Fund Quarterly* 58, 3: 386–415.
Yuker, Harold
   1977   "Attitudes of the General Public toward Handicapped Individuals." In *The White House Conference on Handicapped Individuals*, ed. J. K. Weston, vol. 1. Washington, D.C.: U.S. Government Printing Office.
Yuker, Harold, J. R. Block, and Janet Young
   1966   *The Measurement of Attitudes toward Disabled Persons*. Albertson, N.Y.: Human Resources Center.
Zadny, Jerry
   1979   "Employer Reactions to Efforts to Place Disabled and Dis-

advantaged Workers." Regional Rehabilitation Research Institute, Portland State University.

Zeckhauser, Richard
1970   "Medical Insurance: A Case Study of the Trade-Off between Risk Spreading and Appropriate Incentives." *Journal of Economic Theory* 2 (March): 10–26.

INDEX

CONTRIBUTORS

David Appel is vice president for economic and social research of the National Council on Compensation Insurance (NCCI). He received his Ph.D. from Rutgers University, where he also taught before joining NCCI. Mr. Appel has written extensively on workers' compensation insurance and testified frequently in regulatory hearings. His work has appeared in the *Journal of Risk and Insurance* and the *Journal of Insurance Regulation*.

Monroe Berkowitz is a professor in the Department of Economics and head of the Disability Economics section of the Bureau of Economic Research at Rutgers University. He received his Ph.D. from Columbia University. Mr. Berkowitz has written numerous books and articles on workers' compensation and disability economics.

Richard V. Burkhauser is a professor of economics and senior research associate at the Institute for Public Policy Studies at Vanderbilt University. He has published widely on the behavioral and income distribution effects of government policy toward aged and disabled persons. He is coauthor of *Disability and Work: The Economics of American Policy* (Johns Hopkins University Press, 1982), a critical analysis of the U.S. disability system, and of *Public Policy toward Disabled Workers: A Cross-National Analysis of Economic Impacts* (Cornell University Press, 1984), which compares the U.S. disability system with those of seven industrial countries of Western Europe.

Richard J. Butler is an associate professor of economics at Brigham Young University. He received his Ph.D. in economics from the University of Chicago. He has published articles (with John D. Worrall) on workers' compensation in the *Economic Journal*, the *Journal of Risk and Insurance*, the *Review of Economics and Statistics*, and the *Journal of Law and Economics*, as well as chapters in several books. Besides his interest in workers' compensation, he has published work in the economics of discrimination and inequality.

Frederick C. Collignon is an associate professor in the Department of City and Regional Planning at the University of California, Berkeley, and president of Berkeley Planning Associates. He received his Ph.D. in political economy and government from Harvard University.

M. Anne Hill is an assistant professor of economics at Rutgers University. She received her Ph.D. in economics from Duke University and has written on the economics of disability, vocational rehabilitation, and labor supply. Her writing has been published in the *Review of Economics and Statistics*, the *Journal of Human Resources*, the *Southern Economic Journal* and the *Journal of Development Economics*.

William G. Johnson is a professor of economics at the Maxwell School and senior research associate of the Metropolitan Studies Programs at Syracuse University. He has written widely on the economic aspects of death and disability; his most recent work on this topic has been published in the *Journal of Human Resources* and the *Industrial and Labor Relations Review* (1984).

James Lambrinos is an associate professor of administration and management and director of the Program in Health Systems Administration at Union College. He has published articles on the economics of disability and the economics of medical care in the *Review of Economics and Statistics*, the *Journal of Human Resources*, *Harvard Business Review*, and the *Journal of Health Economics*. He is currently working on a classification system for disability called Disability Related Categories, which is similar to the Diagnostic Related Groups used in the Medicare program.

Jonathan S. Leonard is an assistant professor in the Organizational Behavior and Industrial Relations Group of the School of Business Administration, University of California at Berkeley. He is also a research associate of the Institute of Industrial Relations at Berkeley, and a research fellow of the National Bureau of Economic Research in Cambridge, Massachusetts. His primary areas of research include the impact of antidiscrimination and affirmative action policies, employment growth and variability, trade unions, and disability and labor supply. This work has been published in the *Industrial and Labor Relations Review*, the *Journal of Human Resources*, and the *Journal of Labor Economics*.

Rebecca Maynard is vice president and deputy director of research at Mathematica Policy Research (MPR), and has spent most of her career designing and evaluating employment training programs and welfare policies aimed at promoting economic self-sufficiency among disadvantaged and disabled populations. Subsequent to joining MPR, she managed the impact analysis of the National Supported Work Demonstration and has played major roles in designing numerous experimental and quasi-experimental programs and program evaluations including the Structured Transitional Employment Training Service (STETS) demonstration, which focused on mentally retarded young adults and programs for youth, welfare recipients, and dislocated workers.

Robert S. Smith is a professor of labor economics at the New York State School of Industrial and Labor Relations, Cornell University. He received his Ph.D. in economics from Stanford University in 1971. He has published extensively on topics related to occupational safety and health and is coauthor of a textbook on modern labor economics.

Craig Thornton is a senior economist at Mathematica Policy Research (MPR). He has worked on numerous evaluations of social programs including employment and training programs, offender-rehabilitation programs, and health-related programs. In the past five years he has been studying transitional and supported employment programs for persons with disabilities, and is currently directing an evaluation of the Social Security Administration's Transitional Employment Training Demonstration. He has made numerous professional presentations and extensively published his findings. His benefit-cost studies have gained national acclaim.

Carolyn L. Weaver is a senior research fellow at the Hoover Institution at Stanford University, conducting research on social security retirement and disability policy and collective choice. Prior to joining the Hoover Institution in 1984, Dr. Weaver served as chief professional staff member on social security programs to the U.S. Senate Committee on Finance and as senior advisor to the National Commission on Social Security Reform. She has been a member of the economics department and the Center for Study of Public Choice of Virginia Polytechnic Institute and State University, where she received her Ph.D., and has also taught at Tulane University. Dr. Weaver has published articles in professional journals on the history and political economy of social security as well as the effects of agenda control and spending limitations in the public sector.

John D. Worrall is an associate professor of economics at Rutgers University, where he also received his Ph.D. He has written extensively on workers' compensation, safety incentives, the economics of disability, and vocational rehabilitation. His work has appeared in the *Economic Journal*, the *Journal of Law and Economics*, the *Review of Economics and Statistics*, the *Journal of Human Resources*, and the *Journal of Risk and Insurance*. He is also the editor of *Safety and the Work Force: Incentives and Disincentives in Workers' Compensation Insurance* (ILR Press, 1983) and coeditor with David Appel of *Workers' Compensation Benefits: Adequacy, Equity, and Efficiency* (ILR Press, 1985).